The Public Financing of Pharmaceuticals

The Public Financing of Pharmaceuticals

An Economic Approach

Edited by

Jaume Puig-Junoy

Research Centre for Economics and Health (CRES), Department of Economics and Business, Pompeu Fabra University, Spain

Edward Elgar

Cheltenham, UK • Northampton, MA, USA

Published by
Edward Elgar Publishing Limited
Glensanda House
Montpellier Parade
Cheltenham
Glos GL50 1UA
UK

Edward Elgar Publishing, Inc.
136 West Street
Suite 202
Northampton
Massachusetts 01060
USA

A catalogue record for this book is available from the British Library

Library of Congress Cataloguing in Publication Data
The Public financing of pharmaceuticals : an economic approach / edited by Jaume
    Puig-Junoy.
        p. cm.
        1. Pharmaceutical industry—Government policy—United States. 2.
    Pharmaceutical industry—United States—Finance. 3. Drugs—Research—United
    States—Finance. I. Puig-Junoy, Jaume.

HD9666.6.P83 2005
338.4′7615′0973—dc22

                                                                                        2004058627

ISBN 1 84542 088 8

Typeset by Cambrian Typesetters, Frimley, Surrey
Printed and bound in Great Britain by MPG Books Ltd, Bodmin, Cornwall

Contents

v

Figures

Tables

Contributors

X. Badía Llach   Consultant, Clinical Epidemiology and Public Health Department, Health Outcomes Research Unit, Sant Pau Hospital, Barcelona

J.R. Borrell Arqué   Interim full lecturer, Faculty of Economic and Business Sciences, University of Barcelona

M. Cabañas Sáenz   Documentalist, Health and Pharmaceuticals Social Studies Seminar, Carlos III University, Madrid

L. Cabiedes   Full lecturer, Applied Economics, University of Oviedo

A. Costas Comesaña   University professor, Faculty of Economic and Business Sciences, University of Barcelona

J. Darbà Coll   Full lecturer, Department of Economic Theory, University of Barcelona

B. González López-Valcárcel   University professor, Faculty of Economic and Business Sciences, University of Las Palmas de Gran Canaria

R. González Pérez   Research assistant, Health and Pharmaceuticals Social Studies Seminar, Carlos III University, Madrid

P. Ibern Regàs   Research Centre for Economics and Health (CRES); associate lecturer, Department of Economics and Business, Pompeu Fabra University, Barcelona

F. Lobo   Director of the Health and Pharmaceuticals Social Studies Seminar, Carlos III University, Madrid

G. López-Casasnovas   Research Centre for Economics and Health (CRES); university professor, Department of Economics and Business, Pompeu Fabra University, Barcelona

R. Nonell Torres   Full lecturer, Faculty of Economic and Business Sciences, University of Barcelona

V. Ortún   Research Centre for Economics and Health (CRES); full lecturer, Department of Economics and Business, Pompeu Fabra University, Barcelona

J.L. Pinto Prades Research Centre for Economics and Health (CRES), Department of Economics and Business, Pompeu Fabra University, Barcelona; university school professor

J. Puig-Junoy Research Centre for Economics and Health (CRES); university school professor, Department of Economics and Business, Pompeu Fabra University, Barcelona

J. Rovira Forns Senior health economist, The World Bank Health, Nutrition and Population, Washington and lecturer, University of Barcelona

Abbreviations

AES	*Associación de Economía de Salud*
AIDS	acquired immune deficiency syndrome
ASTRO-PU	age, sex and temporary resident originated prescribing unit
BOE	*Boletín Oficial del Estado*
CBA	cost–benefit analysis
CEA	cost-effectiveness analysis
CMg	constant marginal cost
COPD	chronic obstructive pulmonary disease
CP	price paid by the consumer
CPI	consumer price index
CRES	Research Centre for Economics and Health
CS	consumer surplus
CUA	cost-utility analysis
DDD	defined daily dose
DH	Department of Health
EE	economic evaluation
EFG	*especialidad farmacéutica genérica*
EFP	ex-factory price
EU	European Union
FDA	Food and Drug Administration
GATT	General Agreement on Tariffs and Trade
GDP	gross domestic product
GP	general practitioner
HMO	health maintenance organization
IMS	Intercontinental Medical Systems
INE	*Instituto Nacional de Estadística*
INN	International Non-proprietary Name
Insalud	*Instituto Nacional de Salud*
MAC	maximum allowable cost
MOH	Ministry of Health
MUFACE	Mutualidad de Funcionarios de la Administración Central del Estado
NHS	National Health Service
NSEA	non-safe and effective drug approved
NSER	non-safe and effective drug rejected

OECD	Organization for Economic Co-operation and Development
OTC	over the counter
PA	probability of the drug being accepted
PBM	Pharmacy Benefit Management firm
PCG	primary care group
PCR	price-cap regulation
PNSE	probability of the drug not being safe and effective
PPP	purchasing power parity
PPRS	Pharmaceutical Price Regulation Scheme
PR	probability of the drug being rejected
PSE	probability of the drug being safe and effective
QALY	quality-adjusted life-year
R&D	research and development
RORR	rate of return regulation
RP	reference price; reference pricing
SEA	safe and effective drug approved
SER	safe and effective drug rejected
SNS	*Sistema Nacional de Salud*
SS	*Seguridad Social*
TRIP	Trade-related aspects of intellectual property
UK	United Kingdom
USA	United States of America
WHO	World Health Organization
WTO	World Trade Organization

1. Introduction: Public pharmaceutical expenditure

J. Puig-Junoy

PHARMACEUTICALS AND EFFICIENT HEALTH PRODUCTION

In the analysis of health care the price of care is often confused with the level of expenditure, particularly so in the analysis of the cost of pharmaceuticals. Pharmaceutical cost containment should never be the exclusive goal of public policies: emphasis on costs without paying attention to the value of the products may lead to inefficient policies. The value of a new pharmaceutical resides in its ability to improve health, not just in its contribution to the decrease or increase of health care costs. Increased spending on health care and pharmaceuticals is therefore compatible with a reduction in their price, if the resulting value increases more than the expenditure.

According to a common cliché, health care spending on pharmaceuticals is excessive in Spain, although the figures do little to endorse this idea, and moreover do not in themselves serve to lay blame or pinpoint inefficiencies. Public and private pharmaceutical spending per capita in Spain is not among the highest in the European Union (EU): it is almost 10 per cent lower than the European average, and lower than the figure for nine of the 15 Member States. The proportion of spending on pharmaceuticals within health care expenditure as a whole stands at around 20 per cent (20.7 per cent in 1997), according to data published by the Organization for Economic Co-operation and Development (OECD). This indicator shows wide variation internationally, from less than 10 per cent in Denmark, Ireland and Switzerland to 26.5 per cent in Hungary and 35 per cent in Bulgaria. The proportion is greater in lower-income countries than in higher income ones.

The allocation of a greater or lesser proportion of the total health expenditure to pharmaceuticals merely indicates that there are different ways of combining resources to produce health care. The superiority of one combination of resources over another can only be established by examining the aggregate results of the resources used on the health status of the population.

The economic cost of the pharmaceuticals for the patient and society as a

whole is not well represented by the observation of higher or lower pharmaceutical expenditure. The opportunity cost of pharmaceuticals must take into
account the benefit they provide, and also the problems that may arise from
pharmacological treatment (prescription and medication errors and various
types of interaction, incomplete treatment, adverse reactions to pharmaceuticals and bacterial resistance). The degree of suitability of the prescription is an
illustration of problems related to the benefits of pharmaceuticals.

INTERPRETING MEASURES OF HEALTH CARE SPENDING ON PHARMACEUTICALS

The interpretation of the available empirical evidence of the absolute and relative magnitude of pharmaceutical expenditure on an aggregate or macroeco-
nomic level is often prone to the effects of confusing the level of expenditure
with the cost or price of care. It is of great value to identify two very important aspects for measuring and interpreting pharmaceutical expenditure.

Firstly, we should review the problems associated with the available
empirical evidence in aggregate-level statistical sources for the health system
that are used most frequently in the analysis of pharmaceutical expenditure.
Secondly, the conditions to be fulfilled by the measures of the relative importance of pharmaceutical spending within health care spending should be clearly
established, thus enabling us to observe what type of variation is occurring,
and the nature of the underlying explanatory factors that are responsible for
the evolution of the observed spending. This would allow valid comparisons
between forecast and actual spending.

According to OECD figures, pharmaceutical spending accounted for 22 per
cent of Spain's public health care expenditure in 2001. This is considerably
more than in a large number of countries, only Portugal (24 per cent in 1997),
and Hungary (25.3 per cent) registering higher percentages. Furthermore, this
2001 figure for Spain represented a considerable increase over the figure for
1987 (14.9 per cent). However, at present the proportion is clearly smaller than
that observed in Spain at the beginning of the 1970s (34.8 per cent in 1973),
and it remained steady from 1979 to 1994 (see Table 1.1).

Yet public pharmaceutical expenditure per capita is lower in Spain than in
many OECD countries. In 2001 public spending on pharmaceuticals stood at
US$251 per person, less than in countries such as France (US$354) Germany
(US$284), Japan (US$269) and Luxembourg (US$268 in 2000).

These examples highlight that the interpretation of this relative magnitude,
chosen by many authors as an indicator of the exception that Spain constitutes
as regards pharmaceutical drug consumption, is questionable at best. This
empirical measure is far from representing the combination of pharmaceutical

and non-pharmaceutical resources adopted by each health system (relative amount of resources or technology) for several reasons. The participation and contribution of the pharmaceutical resource to health production should be evaluated on the basis of data indicating the consumption of factors of production that are not contaminated by the origin of the funding. Thus, for example, cross-national comparisons of public pharmaceutical spending at a particular time are affected by major differences in levels of co-payment (that is, user participation in the funding of pharmaceuticals) between countries (see Table 1.2). The variation over time of the level of co-payment in Spain (a markedly decreasing trend) is bringing about changes in the share of public health expenditure devoted to pharmaceutical spending that do not reflect any rise in relative consumption of the pharmaceutical resource but rather private financing that is not only one of the lowest in the EU but moreover is decreasing.

Given that there is a crossover between public and private pharmaceutical financing in the production of health services (users with coverage who prefer to pay the retail price of the drug to the inconvenience of obtaining the prescription from the public primary care provider; direct-payment prescriptions made out in a private surgery that are subsequently reclassified as prescriptions made out by a public primary care provider), the observation of empirical data on public pharmaceutical spending is not meaningful as an indicator of resource combination in health production. There are more advantages to be had in observing the total pharmaceutical expenditure as compared to the total health expenditure (Table 1.3). If we observe the behaviour of this indicator, we can see that although the Spanish rate is high (20.7 per cent in 1997), nevertheless: (a) it is lower than or on a par with countries such as France, Greece, Hungary, Japan, Portugal and the Czech Republic, although higher than the rest of the OECD countries, and (b) its 1997 value is still slightly lower than its 1980 value.

Cross-national comparisons of pharmaceutical spending are likewise extraordinarily misleading, as the final pharmaceutical expenditure includes taxes and intermediaries' markups, both of which are very different from country to country.

The analysis of the contribution made by increased pharmaceutical spending to the growth in the per capita intensity of health resources suffers from major measurement problems that deprive available indicators of any value. Traditional pharmaceutical price indexes (such as the Laspeyres index, used to calculate the pharmaceutical component of the consumer price index) provide little relevant information in a market in which the introduction of therapeutic innovations is of prime importance; the indexes show an apparent freeze, and sometimes even a steep drop (as in the Spanish case). However, the steady rise in the average price per prescription paints a very different picture.

The rise in the average price of medicines can be attributed to any of

Table 1.1   Public pharmaceutical expenditure as a percentage of public health expenditure

	1960	1961	1962	1963	1964	1965	1966	1967	1968	1969
Australia	16.3			18			17.6			14
Austria										
Belgium										
Canada	0.2					0.2				
Czech Rep.										
Denmark										
Finland					1.4	5	4.9	5	5.5	5.4
France										
Germany										
Greece										
Hungary										
Iceland	11.1	14.7	12	9.8	9.5	10	9.4	9.7	8	11.9
Ireland										
Italy										
Japan										
Korea										
Luxembourg										
Mexico										
Netherlands										
New Zealand										
Norway						2.4	2.6	3	3.2	3.2
Poland										
Portugal										
Spain										
Sweden	11.2	11.2	12.5	13.1	12	17.2	21.2	27.6	31.3	32.7
Switzerland										
Turkey										
UK										
USA	8.1	5.9	5.9	6.3	7.4	12.2	11.6	11.5	10.3	10.5

	1980	1981	1982	1983	1984	1985	1986	1987	1988	1989	1990
Australia	5.5	6.1	6.1	5.7	5.4	5.3	5.7	6.4	6.3	6.6	6
Austria											
Belgium											
Canada	2.8	2.9	2.9	3.1	3.4	3.8	4.1	4.3	4.5	4.8	5.1
Czech Rep.											19.2
Denmark	3.4	3.3	3.1	3.3	3.4	3.5	3.7	3.6	3.9	3.6	3.1
Finland	6.3	6.1	5.7	5.7	5.6	5.5	5.4	5.6	5.5	5.5	5.5
France											13.6
Germany	12.5	12.5	12.4	12.6	12.8	12.8	13	13.5	13.6	13.7	13.7
Greece	20.3								15.4	14.7	15.1
Hungary											
Iceland	9.2	8.9	9.5	12.5	11.3	11.8	11.2	10.2	10	11.3	12.8

1970	1971	1972	1973	1974	1975	1976	1977	1978	1979
	12.3	11.1	11.1	10.2	7.6	6	6.3	6	5.6
0.3	0.5	0.6	0.8	1.1	1.7	2	2.2	2.5	2.7
5.8	6.6	7.2	7.2	7.5	7.1	7.1	7	6.8	6.6
14.1	13.5	13.4	13.1	13	12.7	12.8	12.4	12.4	12.5
36									
11.2	10	7.3	7.2	7.5	9.2	7.6	7.2	8.9	7.9
13.6		2.7	4.8	5.7	7.5	7.6	7.3	7	6.9
18.5					15.4	15.5	14.5	14.3	14
		10.2	10	9.2	8.9	8.6	8.4	8.2	7.9
11.3	11.8	10.6	11	10.1	10.2	11	11.2	10.6	10.3
3.1	3.3	3	3.1	3.4	3.4	3.3	3.3	3.4	3.6
15.6		19.6		19.1		19.7		21.4	
32.3	34	33.4	34.8	29.5	27	20.6	18.8	18.9	17.7
4.8	5	5.5	6.2	5.9	5.9	5.6	5.5	5.4	5.3
10	9.8	9.7	9.4	10.3	8.7	9.5	10.3	10.6	10

1991	1992	1993	1994	1995	1996	1997	1998	1999	2000	2001	2002
6	7	7.9	8.2	9.1	9.2	8.7	8.9	9.3	10.7	10.9	
				11	11.3	13.6	14.8	15.5	16.2	17	17.3
				10.1	9.9	10.3	11.2	11.5			
5.3	5.7	5.9	5.9	6.4	6.4	6.6	6.9	7.3	7.8	8.2	8.4
16.9	19.7	17.8	22.7	23.1	22.9	22.3	22.7	19.6	18.8	18.4	
4.7	5	5	5.1	5.3	5.2	5.2	5.4	5.2	5.2	5.5	
5.9	6.2	7.2	8.1	8.4	8.8	9.3	9.2	9.8	10.4	10.7	
13.8	13.8	14.1	13.8	14.2	14.3	14.8	15.4	16.4	17.4	18.2	
	14	11.6	11.4	11.4	11.5	11.2	11.6	12.3	12.6	13.5	
18.9	20	20.5	21.9	21.4	22.3	22.9	18.6	18.9	17.4	18.9	
24.5	21.4	22.5	21.9	19.9	20.8		26.4	24.8	24.9	25.3	
11	11.9	10.8	11.9	12.4	13	12.3	11.5	11			

Table 1.1   (*continued*)

	1980	1981	1982	1983	1984	1985	1986	1987	1988	1989	1990
Ireland	7.1	8	8.5	7.7	7.9	7.9	8.5	9	9.9	11.2	11
Italy									16.7	16.9	16.8
Japan					16.5	15.4	16.1	17.2	16.9	18.1	16.9
Korea										0	0.3
Luxembourg	13.5	13.4	13.6	13.3	13.7	14.2	14.6	13.9	14.1	14.3	13.6
Mexico											
Netherlands	7.7	7.6	7.8	7.2	7.9	8.3	8.6	8.9	9.1	8.6	9.5
New Zealand	10.9	9.3	10.4	10.6	11.4	12.3	13.8	14	13.8	14	12.5
Norway	4.3	4.3	4.4	4.4	4.5	4.6	4.4	4.2	6	6.3	6.9
Poland											
Portugal	21.2		22.6	22.5	21.9	30.1	29.4	33.9	27.5	28	23.7
Spain											
Sweden	16.8	16.6	17	15.6	15.1	15.7	14.9	14.9	17.5	16.7	16.2
Switzerland	5	4.7	5.2	5.4	5.1	5.4	5.6	5.9	5.1	6.3	6.4
Turkey											
UK					21.3	22.6	24.3	28.1			29.6
USA	9.7	9.6	10.5	10.3	10.5	10.5	10.7	10.6	11	11.1	10.8

Source: OECD Health Data (2003).

several factors: (a) 'pure' variations in the price of existing products, (b) the appearance and spread of the consumption of new products with a higher than average price and a greater or lesser degree of therapeutic innovation, and (c) a shift in consumption from low-priced products to products with a higher price than those consumed previously, which may entail a greater or lesser degree of therapeutic innovation (shifts between different presentations, between different brands with the same active ingredient, and between different therapeutic subgroups).

The important question to answer is to what extent the increase in pharmaceutical prices involves an increase or a decrease (and of what magnitude) in the cost of health care. In other words, to what extent is the rise in pharmaceutical expenditure contributing to increase, maintain, or reduce the cost of obtaining an additional quality-adjusted life-year (QALY)? The first indispensable step towards eradicating the confusion that exists between pharmaceutical expenditure and cost of care is, in addition to choosing the right monetary magnitude, to avail ourselves of appropriate price indexes for drug consumption.

An accurate measure of the apparent causes of the evolution of pharmaceutical expenditure could be obtained by taking chain-linked Laspeyres price indexes for each therapeutic group with a suitable level of disaggregation. In this situation, ideally we would have monetary measures of willing-

1991	1992	1993	1994	1995	1996	1997	1998	1999	2000	2001	2002
10.6	11.1	10.7	11.1	11.3	11.7	11	11.4	11.8	11.6	12.7	
15.6	14.6	13.2	11.1	11.1	11.3	11.4	12	12.7	13.4	16	15.5
18.7	18	18.5	17.6	19.5	18.8	17.9	15.7	15.1	15.5	16.2	
0.3	0.3	0.6	1.1	1.6	1.6	1.6	1.5	1.8	6.2		
13.7	14.2		10.8	10.6	10	11.2	10.7	11	11.2		
								0	0.1	0.2	
9.3	13.2	13.6	13.5	13.7	10.5	10.4	9.3	9.7	9.7	9.7	
12.6	12.7	13.3	13.5	13.4	13	13.1					
21	18.1	17.2	18.1	20.3	19.6	13.3	12.5	13		15.7	15.8
24.4	25.5	25	24.8	23.8	23.6	24					
								28.9	31.4	31.5	
16.9	17.2	17	17.8	19	19.6	20.9	21	21.6	21.8	22	
7	7.9	8.8	10	10.4	11.6	9.6	10.9	11.4	11.4	10.9	
				9.9	10	10.4	10.6	11		11.7	11.6
			4								
10.7	10.6	11	11.3	11.5	11.8	12.7					

ness to pay for the improvement in quality of the main products, resulting from economic evaluations carried out using techniques such as contingent valuation, or by estimating the statistical value of life by means of hedonic prices. In this way we could determine the part of the price increases that are attributable to improvements in the quality of the products on the one hand and pure price rises on the other. The problems to solve in the construction of pharmaceutical price indexes are biases that are well known from the construction of inflation and welfare indexes: substitution bias, bias due to the appearance of new goods or services, and the consideration of changes in quality.

A number of empirical approaches have been put forward to quantify the price level and changes in prices of a treatment or a QALY: constructing price indexes (that is, learning to separate inflation from better inputs) for pharmaceuticals for a given disease taking into account the value of the innovation, changes in the structure of consumption, and so on; avoiding intertemporal comparisons of pharmaceutical cost per person, per stay, per illness, and so on, which add to the confusion between expenditure and the price of health; and developing measures of the monetary value of improvements in the quality of pharmaceutical innovations in order to establish the right relationship between spending and the price we are paying for additional QALYs (the true index of variation in the cost of health or life).

Table 1.2 Cost sharing in the health systems of western European countries

Country	First contact with the system	Referrals (within the system)	Pharmaceuticals
Austria	Does not affect 80% of the population. A percentage rate of co-payment for health care is applied to the rest, unless exempted for reasons of low income	Combination of co-payment and percentage rate (with exemptions). The scheme of direct payments by the patient is limited to the first 28 days of hospitalization	Co-payment for prescription drugs. Drugs not prescribed by health professionals are excluded
Belgium	Wide range of co-payments and percentage rates of cost sharing, with the exception of the low-income bracket. Patients are entitled to opt for an extra billing system[a]	Co-payment varying with the systems of payment of the professionals. Benefits are reduced after 90 days, less so for the low-income bracket	Co-payment and percentage rates of cost sharing that range from 0% to 85% according to the type of drug consumed. Pharmaceuticals not included in the system's positive financing list are not covered in any way
Denmark	None	None	Variable percentage rate of cost sharing (0–50%) applied on the basis of drug reference prices (RP). Drugs outside the MOH formulary are excluded from the coverage of the system
Finland	None. A choice is made between: a prior annual payment, a co-payment, and a co-payment with a maximum in the user-shared bill for the annual cost. Varies according to the municipality	Maximum payment levels for (daily) hospital stays and for specialist visits	Percentage rates of user sharing in pharmaceutical costs
France	Percentage rates of cost sharing. Extra billing is permitted for certain categories of doctors	Percentage rates of cost sharing per diem, together with co-payments covering meals. Direct payments by the user are not applicable after the first 30 days	Mostly subject to percentage rates of cost sharing. There is a positive list of pharmaceuticals with public coverage
Germany	None.	Flat rate of co-payment for the first 14 days per year of hospitalization, after which there is no cost sharing of any sort	Variable co-payment. RP system. No coverage is applied to those pharmaceuticals on public financing negative lists
Greece	None, although extra billing is common practice among private doctors	None for hospital stays. Some schemes practice shared financing through user cost-sharing rates for diagnostic services	Percentage rates of user sharing in pharmaceutical costs

Country			
Iceland	Co-payments, with higher rates for visits outside normal working hours. Larger co-payments for house calls. A maximum is set for the financial participation of the user	None for hospital stays. Combination of co-payment and percentage rate of cost sharing for specialist care and out-patient visits. Co-payment in diagnostic services. A maximum is set for the financial participation of the user	Combination of daily deductibles per prescription and percentage rates of cost sharing up to a maximum level. Some medicines are completely free, while others are excluded from public coverage
Ireland	None for category I of the population (represented 37% in 1987). The participation is 100% for the rest of the population unless they take out health insurance against it. An annual deductible is applied to insured groups which also acts as a maximum level of user participation	None for category I in public hospitals. For the rest, co-payments are applied for the first out-patient visit per episode, and there is a per diem co-payment for the first 10 days of hospitalization per year. Insurers buy free care for both public and private hospitals	None for population category I. Deductibles are applied to the rest of the population which also act as monthly maximum levels of user participation. Pharmaceuticals included in the negative list of public funding are not covered
Italy	None	None for in-patient care. Cost sharing was introduced in 1990 for public hospitals. Most of the rest are with regard to diagnostic procedures, hospital visits and spa treatments	Deductibles are only applied for medicines that are considered essential. Most of the rest are financed through a combination of deductibles and percentage rates of cost sharing. Some pharmaceuticals are excluded from public coverage
Luxembourg	Percentage rates of user sharing in the cost of services	Inflation-linked per diem co-payments	Percentage rates of cost sharing, except in the case of 'special diseases'. Medicines are free during hospitalization
Netherlands	None for public insurance, but varies in the case of private insurance	None for public insurance, but varies in the case of private insurance	RP system, with the exclusion of some pharmaceuticals
Norway	Cost sharing, with a maximum annual contribution for all services as a whole	None for in-patient care. Cost sharing for diagnostic services	RP system for medicines that are considered essential
Portugal	Cost sharing	Cost sharing	Two percentage cost sharing rates, depending on the type of pharmaceuticals involved. Some pharmaceuticals are free, while others are excluded from public coverage
Spain	None	None	Percentage rates of sharing in the cost of pharmaceutical consumption. Positive list of pharmaceuticals with public coverage

Table 1.2 (continued)

Country	First contact with the system	Referrals (within the system)	Pharmaceuticals
Sweden	Co-payment, with maximum levels of sharing in health service bills, with the exception of hospital in-patient bills	Per diem co-payment for in-patient services. Co-payment for therapeutic referrals	Co-payment for the first drug prescribed, with significantly lower co-payments for subsequent prescriptions. RP system for medicines with 'generic' equivalents
Switzerland	Combination of annual deductibles and percentage cost-sharing rates	Per diem co-payments for hospitalization	User sharing in drug consumption costs, which varies between different health insurance schemes. Negative lists of medicines exclude consumption from public coverage
Turkey	Mostly private providers who apply 'payment per act' (FFS) schemes in their bills	Social health insurance covers the totality of costs, although specific rates are applied to uninsured groups	All social health insurance schemes apply percentage rates of user participation for medicines (in out-patient visits)
UK	None	None, except for hospital rest beds	Co-payments, although 83% of prescriptions are exempt. Negative lists of medicines exclude NHS coverage

Notes: a. Extra billing is that which exceeds the maximums (of coverage) set by the insurance scheme (to which the patient belongs), and which the ultimate provider of the services charges directly to the patient.

Source: López-Casasnovas, G., V. Ortún and C. Murillo (1999), *El sistema sanitario español: informe de una década*, Bilbao: Fundación BBV.

THE CONTENTS OF THIS BOOK

This book consists of a series of works that evaluate various aspects related to the public financing of pharmaceuticals. In all health systems with majority public funding, the financing of pharmaceuticals constitutes one of the key factors in reform policies and health cost containment measures. This import- ance of pharmaceutical spending can be explained by both its relative size (its share within health expenditure as a whole), and its rapid growth, which is closely related to the constant incorporation of therapeutic innovations.

The credibility of the commitment to maintain and even improve the public funding of medicines in the short and long term renders it necessary to take measures aimed at reducing the imperfection and inequality of users'/voters' information about the fact that not all pharmaceuticals are equally effective or necessary, and that there is no worse enemy for the public provision of phar- maceuticals (and indeed one's state of health) than the illusion that it is poss- ible to indiscriminately continue to provide any drug to anyone regardless of its effectiveness and cost.

An efficient pharmaceutical policy should go beyond the partial regulation of drugs, industry and prescribers. Its makers should learn how to combine these instruments, by explicitly recognizing the conflicts of interests that are at work in the sector. This involves making the effort to find the right dose of each regulatory measure, to underline that public financing must be based on cost-effectiveness criteria, and that these criteria must be applied in such a way as to create a stable framework for industry and thus encourage innovation.

The contributions included in this book seek to provide economic keys for a better understanding of both the dynamics of public pharmaceutical spend- ing and the effects of public policies in this area. We see these economic keys as indispensable for overcoming clichés and truisms and building the debate on public pharmaceutical funding on theoretical and empirical findings. In this respect, the public policies implemented in recent years with a view to ration- alizing and containing the growth rate of expenditure should in no way be regarded as useless or ineffective. However, we find that these measures can only be effective if coordinated and integrated policies are adopted that take into consideration the overall effect on the role of pharmaceuticals, and if the best knowledge available is taken as the point of reference. The effectiveness of partial measures depends on the integration and coordination of the incen- tives present on the various fronts of pharmaceutical policy. One key factor for an integrated pharmaceutical policy is to be found in action on the economic and non-economic incentives of prescribers (self-regulation, controls by health authorities, budgets, prescription guidelines, information and pharma- cological counselling).

The first group of contributions focus on regulation and competition in the

Table 1.3 *Pharmaceutical expenditure as a percentage of total health*
expenditure

Years	1960	1961	1962	1963	1964	1965	1966	1967	1968	1969
Australia	22.6			22.2			21.6			17.8
Austria										
Belgium										
Canada	12.9	12	11.7	11.7	11.7	12.1	11.7	11.7	11.4	11.4
Czech Rep.										
Denmark										
Finland	17.1	17.1	15.8	15.3	14.8	14.8	14	13.4	13.1	12.5
France										
Germany										
Greece										
Hungary										
Iceland	18.5	19.2	19.9	18.4	18.2	17.7	16.3	17.4	16.7	18.9
Ireland										
Italy										
Japan										
Korea										
Luxembourg										
Mexico										
Netherlands										
New Zealand										
Norway			9.7	10	9.5	8.9	8.7	8.9	8.7	8.6
Poland										
Portugal										
Spain										
Sweden										
Switzerland										
Turkey										
UK										
USA				12.9	13.5	15.8	15.1	14.9	14.6	15.2

Years	1980	1981	1982	1983	1984	1985	1986	1989	1990	1991
Australia	8	8.1	8	8.3	8.1	8.1	8.1	8.1	8.4	8.8
Austria										
Belgium	17.4	16	15.4	15.6	15	15.7	15.7	16	16.5	16.2
Canada	8.5	8.9	8.6	8.7	9.1	9.6	10.3	10.6	11	11.2
Czech Rep.										
Denmark	6	5.9	6	6.2	6.4	6.6	7	6.7	7.1	6.8
Finland	10.7	10.3	9.8	10	10	9.7	9.6	9.6	9.5	9.4
France										
Germany	13.4	13.5	13.4	13.7	13.8	13.8	13.9	14.1	14.2	14.3
Greece	18.8							13.3	14.8	13.6
Hungary										
Iceland	15.9	14.7	15.2	17.4	16.5	16.6	15.8	14.7	14.2	14.8

1970	1971	1972	1973	1974	1975	1976	1977	1978	1979
	13.7	12.9	13	12.6	9.8	9.1	8.5	8.5	7.7
28.1	28.3	27.6	27.5	26.8	21.9	18.9	18.3	17.8	17.4
11.3	10.8	10.4	10.4	9.5	8.9	8.6	8.6	8.5	8.7
12.6	13.6	13.5	12.8	12.4	11.9	12	11.9	11.9	11.4
16.2	15.5	15.2	14.6	14.2	13.7	13.7	13.4	13.4	13.4
25.5									
17.1	17.3	17.8	16.6	13.8	16.2	14.8	14.6	14.5	13.5
22.2		18.8	17.8	14.9	13.8	13.5	13.4	12.9	12.3
19.7	19.3	18.8	19.6	19	16.6	16.4	15.3	15.2	15
		10.3	10.3	9.7	9.3	9.1	8.7	8.5	8.3
	11.4					10.6			
7.8	7.3	6.5	6.4	6.5	6.4	6.1	5.7	5	5.3
13.4							19.8	22.9	23.7
6.6	6.9	7.6	8,5	8.3	7.9	7.5	7.2	7	6.9
14.7	14.8	14.4	13.8	13.9	11.8	12.3	12.8	13	12.9

1992	1993	1994	1995	1996	1997	1998	1999	2000	2001
9	9.5	9.9	10.4	11	11.2	11.5	11.7	11.9	12.4
					11.1	11.2	13.1	14	14.5
15.5	15.6	16.3	17.4	17.5	16.5	15.8	16.5		
11.5	11.8	12.4	13	13.1	13.8	14	14.7	15.2	15.3
21	18.4	21.1	19.4	24.7	25.6	25.5	25.3	25.5	22.7
7.5	8	7.9	8.5	8.8	9.1	8.9	9	9	8.7
9.4	9.9	10.8	12.3	13.4	14.1	14.4	14.8	14.6	15.1
16.9	17.2	17.1	17.5	17.4	17.6	17.6	18	18.6	19.5
14.3		14.7	13.2	12.9	12.7	12.8	12.9	13.4	13.5
14.3	16.3	17	16.6	16.1	15.7	16.1	16.2	13.9	13.8
	27.6	26.5	28.4	28	25	26	25.9		
15.7	14.2	14.9	14.3	15	15.5	16.5	16.1	15.3	14.5

Table 1.3   (continued)

Years	1980	1981	1982	1983	1984	1985	1986	1989	1990	1991
Ireland	10.9	9.7	9.8	9.4	9.9	9.9	10.4	10.8	11.4	12.3
Italy									21.1	21.3
Japan	21.2				19.5	18	18.9	20.3	20.6	22.3
Korea						28.7	29.5	31.1	29.4	29.4
Luxembourg	14.5	14.4	14	13.8	14.2	14.7	15.2	14.9	15.5	15.7
Mexico										
Netherlands	8	8	8.2	8.2	8.9	9.3	9.6	10	9.9	9.3
New Zealand	11.9	10.8	11.4	12	12.4	13.3	14.5	14.7	14.2	14.3
Norway	8.7	8.9	9.1	9	9.1	9.1	9	8.6	6.4	6.7
Poland										
Portugal	19.9	18.2	18	19.2	19.9	25.4	22.5	24.9	22.9	23.9
Spain	21.0	20.6	21.2	20.0	18.6	20.3	19.0	18.1	17.8	18.3
Sweden	21	20.6	21.2	20	18.6	20.3	19	18.7	17.8	18.1
Switzerland	6.5	6.5	6.8	6.9	6.6	7	7.2	7.5	6.9	7.9
Turkey						11.3	11.8	10	10.4	10
UK		10.2	11.6	10.9	10.6	13.2	11.8	12.6		
USA	12.8	12.7	13.6	13.5	14.3	14.1	14.1	13.6	13.8	13.8

Source: OECD Health Data (2003).

pharmaceutical sector as a whole, and its effects on the introduction of innovations and the level of pharmaceutical prices.

In Chapter 2, Pompeu Fabra University lecturer P. Ibern Regàs offers an analysis of the advantages and the limitations of the financing of innovation in the pharmaceutical sector based on protection through patents. The author observes that, although patents have indisputably contributed to the development of innovation (with private financing of a public good), economic theory yields results that cast doubt on the suitability of this instrument when applied uncritically throughout the whole pharmaceutical sector. Several studies have shown that the marginal extension of patents to developing countries, when an innovation has already become widespread in the major pharmaceutical markets, can result in welfare losses. The author suggests that it would be advisable to revise the situation of patents as a mechanism for promoting innovation when there are alternative proposals that are firmly founded on theory, along the lines of the acquisition of patents by governments.

In the sphere of price regulation, professor J. Puig-Junoy of Pompeu Fabra University analyses in Chapter 3 the price regulation systems used in the OECD countries and their main effects. Theoretical justifications for price regulation in markets of prescription drugs whose patent has expired are scarce, and therefore price regulation in these cases is generally speaking unjustified. The author argues that individual price regulation systems for each

1992	1993	1994	1995	1996	1997	1998	1999	2000	2001
12.2	11.6	11.1	10.7	10.6	10.4	10.5	10.2	10.4	10.5
21.2	20.4	20.4	19.9	19.9	20.9	21.1	21.3	21.8	22.3
21.4	22.9	22	22.3	21.1	22.4	21.8	20.8	18.9	18.1
25.7	26.8	25	24.3	22.7	21.9	19.8	17	13.8	13.9
14.9	15			12.2	12	11.5	12.6	12.3	12.1
									18.6
9.6	9.6	10.5	11	10.9	11	11	11	9.7	10
13.8	14.1	14.2	14.9	15.8	14.8	14.5	14.4		
7.2	7.3	7.5	9.6	8.8	9	9.1	9.2		
24.9	24.3	24.7	25.6	25.2	23.2	23.6	23.5	22.8	
18.6	18.6	18.5	19.6	20.0	20.7				34
17.8									
8	8.7	9.7	10.7	11.8	12.3	13.6	12.4	13.6	13.9
10.2	9.8	9.4	9.7	9.8	10	10	10.3	10.2	10.5
20.5				31.6					
13.5	13.8	14.2	14.8	15.1	15.3	15.6	15.8		

product are ineffective as a system for controlling the profits of pharmaceutical companies. The rate of return regulation system that operates in the UK gives firms a certain amount of leeway in the pricing of individual products, but it still suffers from the inefficiency problems attributed to this public service regulation system by economic theory.

The price intervention system that has operated in Spain since 1991 is based on the fixing by the health authorities of the price cap for each product, calculated according to what is called its 'cost'. The application of this system, together with the restrictive criteria used in price revisions, has brought about a situation in which the relative price level of pharmaceuticals that have been on the market for some time would appear to be lower in Spain than in other countries, although this trend is being offset by the faster rate at which new and more expensive products are being introduced onto the market. This situation has led the health authorities to apply other measures on the supply side, such as agreements with Farmaindustria and reference pricing.

The present Spanish system of price control is inefficient, as it provides notable negative incentives for pharmaceutical consumption and expenditure; it would be desirable to replace it with a more flexible system such as an overall profit control system, or a combination of price-cap regulation and rate of return regulation.

In Chapter 4, University of Barcelona lecturers J.R. Borrell Arqué, A.

Costas Comesaña and R. Nonell Torres look at the extent to which pharmaceuticals are withstanding competition from therapeutic substitutes and generics, and how necessary price regulation is. This chapter provides empirical evidence on competition between rival pharmaceuticals in England and Spain, and shows the number of pharmaceuticals on the market, the position of dominance occupied by products in relation to their substitutes, and the prescription concentration at various levels of therapeutic and generic differentiation. The authors conclude that the different national regulations have shaped markets that differ greatly in the type of competition between substitute drugs. Generic competition between products/drugs containing the same therapeutic substance is seen to be keener in England, whereas therapeutic competition between products containing different substances is more intense in Spain.

In the same sphere, in Chapter 5, University of Barcelona lecturers J. Rovira Forns and J. Darbà Coll analyse mechanisms designed to encourage price competition in the pharmaceutical market and their effects on efficiency and welfare. The authors first study the supply factors that restrict competition (patents, brands, registration and marketing authorization) and also the demand factors (absence of incentives). They then go on to conclude that price discrimination between market segments may provide a solution by bringing together the interests of the various economic agents involved. From this point of view, the establishment of a single price internationally for a product under patent is not the optimal solution, and welfare gains can be generated by means of price differentiation in each market (Ramsey prices). Nevertheless, both the phenomenon of parallel imports and national price regulation on the basis of the observed price in other countries tend to work for the smoothing of prices.

The second series of contributions focus on the analysis of the application and effectiveness of the main instruments public financing agencies use to regulate pharmaceutical expenditure, on both the demand side and the supply side.

Reference pricing as a mechanism for pharmaceutical reimbursement by public insurers is the subject of Chapter 6, by professors G. López-Casasnovas and J. Puig-Junoy of Pompeu Fabra University. A reference pricing system operates by classifying pharmaceuticals into equivalent groups, and fixes a maximum reimbursement level for drugs that are classified within the same group and an (avoidable) co-payment equivalent to the difference between the retail price and the maximum reimbursable level. The application of the reference pricing system in Spain is limited to bio-equivalent drugs, in which area very little doubt can be cast on the justification and effectiveness of this mechanism.

The greatest effectiveness of reference pricing as a public spending control mechanism is achieved in health care environments in which the problem of pharmaceutical expenditure lies in high unit prices and the prescribed product is easily substituted by the pharmacist. Reference pricing can be useful for encouraging price competition in products whose patent has expired. It can result in a larger market share for generics and a drop in prices for brand products that are unprotected by patents.

Reference pricing was not introduced in Spain until December 2000. The fact that it is applied exclusively to bio-equivalent products leads, in the opinion of the authors, to the assumption that its effect on expenditure is limited, as a major market share is acquired by recently introduced drugs. The level at which the reference price is fixed is an important factor. For non-patented products, price competition should push the price towards the marginal cost, and therefore a reference price that is clearly higher than the cheapest generic could actually become a barrier to price competition in this case.

Empirical evidence suggests that the price paid by the patient should not be given a predominant role in the regulation of pharmaceutical expenditure. Available studies on the effects of co-payments indicate that they are more useful for increasing the financing of the user in the cost of the service than for reducing consumption, and therefore the reduction is not very great, as the demand is fairly inelastic. Furthermore, the application of co-payments with exemptions in order to attenuate the negative effects on equity is generally complex and costly.

In Chapter 7, professor B. González López-Valcárcel of the University of Las Palmas de Gran Canaria analyses the participation of the insuree in the payment of the price of the pharmaceutical. In spite of the widespread application of pharmaceutical co-payment in European health systems, the author observes that this mechanism does not appear to have been very effective in cost containment. Co-payments represent a way of making the user share the burden of the cost rather than an essential source of income for the public system. Theory and comparative experience of the system alike indicate that the indiscriminate application of co-payments is a source of inequalities, and that in any event its effects on consumption depend largely on prescriber incentives. For this reason the author recommends that co-payments should not be uniform for different population groups, and that they should not be applied in isolation, as their effectiveness is enhanced in combination with other instruments.

In Chapter 8, professor J.L. Pinto Prades of Pompeu Fabra University and X. Badía Llach of the Health Outcomes Research Unit at Santa Creu i Sant Pau Hospital take a look at the potential contribution of economic evaluation to the regulation and control of public spending on pharmaceuticals. The authors focus on observing how economic evaluation can be used in pharmaceutical policy. To this end, they distinguish and analyse the potential this instrument has in six distinct areas: the approval of pharmaceuticals by health authorities, drug prices, financing, medical treatment guidelines, reimbursement and patent policy. The authors' thesis is that economic evaluation can help to design more efficient policies in all these areas of the pharmaceutical regulation process.

In Chapter 9, lecturers V. Ortún Rubio of Pompeu Fabra University and L. Cabiedes Miragaya of the University of Oviedo address the subject of measures intended as a way of influencing prescriber decisions. The authors place special emphasis on analysing prescriber incentive policies, distinguishing between incentives of a financial nature (both coercive and non-coercive) and non-financial incentives (information, training, treatment protocols, monitoring of prescription practices, cost-effectiveness guidelines, interaction with other professionals, pressure from patients and so on). The authors advocate incentive policies based on a combination of financial and non-financial incentives.

The third group of contributions consists of the two final chapters that focus specifically on the present situation and the outlook for the future of pharmaceutical expenditure within the Spanish health system.

In Chapter 10, professor G. López-Casasnovas of Pompeu Fabra University provides evidence of expenditure behaviour and the evolution of the public financing of pharmaceuticals in the context of Spanish public health expenditure. Empirical evidence based on simple data may lead to excessively direct and contradictory conclusions as to the situation of Spanish pharmaceutical spending. Such would be the case of the figures for the share of health expenditure devoted to spending on pharmaceuticals (the Spanish figure is above the average for Western countries), whereas expenditure per capita is below the EU average. The author notes that although pharmaceutical expenditure has been subjected to all possible containment measures, to date no decrease has been forthcoming in Spanish pharmaceutical spending; indeed, quite the contrary. In López-Casasnovas' opinion, the sector requires the adoption of a stable 'legal' framework with a broad consensus, in order to lay down guidelines for the public financing of pharmaceutical expenditure in the mid-term.

Lastly, F. Lobo of Carlos III University, M. Cabañas Sáenz and R. González Pérez present in Chapter 11 the results of a review of the research done by Spanish economists on the economics of pharmaceuticals since 1980.

ACKNOWLEDGEMENTS

This book is a revised and updated translation of a previously published volume entitled *Análisis económico de la financiación publica de medicamentos*, published in Spanish in 2002 by Masson S.A. Barcelona, Spain.

This book has been translated into English by Tobias Willett, and revised by the authors.

PART I

2. Incentives for innovation in the pharmaceutical market

P. Ibern Regàs

INTRODUCTION

The production of goods and services requires technical information, that is, the necessary knowledge for the production process. Information is an economic good in its own right with characteristics that differentiate it from other goods, and also a differential factor for businesses in an industrial sector.

The first unique characteristic has to do with how information is produced. As Arrow points out,[1] unlike with other goods, once we have produced technical information we can use it continuously for the production process, but the reproduction of the same process of obtaining technical information adds nothing new. The second characteristic has to do with its use. Once technical information has been obtained it can be used by others, even though the original owner still possesses it. The property rights on information are difficult to define. Patents were developed in order to induce an artificial shortage, with the aim of creating incentives to acquire information. Arrow also states that these intellectual property rights not only entail inefficiencies but at the same time can only offer partial protection.

Economic growth ultimately depends on the production of new ideas, yet a competitive market is unable to offer suitable incentives for the production of such ideas.[2] Patents are not the only mechanism that society has developed to meet this need for new ideas; governments have attempted to promote the production of innovation by means of public subsidies. However, both these instruments give rise to inefficiencies, as we will see below.

The pharmaceutical industry is precisely one of the sectors in which patents have most impact. The general arguments that are formulated on the subject of technical information are fully applicable to the pharmaceutical environment. Thus in Spain, for example, pharmaceuticals are the third sector in terms of investment, behind automobiles and food. The two questions we must ask are: whether there would be less investment and poorer results if patents did not exist, and to what extent results are achieved with the existing patent protection. Nevertheless, these two questions are not easy to answer. Furthermore, the key issue is not the amount invested but rather the return on the invest-ment. Empirical research in the US market has for the most part sought to measure the internal rate of return in the pharmaceutical industry from a finan-cial perspective, and there are few examples of research works that attempt to relate pharmaceutical innovation to improvements in the aggregate health status of a population.[3] Seen in this light, the contribution of pharmaceutical patents should be evaluated as a function of how they have helped to develop new medicines that have improved the health of citizens, and in particular from a perspective of opportunity cost. Unfortunately, studies along these lines are infrequent.

This chapter offers an overview of the role played by technical information in the development of innovation and the necessary incentives for its creation, and at the same time the implications for the pharmaceutical sector. To this end, we present the basis and the significance of the patent system, we offer an analysis of the impact of this system, and lastly we present a reflection on the future of the system and its relationship with the pharmaceutical industry.

INCENTIVES TO INNOVATE

Insofar as information is a good with unique characteristics, which cannot be allocated in a competitive market, whoever possesses information is seeking to obtain an advantage, and a priori is a monopolist. However, owners of infor-mation cannot sell it in an open market, because by doing so they would break their own monopoly, as information can be reproduced at no or very little cost. As a result, information would only be used by whoever first held it, and there would be no possibility of trading in it. In this situation, the development of new ideas and knowledge, which is the driving force of economic growth, would be blocked. Not only would it be socially inefficient but furthermore it would hinder incentives to create new knowledge.[2]

The legal protection of inventions by means of patents is a necessity in order to be able to exert the monopolistic power mentioned above and to provide incentives for its continual creation.

Effective protection requires at the very least reimbursement for innova-tors' development costs, that is, the costs of producing an original innovation which are not incurred again when the innovator produces new units, and which competitors will not incur even in the first unit they produce. An opti-mal protection system should offer additional incentives. It should compensate not only development costs but also the risk involved in innovating, and it should internalize society's preferences for certain types of good. Society values some innovations more than others, and thus reward merely for the risk involved in innovating would be insufficient. The size of this additional reward on top of that corresponding to development costs is an issue that has more to do with politics than with economics. It should also be borne in mind that not all innovations are beneficial. If the development costs of a given innovation exceed its value for society, the patent system should not provide backing for its development, or once it has produced it should not provide compensation for the entirety of its costs.

If we consider that at least development costs should be reimbursed, an efficient protection system will give rise to a set of broad values. Innovations with development costs x would result in compensation amounting to at least x. Once incurred, development costs are irrecoverable; they are sunk costs. Any discontinuity in the relationship between development costs and their reimbursement would give rise to inefficiencies; capital would be attracted to a greater or lesser extent towards certain innovative projects.

All patents create a monopoly, guaranteeing the innovator's exclusive rights to use and sell the innovation for a fixed period of years. The monopoly revenue during this period is what provides the compensation for the initial investment. Ultimately, the market determines the size of the reward.

While the public powers guarantee the monopoly, the consumers determine the final value of the innovation. In order to understand this process we must define four concepts in a competitive market environment:

1. Consumer surplus as the difference between what consumers would be willing to pay for a good and the price they actually pay.
2. Producer surplus as the equivalent concept for the producer. It is the difference between the price and the cost.
3. Social or aggregate surplus as the sum of the consumer surplus and the producer surplus. It is the inherent value of the good, the benefit that society receives from the innovation.
4. Welfare loss means any social value that could be gained in theory but is lost due to the market structure.

In order to estimate the welfare loss we must be able to quote a monopoly price (p_1 in Figure 2.1) and also an estimate of the price as it would have stood had the sector been competitive (p_2 in Figure 2.1). We also need an estimate of the demand curve in order to know what quantity consumers would buy at each price, q_1 when the price is p_1 and q_2 when it is p_2. A monopoly situation involves a shift from B to point A, which causes a welfare loss equivalent to triangle ABC.

Social value is created insofar as an innovation reaches the marketplace, and consumers buy it insofar as it meets their needs. The producers who can manufacture it at a cost that is lower than the price sell it. In a competitive market, this process forces prices down to a point of maximum consumer

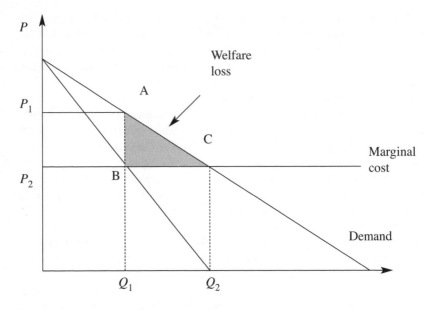

Figure 2.1   Welfare loss of a monopoly

surplus. For producers of innovations, however, this result may not provide sufficient compensation for their development costs. If we introduce patents, this situation changes significantly. Patents, and monopolies in general, turn consumer surplus into producer surplus. Yet the transformation is imperfect, as part of the consumer surplus is lost; in other words, it gives rise to a welfare loss in the terms described above.

Over the years many economists have stated their positions in the debate as to whether patents are the best instrument for resolving the inexistence of a competitive market for technical information. For example, Plant,[4] Breyer[5] and Samuelson[6] form part of a minority who have voiced their opposition to the existing protection mechanisms. These authors consider that patents are unnecessary because in their opinion most creative and inventive activity is carried out aside from financial compensation. They also claim that other mechanisms of legal protection could be applied in order for inventors to benefit from their work before others copy it. For them, the present systems are inefficient because they have been applied across the board to all inventions, whereas such protection is only justified in some cases. A recent example that would support this thesis is the case of the meningitis B vaccine.[7] A group of Cuban researchers developed a highly effective vaccine during the 1980s; it was supplied to the population and the disease practically disappeared. Now, 20 years later, the Western pharmaceutical industry has acquired the licence in order to conduct trials and market the vaccine. In this case the professional incentives to develop the innovation, and not the patent system, were the determining factor in achieving the results.

Levin[8] prepared a survey for research and development R&D heads in which they were asked about the effectiveness of different methods for protecting products and processes: patents, industrial secrecy, rapidity in the learning curve and sales efforts. The results showed that product patents were considered to be more effective than process patents, but in general all the other methods were regarded as more effective than the protection provided by patents, in a general survey that was not addressed to any particular sector.

Thus, if we consider that some sort of protection is necessary, the problem is to find out how to establish it in such a way that the alteration of incentives and of the level of competition is manageable. One of the key issues in achieving this is the length and scope of the patent.

DETERMINING THE PERIOD AND SCOPE OF PROTECTION

The appropriate period for which an invention should be protected is that which allows the recovery of the costs of the innovative activity adjusting for the risk incurred. But this can only be considered in an ideal situation with a single isolated innovation that does not affect other possible innovations and in which the innovation process cannot be speeded up with additional resources. If a shorter period of protection were given instead of this ideal period in ideal conditions, the innovation would not be developed. And if the period were longer, there would be an unnecessary delay in the supply of innovations that would effectively create a welfare loss.

The optimal protection period of a patent is one of the crucial aspects of the debate on this issue. Choosing the right period involves weighing up the benefits of promoting more innovative activity on the one hand and the social costs of delaying the supply of innovations to the marketplace on the other. A system that endows all innovations with the same period of protection (the usual case) actually gives too much protection to some types of innovations and too little to others. An ample level of protection gives rise to efforts in complementary developments that in some cases add very little value and in others originate new ideas. The key, according to some authors, is to attach less importance to the length and concentrate more on the scope of the patent. This approach is built on the fact that not all innovations are equal. There are innovations that 'trigger' new inventions. Therefore, the protection should not be the same. There should be less protection for 'breakthrough' innovations because they encourage the appearance of new innovations that can otherwise be strategically delayed by the main patent holder. The social value of 'breakthrough' innovations is greater the sooner they are made available to other companies in order for them to generate new developments.

Thus, for example, Matutes et al.[9] show in a formal model that in basic or 'breakthrough' innovations, protection on the basis of scope generates higher levels of welfare than period-based protection. The reason for this is that the period in which rivals can introduce applications is shorter and the patent holder can decide when to exert his or her rights. Nevertheless, it is also true that this can accelerate developments that do not generate additional value if the calculation of the reward given to the second-level innovator is excessive. The concept of the right reward for the two types of innovation is not easy to put into practice.

Klemperer[10] and Gilbert and Shapiro[11] follow a similar line. The application of the concept of scope patents in the biotechnology sector is studied by Lerner.[12] According to his estimate, broad patents are more valuable when there are multiple substitutes, which confirms theoretical findings.

The theoretical model devised by Horowitz and Lai[13] is an attempt to summarize the effects of patent length on the rate of innovation and welfare. Greater length is associated with more important or groundbreaking innovations, but also with less frequency of innovation. Finding the patent length that maximizes the rate of innovation and welfare means striking a balance between importance and frequency. From a welfare point of view, the point of equilibrium is to be found in short-duration patents. The duration that maximizes consumers' welfare is shorter than that which maximizes the rate of innovation.

BASIC RESEARCH AS A PUBLIC GOOD

Those inventions that are valuable for society, which include innovative pharmaceuticals, generate positive externalities, that is, the benefits falls to society at large. The sum of these benefits gives the social benefit or value of the invention. In this way, patents represent the appropriation of part of this social value. Naturally, when businesses decide to undertake a project they do so with their own benefit in mind. Some research, particularly basic research, might not be undertaken in these circumstances, and therefore governments decide to invest to fill the gap that may be left by the patent system. Basic research allows the development of multiple applications and the discovery of scientific principles. The field of genetics is a prime example of this.

Basic research can be regarded as a public good; it is difficult to prevent a person from benefiting from it, and the marginal cost of another person enjoying it is zero. Basic research is not patentable, even though private companies

fight for it. And despite the attempt to patent the human genome, the international public consortium was able to publish its content a matter of days before
the private company Celera, which was also struggling to do so. The fact of
basic research being considered a public good would cause private enterprise
to avoid undertaking it, and this would be the justification for public spending
on R&D.

Society as a whole gains from being able to access the knowledge that
arises out of basic research, and in particular it gains more to the extent that
applications are developed. This is why we say that the marginal cost of a
person having access to this knowledge is zero once it has become available.
If basic research were fenced in by a patent it would not allow this access.

PATENTS AND THEIR EFFECTS

The distortions that patents provoke were reviewed recently by Kremer.[14]
Monopoly prices create both static and dynamic distortions. On the one
hand, some consumers will not be able to pay prices that are fixed above the
marginal cost in order to recover the investment in R&D. On the other hand,
potential investors will not necessarily take the consumer surplus into
account when they decide to carry out research projects. The value of a
patent – and in this case of a pharmaceutical – may be very different for
different consumers, but price discrimination is impossible. The industry
may shelve certain projects owing to the lack of a satisfactory return,
because of the difficulty of price discrimination. Kremer even claims that the
welfare loss due to monopoly prices is in the region of a quarter of the sum
of the profits and the consumer surplus. Other authors, such as Güell and
Fischbaum,[15] estimate welfare loss as being around 60 per cent of the sales
figure.

Kremer[16] then went on to make a precise estimate of the social value of an
innovation or surplus under a situation of competition and under a monopoly.
Thus, for example, for a price five times higher than the price fixed according
to the marginal price, we detect a static distortion of 1.5, that is, the social rate
of return of an innovation in a situation with marginal cost prices will be 1.5
times the return on the investment under monopoly prices. In this situation the
social value of an innovation in a competitive environment would be 9.35
times the social value in a monopoly, that is, when there is no welfare loss.
Kremer thus provides an estimate of welfare loss from a more thorough
analytical perspective, and shows that it can be sizeable.

Patents make it difficult to take advantage of positive externalities – by
means of developments of knowledge – and promote negative externalities
through 'patent races'. So, while research provides more knowledge to others,

thus encouraging development, it also gives rise to an excessive incentive to develop substitutes for patented products and too little incentive to create complements. As companies develop substitutes, the revenues of patent holders are eroded.

Cockburn and Henderson[17] showed that the positive externality effect is stronger than the patent race. Although their results are not conclusive and they state clearly that it is impossible to say whether there is an excess or a shortage of research, this is an interesting example of analysis of competition in innovation and its effects on ten major US pharmaceutical corporations.

Thus, we see that the protection of innovation by means of patents affects the costs of innovating in both directions. However, these costs are also affected by the length of the patent. A long protection period increases the reward for the innovator, and encourages his or her activity. Given that many developments are cumulative, some subsequent innovations depending on their predecessors, the result is increased costs for the remainder or a restriction in terms of time.

In 1996, the cost of developing a new pharmaceutical in Spain was estimated at 25 000 million pesetas. Considering that the development period lasts on average 12 years, and that patents are for 20 years, only eight years remain to recover the investment.[18] In the USA, in contrast, it takes only eight years for a drug patent to reach the marketplace, and in 1990 the process cost $126 million.[19] This is one of the issues in the debate that has often raised pleas for patent extension. However, development period patterns are currently undergoing radical changes, and moreover the problem is not so much the patent length as the size of the potential market, the prevalence of the disease. A short patent with a large market may be enough to recover the investment. Thus, the issue of patent length remains open for subsequent analyses.

PATENTS AND THE WORLD TRADE ORGANIZATION (WTO)

At the end of 1993 an agreement was reached on patent protection in the Uruguay round of the General Agreement on Tariffs and Trade (GATT), entitled 'Trade-related aspects of Intellectual Property' (TRIPs). This agreement induced major changes in the level of protection, as a result of pressure by the USA. The main points addressed in the agreement are as follows:

1. All commercial technology areas are considered as patentable technologies. The most important effect of this was precisely in the field of pharmaceuticals, as non-recognition of patents was prohibited.
2. Patents were fixed at 20 years.

3. Patent holders were given the right to ban imports of products that infringe the law.
4. Limits were imposed on the circumstances in which governments can enforce the licensing of patents.

In practice, future development will depend on how the TRIPs agreement is applied. Developing countries have until 2005 to comply to it. As of 2005 they are obliged to accept the patent application for new pharmaceutical products and to guarantee exclusive marketing rights for products obtaining a patent in another GATT country. For the USA it meant the extension of patents in 1994 from 17 to 20 years from the patent application date.

However, the application of this TRIPs agreement is not free of controversy. The opinion has been voiced recently in the scientific community that although patents may stimulate research, they may be counter-productive if taken to an extreme.[20] According to this view, patents are just one of several ways of promoting inventions, and a revision of the TRIPs agreement is sought with the aim of safeguarding access to medicines. Some of the large pharmaceutical corporations admit these difficulties in part, observing that 80 per cent of world production is directed at 20 per cent of the population, and consider that radical solutions are necessary.[21]

THE FUTURE OF PATENT PROTECTION

Patents are not the only option to promote innovation. Systems of research grants awarded by governments have existed for centuries. Such systems enable innovations to reach the public domain, making them accessible for everyone.

A formal comparison between a system of grants or rewards and that of patents was presented recently by Shavell and Ypersele.[22] In their article they present a review of the two systems and the theoretical positions of each of them. They state that under the system of grants, insofar as there would be no welfare loss as a result of monopoly prices, the only deviation from optimal allocation would be in relation to the incentive to invest in research. This incentive can be ambivalent. If the social or aggregate surplus is greater than the reward or grant there will be insufficient incentives, and vice versa. Either of these two possibilities may occur, as the optimal reward is equal to the expected surplus under different demand curves.

On the other hand, under the patent system, incentives to carry out research come from the expected monopoly revenue. This leads to two imperfections. First, the incentives to do research are inadequate, because the monopoly benefits are less than the social surplus generated by the innovation. Second, if the innovation is achieved there is a welfare loss, because a smaller quantity is sold as a result of the monopoly price (as mentioned above).

Shavell and Ypersele focus on a model in which there is a potential innovator who knows the demand curve before investing in research, whereas the government only knows the probability distribution of the demand curves. Although this is a restrictive model, they go on to develop the case for which the government observes the quantity sold ex post, and establish inferences on how the grants could be formulated.

A straightforward comparison between the two systems would show first of all the superiority of the grant system, as the welfare loss due to monopoly prices is diluted. However, the incentives to carry out research are imperfect in both systems, although in a different way. In the patent system they are always inadequate because the monopoly benefits are less than the social surplus. In the grant system, the incentives to invest are not systematically inadequate, as they are related to the reward received rather than to the real surplus.

Nevertheless, as patents safeguard the innovator's private information as to the value of the innovation, incentives to innovate would be greater with patents than with grants. There is no a priori argument to tip the balance towards one alternative or the other. It is necessary to develop a formal model, as proposed by Shavell and Ypersele.

The theoretical conclusion they reach is that the system of grants, or optional grants, especially those related to sales information, is an alternative that represents an improvement on the patent system inasmuch as it allows incentives to be attached to innovation without the need for a monopoly power. Further research will be necessary before this method can be adopted on a practical and experimental level.

Beyond the formal comparison of different methods, Kremer[16] has put forward an original system whereby governments would acquire the patent from its creators at its social value and transfer it to the public domain. The author acknowledges the difficulty of establishing the social value of an innovation, but proposes an invitation to tender to determine the private value of a patent.

The system would work as follows. The holder of the patent would invite tenders from both governments and companies. The government would offer to buy the patent at a higher price than the private value with the aim of reflecting its social value. In order to provide private participants with an incentive to reflect its real value, the awards would go at random to the highest bidder. The patent holders would have the option of accepting or rejecting the government's offer. They could even be allowed to decide if and when the invitation to tender should be made, although the author considers that a period of three to five years would be appropriate.

Kremer proposes sealed-envelope tenders in which the successful bidder is the one offering the second highest price, as this mechanism would best show the bidders' preferences. A great number of key details come into play in order for the mechanism to work correctly, all of which are clearly set out in the article. Issues such as the relationship between substitutes and complements with a patent in private hands, the interrelation with existing patent holders, the size of the margin to pay above the private value, and how to avoid collusion, are also dealt with in the article.

One interesting observation is that this method would not be appropriate for those sectors in which innovators have a sizeable advantage in costs that might even enable them to approach monopoly prices in the absence of patents. In the event of significant market imperfections, or a shortage of bidders, random adjudication might return the patent to the original innovator, who would then be obliged to provide information allowing the estimation of the product's profitability.

Kremer notes that this mechanism would be particularly suitable for experimental application in the pharmaceutical industry. Güell and Fischbaum had proposed a similar but less elaborate mechanism. Their approach assumed the government to have the right to acquire patents. Under this mechanism, adverse effects might be generated for the development of new innovations, whereas Kremer states that the patent holder could sell at a price higher than the private value and close to what would amount to the social value. Furthermore, Kremer's proposal has a different pricing mechanism, and in order to avoid ultimately discretionary behaviour by the government, it includes a carefully designed tendering system. And finally, Kremer provides solutions for complementary and substitute innovations, whereas Güell and Fischbaum did not take this issue into account. In a subsequent article, Güell[23] stressed the importance of negotiation between enterprise and government in order for the proposal to be put into practice, although a number of questions are left unresolved.

Kremer's proposal, like those of Güell and Fischbaum, stands midway between patents and grants.[24] One of the objections raised by *The Economist* to Kremer's proposal is that the government would end up paying more than the consumer surplus and the welfare loss (triangles ABC and pp_1A in Figure 2.1). In the face of this situation, the new method would be clearly detrimental because it would force a tax increase to pay for the patent. Furthermore, the international nature of patents would require the existence of some kind of international coordination, not an easy task to accomplish. We are dealing, therefore, with a theoretical proposal that needs further contributions.

Then there are other proposals that, despite having been developed in other environments, display characteristics that make them relevant in part to the pharmaceutical industry; one such case is Rogerson's.[25] His analysis concentrates on prizes for innovation with contractors in the defence sector. The particularity of his proposal is that it deals with an atypical sector in which the number of suppliers and demanders is highly limited, resulting in situations of bilateral monopoly. As there is a single buyer, the problem of incentives for innovation is particularly acute. Given that companies have private information on potential developments, the existence of prizes for innovation helps to promote development. In many countries the final buyer for the pharmaceutical industry is the government, in that it is the government that finances the drugs. In this sense, the situation described by Rogerson, in which the government is the buyer, is similar to the case of the pharmaceutical industry.

CONCLUSIONS

Patents have contributed to the development of innovation. In spite of the difficulty of estimating the magnitude of its impact, nobody doubts that this is the case. Yet at the same time new questions are now being raised. To what extent might other mechanisms achieve better results? For the time being, this question remains unanswered. Proposals made recently by several authors are still on a theoretical and speculative level. Despite clear indications that revision is necessary, there is no obvious direction in which to work.

Over the last two decades, patents have played an increasingly important role in international trade and the protection they afford has been extended. Yet parallel to this, economic research on the impact of patents has been emphasizing that this is only one of the mechanisms for encouraging innovation. Furthermore, the extension of patent protection in publicly funded research is bearing fruit.

Pharmaceutical innovation has made a decisive contribution to the reduction of mortality and the improvement of quality of life. The role of patents in providing incentives for innovation has been crucial. Yet at the same time there are limitations that need to be overcome in the future. Here we will mention just two examples: orphan drugs and parallel imports. Patents do not offer incentives to develop drugs for low-prevalence diseases, known as orphan drugs. Governments are sometimes faced with the option of public production, as the private sector does not invest in them. Yet these would be precisely the cases in which experiments would be conducted with new models for promoting innovation, as discussed in this chapter.

The case of parallel imports presents a serious challenge for many governments, in that patent protection is unequal between countries, a fact that gives rise to trade between countries that fails to respect the necessary protection to provide incentives for innovation. The standardization of patent systems has become a priority for the WTO. The EU has published the Green Paper on Patents, in an attempt to contribute towards the development of a homogeneous system beyond the advances achieved to date.

Development in the field of genetics and biotechnology are adding further complexity to the mechanism of patents. The role to be played by new drugs and biochips may spell a radical change in the patent system, pharmaceutical prices and public financing as we have known them until now.[26] Governments will be faced with a new reality in which a limited number of suppliers may contribute significantly to the health of citizens by means of personalized solutions. The role of the market and competition will be completely different from what we have seen up to now. While we await this evolution, we need the patent system to be effective and the necessary improvements to be implemented without delay.

REFERENCES

1. Arrow, K.J. (1996), 'Technical information and industrial structure', *Industrial and Corporate Change* 5, pp. 645–52.
2. Arrow, K.J. (1962), 'Economic welfare and the allocation of resources for inventions', in R.R. Nelson (ed.), *The Rate and Direction of Inventive Activity*, Princeton: Princeton University Press.
3. Grabowski, H.G. and J.H. Vernon (1994), 'Return to R&D on new introductions in the 1980s', *Journal of Health Economics*, 13, pp. 383–406.
4. Plant, A. (1934), 'The economic theory concerning patents for inventions', *Economic NS*, 1, 30–51, reprinted in A. Plant (1974), *Selected Economic Essays and Addresses*, London: Routledge & Kegan Paul, pp. 35–56.
5. Breyer, S. (1970), 'The uneasy case for copyright: a study of copyright in books, photocopies and computer programs', *Harvard Law Review*, 84, pp. 281–351.
6. Samuelson, P. (1984), 'CONTU revisited: the case against copyright protection for computer programs in machine readable form', *Duke Law Journal*, pp. 663–769.
7. *The Financial Times* (2001), 'Cuba's medical revolution', *The Financial Times*, 13–14 January, p. 10.
8. Levin, R.C. et al. (1987), 'Appropriating the return from industrial research and development', *Brookings Papers on Economic Activity*, 3, pp. 783–820.
9. Matutes, C., P. Regibeau and K. Rockett (1996), 'Optimal patent design and the diffusion of innovations', *Rand Journal of Economics*, 27, pp. 60–83.
10. Klemperer, P. (1990), 'How broad should the scope of patent protection be?', *Rand Journal of Economics*, 21, pp. 113–30.
11. Gilbert, R. and C. Shapiro (1990), 'Optimal patent length and breath', *Rand Journal of Economics*, 21, pp. 106–12.
12. Lerner, J. (1994), 'The importance of patent scope: an empirical analysis', *Rand Journal of Economics*, 25, pp. 319–25.
13. Horowitz, A. and E. Lai (1996) 'Patent length and the rate of innovation', *International Economic Review*, 37, pp. 785–801.

14. Kremer, M. (1997), 'Patent buy-outs: a mechanism for encouraging innovation', *Cambridge: National Bureau of Economic Research (NBER), working paper no 6304.*
15. Güell, R.C. and M. Fischbaum (1996) 'Toward allocative efficiency in the prescription drug industry', *The Milbank Quarterly,* 73, pp. 213–30.
16. Kremer, M. (1997), 'A mechanism for encouraging innovation', *Massachusetts Institute of Technology, NBER working paper no 6304.*
17. Cockburn, I. and R. Henderson (1994), 'Racing to invest? Dynamics of competition in ethical drug discovery', *Journal of Economics and Management Strategy,* 3, pp. 481–519.
18. *El País* (1996), 'Poner en la calle un nuevo medicamento cuesta en España 25.000 millones de pesetas', *El País,* 22 October, p. 29.
19. Dimasi, J. (1991), 'Cost of innovation in the pharmaceutical industry', *Journal of Health Economics,* 10, pp. 107–42.
20. *The Financial Times* (2001), 'Strong global patent rules increase the cost of medicines', *The Financial Times,* 14 February, p. 20.
21. *The Financial Times* (2001), 'Patents and patients', *The Financial Times,* 17 February.
22. Shavell, S. and T. Ypersele (1999), 'Rewards versus intellectual property rights', *Cambridge: NBER working paper no 6956.*
23. Güell, R.C. (1997), 'Haggling for a patent: what a government would have to pay for prescription drug patents', *Health Economics,* 6, pp. 179–85.
24. *The Economist* (1996), 'A patent cure all', *The Economist,* 15 June, p. 93.
25. Rogerson, W.P. (1987), 'Profit regulation of defense contractors and prizes for innovation', *Journal of Political Economy,* 97, pp. 1284–395.
26. *The Economist* (1998), 'The alchemists', *The Economist,* 21 February, p. 18.

3. Price regulation systems in the pharmaceutical market

J. Puig-Junoy

INTRODUCTION

Three submarkets of the pharmaceutical market can be distinguished: innovative patented products sold by prescription, products whose patent has expired and are sold by prescription, and products sold without a prescription. The public regulation of prices in the first of these submarkets, and often also in the second, is a fact that can be observed in most Western countries, with certain notable exceptions such as the USA. Concern about the particular characteristics of the pharmaceutical market (for example, the existence of patents and the pharmaceutical industry's rate of return), together with the desire to provide the majority of the population with access to medicines, regardless of their ability to pay (in many countries the public sector is the main buyer in this market), has led to the fairly widespread adoption of more or less strict price intervention and control policies for pharmaceuticals.

Our aim in this chapter is to analyse the effects of price regulation of prescription drugs. First, we review the reasons traditionally given to justify price control policies from the viewpoint of economic theory. Then we describe the price control systems used in Europe, and particularly in Spain. This is followed by an analysis of the main advantages and disadvantages of the systems of direct price fixing, rate of return regulation and price-cap regulation, and they are compared with the optimal prices. Finally, we take a look at the prospects for deregulation and the encouragement of competition in the pharmaceutical sector by making price control systems more flexible. Interest in the last of these is striking in a context in which the pharmaceutical sector of some European Union (EU) countries, Spain foremost among them, stands as one of the few areas of the economy that is unaffected by processes of deregulation and liberalization.

From the theoretical viewpoint it is useful to separate price regulation and control systems from public reimbursement policies for pharmaceuticals. Strictly speaking, the pharmaceutical reimbursement policies adopted by most public funders as public spending containment policies (for example, the adoption of reference pricing systems) should be distinguished from the regulation of pharmaceutical prices as a whole in each country. However, in practice, when we are dealing with health systems whose public funder is the main buyer in the pharmaceutical market, as in the Spanish case, obviously the distinction between price regulation and the establishment of reimbursement levels is much less clear-cut, and a considerable amount of mutual interaction occurs. This chapter focuses exclusively on the price regulation and control systems that affect the pharmaceutical market as a whole, regardless of who finances or buys the drugs. Chapter 6 of this book deals with the analysis of reference pricing systems as a pharmaceutical reimbursement mechanism.

(UN)JUSTIFICATION OF PRICE REGULATION

There is a long-standing habit in the health economics literature of supporting the need to regulate health care services in market failures such as information asymmetries, complexity and uncertainty, indivisibilities and externalities. These imperfections are also present in the market of a resource that is very important in the health service production process: pharmaceutical products. However, the pharmaceutical market also presents certain specific characteristics that are of particular importance and have been used as arguments in favour of the need to adopt public policies of price intervention and regulation.

Even in an ideal situation in which the doctor is a perfect agent for the patient, the need to regulate prices in the pharmaceutical market may arise from insufficient or very weak competition owing to the temporary market power of the manufacturers, the oligopolistic nature of many therapeutic submarkets, low elasticity of demand and imperfect prescriber information.[1]

The development of a new product requires an ever greater investment in research and development (R&D), which once made represents a sunk cost and furthermore yields an ex-ante return with a high degree of variability and uncertainty. Once the innovation has been developed, the knowledge it contains becomes a 'public good', and can be imitated by competitors at a low marginal cost without the need to bear the sunk costs. The patenting of new products grants a temporary (power of) 'monopoly' for the marketing of the innovation, and represents a second-best solution that is intended to reduce the profit of the imitators and increase that of the innovator, as without the prospect of recovering costs, the incentive to make the initial investment vanishes.

The heavy investment in R&D, together with the increase in the development cost of a new product as the result of the restrictions introduced by the regulation system as regards safety and effectiveness, make for a 'high degree of concentration' in the sector, as these factors act as barriers to entry. The exploitation of economies of scale and scope in the competition for innovation, in combination with the effort required for product differentiation through brands, contributes still further to the trend towards market concentration. This may lead to the creation of 'oligopolistic markets' even in products whose patent has expired. The barriers raised by regulation aimed at effectiveness and safety (for example, the high cost of obtaining a marketing authorization) are a force for the imposition of barriers to entry.

Generally it can be observed that 'price elasticity' is low, a trend that is aggravated by the fact that in most health systems the consumer does not pay the totality of the price. Some authors state that the elasticity of substitution between medicines in different therapeutic groups can be almost nil. The existence of insurance is an incentive for greater consumption and facilitates the application of higher prices (moral hazard).

The number of drugs available is so great and changes so rapidly that few prescribing doctors – the agents who make decisions on behalf of the consumer – are familiar with all the alternatives and the therapeutic value of each of them ('imperfect information'). In this situation, the manufacturers' promotion activities are almost the only information source for the prescribers, and as such can be very profitable (high marginal benefit), especially if the system of financing allows companies to recover their costs (low marginal cost of commercial promotion activities) by transferring them to prices.

The aim of price regulation should be to contribute to an increase in productive and economic efficiency (improvement in welfare), taking into account the conflict of objectives that exists in this market between a moderate price level, which would supposedly improve the consumer surplus (partly at the expense of the manufacturer), and a delay in technical progress, which would limit the availability of innovations providing an improvement in health status, given that R&D is privately financed. The answer lies in assessing in each case whether the effects of a particular price moderation on the consumer surplus and the manufacturer are greater or lesser than the expected gain of the new products. The comparison of these two factors may yield different results in different countries, depending on the influence of national policy on the innovatory activity carried out by industry operating in the country concerned. In practice, regulating pharmaceutical prices means, in all countries, striking a constant balance between health, industrial, employment and public spending objectives.

Despite the existence of direct and indirect mechanisms for pharmaceutical price regulation in most countries, some authors put forward reasons for a growing opposition to the need to regulate prices.[2,3] The discussion on the possible lack of justification for drug price regulation policies to improve welfare can be built on three types of argument, which it is important to understand.

First, the pharmaceutical market failures mentioned above may be empirically inconsequential, which may either render their regulation unnecessary or make it advisable to use more flexible price control policies. For example, justifications for regulation that are based on the virtual absence of competition seem weak when one observes markets with products whose patent has expired. When a patent expires barriers to entry should disappear, since the composition of the active ingredient becomes public, and other companies should not have too many problems to reproduce the production process. The reasons brandished for price regulation when any company can manufacture a generic to compete with the brand product find no justification in theory.

During the period in which a product is protected by a patent, it is not necessarily true to say that the pharmaceutical has a single supplier. The competition exerted by new products that appear in the same therapeutic group and for the same purpose are making the period in which the innovator has no competitor increasingly brief (Calfee[2] presents examples of this cutback in some recent innovations), and the level of competition in the market of patented products can be faster and greater than is often supposed. The greater the incidence of this situation, the greater the difficulties encountered by the initial innovator to maintain monopoly prices.

Some empirical observations are significant in this respect. For example, the demand for brand products is fairly sensitive to the price of generics, and even in some cases to the price of brand name therapeutic substitutes. In an estimate of the parameters of the demand function of brand products and generics in the cephalosporin submarket in the USA, a high price elasticity was observed between brand products and generics, and also in some cases, although to a lesser extent, between therapeutic substitutes.[4]

However, the situation most commonly recognized is that competition in the market of patented prescription drugs is insufficient to produce an optimum level of information or an optimum level of welfare, which makes it necessary to establish some form of regulation. However, price regulation in the markets of non-prescription drugs and drugs whose patent has expired lacks theoretical justification.

Second, the effects of pharmaceutical market failures could be attenuated or mitigated more effectively by means of other types of strategies, such as encouraging competition or the production and dissemination of information on the effectiveness of the medicines, which would be compatible with the existence of a market with non-regulated prices. Thus, for example, the problems of imperfect information can be offset by implementing suitable information policies based on the cost-effectiveness ratio of the drugs and appropriate prescriber incentives, which should not have a negative effect on incentives to innovate, as is the case with price control. Alternatively, demand sensitivity to pharmaceutical prices (price elasticity) could be increased through cost-sharing policies (insurance reduction). In these cases, from the viewpoint of social welfare, the costs and benefits of these measures should be compared with those resulting from price control. The balance of the effects on social welfare can only be established empirically, and the institutional characteristics of each health system are very likely to have a notable influence on this aspect; consequently, the solution cannot be found in universal remedies.

The basic underlying idea of this second line of criticism against price regulation is built on the potential improvement in social welfare that can be provided by measures which, instead of taking for granted that competition is insufficient, actually attempt to increase it. According to this approach, it is not a question of getting rid of regulation but of changing the type of regulatory instrument: less direct intervention in pricing and more dissemination of information on the cost-effectiveness ratio of medicines, or appropriate incentives for patients and prescribers to reduce moral hazard, for example.

And third, given that regulatory intervention generates both benefits and costs, the benefits of price control might be more than cancelled out (welfare loss) by its costs in the form of administrative costs, transaction costs and distortions in incentives derived from the regulation itself.[5] The costs of an imperfect market cannot be compared with those of a perfect one, and pharmaceutical price regulation failures must be taken into account.

In countries where public insurers act as monopsonistic buyers of pharmaceuticals, the price regulation established in the national sphere can result in considerable distortion owing to the significant presence of general sunk costs spread over several countries (R&D). The minimization of the insurer's expenditure may favour the adoption of restrictive price regulation policies allowing the coverage of marginal costs (around 30 per cent of the total cost), and it is taken for granted that someone else will bear the financing of the joint costs (free-rider behaviour). The welfare loss may be caused by the fact that the monopsonist pushes national prices down to the short-term marginal cost, which is insufficient to finance the costs of investment and development (sunk and joint costs). The result of this in the long term can be a poorer (suboptimal) supply of pharmaceutical innovations than is socially desirable.[6,7] Empirical and theoretical analysis of the effects of the price regulation instruments and systems used in the international sphere may offer some useful indications in order to value the contribution of these systems to the improvement of social welfare in the short and the long term.

INTERNATIONAL EXPERIENCE IN PRICE REGULATION

The regulation of drug prices is an instrument that is used in all the countries of the European Union (EU), although in different modes. Table 3.1 shows the

The public financing of pharmaceuticals

Table 3.1 Main forms of price regulation in EU countries in 1997

Country	Price regulation mechanism
Austria	Cost-based prices
Belgium	Prices based on the improvement over existing therapeutic alternatives
Denmark	Free prices and reference pricing that excludes most patented products
Finland	Regulated prices
France	Prices established according to effectiveness and negotiation with each manufacturer
Germany	Free prices and reference pricing that excludes most patented products
Greece	Prices based on cost, transfer price and lowest EU price
Ireland	Danish, French, German, Dutch and UK prices
Italy	Average prices of Germany, Spain, France and the UK, and reference pricing (RP) (proposal)
Luxembourg	Belgian prices, free pricing if no price in Belgium
Netherlands	Price caps equivalent to the average for Belgium, France, Germany and the UK, and RP
Portugal	Lowest price between Spain, France and Italy
Spain	Cost-based prices
Sweden	Negotiated prices and RP that excludes patented products
UK	Rate of return regulation

Source: Mossialos.[9]

various types of price regulation mechanisms at work in Europe, from prices based on the cost of each product to free prices combined with a restriction on the rate of return or with reference prices set by the public sector as the main buyer, and including indexing with the prices of other European countries (price regulation based on cross-national comparisons). Despite the importance attached to price regulation, expenditure per person bears no direct relation with pharmaceutical price levels, which highlights the key role played by demand-related factors in determining expenditure. For example, the relative price in Germany is 2.4 times that of France, whereas expenditure per capita is only 20 per cent higher.[8]

In all EU countries except Germany and Denmark, some form of regulation or intervention in the individual prices of medicines is used as the principal cost containment policy, ranging from systems that fix the price of each product to profit control systems (as in the UK). Price regulation systems are complemented with other measures of a regulatory nature that are related to the public reimbursement systems that are superimposed on them. Some of the more important complementary regulatory measures are across-the-board price cuts or freezes, agreements on limits to total spending, 'voluntary' contributions from industry, control of promotion expenses and so on.

In general terms, international experience in pharmaceutical price regulation enables us to discern two groups of regulation systems: profit control systems and individual price fixing systems. Pricing is free in few countries, although these include some major pharmaceutical markets such as the USA, Germany and Denmark. In the Organization for Economic Co-operation and Development (OECD), individual price fixing systems are applied in Australia, Austria, Belgium, Finland, France, Greece, Hungary, Italy, Japan, Korea, Mexico, Norway, Spain, Sweden and Switzerland.

The criteria used to fix the individual prices of drugs in each country that opts for this type of system are various: the therapeutic value of new products, the cost of comparable treatment, the manufacturer's contribution to the national economy and the observed price in other countries. Table 3.2 shows a comparison of the use of these criteria in several OECD countries according to the answers given to a survey carried out in each country. As can be seen from the table, all the countries that responded to the survey acknowledge use of the comparison of authorized prices in other countries as a price-setting criterion.

Individual prices should be fixed on the basis of a price adjusted according to the milligrams or defined daily dose of each active ingredient, as otherwise strategic changes are induced in the number of units per presentation, the concentration and so on.

The drug price intervention system in place in Spain since 1991 is based on the fixing of the price of each product by the health authorities, calculated according to its 'cost'. This system allows for the possibility of excluding certain products or therapeutic groups from the price intervention system. It would be desirable to apply this exclusion principle to those products that are subject to a reasonable level of competition. Briefly, the main features of the Spanish system of price regulation are as follows:

1. The price of each product is calculated by means of the analytical application of the overall cost including the totality of expenditure on R&D, and incorporating the distribution of commercial and administrative expenses (cost control).
2. The profit on each product is set as a percentage of trading capital of between 12 per cent and 18 per cent depending on the therapeutic use and the cost of alternative treatment (profit control).

Table 3.2   Criteria used in the price regulation of pharmaceuticals in the OECD

Country	Therapeutic value	Cost of comparable treatment	Contribution to the national economy	Price in other countries
Australia	YES	YES	YES	YES
Austria				YES
Belgium	YES	YES	YES	YES
Canada		YES		YES
Czech Republic	YES	YES		YES
Finland	YES	YES		YES
France	YES	YES		YES
Greece				YES
Hungary	YES	YES	YES	YES
Italy				YES
Japan	YES	YES		YES
Korea	YES	YES	YES	YES
Luxembourg				YES
Mexico				YES
Netherlands				YES
Norway	YES	YES		YES
Spain	YES	YES	YES	YES
Sweden	YES	YES		YES
Switzerland	YES	YES		YES
Turkey	YES	YES	YES	YES

Source: Jacobzone.[10]

3.   For advertising and commercial promotion costs that can affect the price of each product, a band is established that ranges from 12 per cent to 16 per cent.

The application of the price control system and the restrictive criteria applied to its revisions together account for the fact that pharmaceuticals have a lower unit price in Spain than anywhere else in Europe. The evolution of sales and public spending have been strongly influenced by the increase in consumption and the launching of new products at higher prices, together with a consumer shift towards higher prices. This situation has led the health authorities to apply other measures on the supply side, parallel to price control, such as agreements with Farmaindustria to limit the annual growth of Social

Security spending. The pharmaceutical industry committed itself to return to the health authorities each year the totality of the gross margin on sales over the allowed growth limit. In exchange, for example, the 1995 agreement guaranteed the industry a price increase for products priced below 300 pesetas (less than €2) and the liberalization of the price of products excluded from public financing.

The main drawbacks to this price regulation system can be summed up as follows:

- A product-by-product profit control system does not allow the control of the company's overall profit, as the average cost depends on the size of the fixed costs and the volume of units sold over time.
- The acute information asymmetry between regulator and companies generates high transaction costs and undermines the usefulness of the whole system, since 'the preparation and presentation of the corresponding costing reports is little more than a ritual'.[11] As a result of this the price is fixed in negotiations that are far removed from transparent, objective criteria,[12] and this high degree of discretionality works in favour of the 'capture' of the regulator by the interests of the regulated.
- The system provides no incentive for cost reduction, as it generously allows expenses incurred through advertising and promotion, or inefficiently managed R&D programmes, to be transferred to prices. Furthermore, the system allows more expensive products to transfer more advertising and promotion expenses to prices.
- The arbitrary restrictions placed on price growth have encouraged an increase in quantities and a shift in consumption towards new, more expensive products, which nevertheless have little added therapeutic value over those already on the market.

PRICE REGULATION SYSTEMS AND OPTIMAL PRICES

The first issue raised by the analysis of the price regulation systems employed internationally from a theoretical viewpoint is that no objective method seems to exist for establishing the 'true' price of a drug on the basis of its average cost.[9] This impossibility, already mentioned in passing in our discussion of the Spanish system of price intervention, is attributable to the significant presence of shared costs in drug production (capital costs, overheads, R&D, promotion expenses) and the fact that the average cost depends on the level of sales because of the importance of the fixed costs.

It is interesting to note that most price regulation systems for new products that are applied in the EU acknowledge either explicitly (criteria or norms used to regulate) or implicitly (practical criteria of application) the use of other criteria complementary to that of average cost (degree of innovation, advantage over existing treatment, comparison with prices in other countries and so on).

The optimal funding of the fixed and sunk costs represented by R&D does not require the imposition of uniform prices in all markets; on the contrary, price differentiation is advisable to maximize welfare. In order to maximize the consumer's welfare, optimal pricing in the presence of heavy fixed costs requires the application of prices that include a contribution to the financing of these costs (above the marginal cost) inversely related to the sensitivity of the consumers to price changes (elasticity of demand). This is what is known as the Ramsey criterion on optimal prices. According to this criterion (see discussion in Chapter 5) uniform pricing on an international scale is not the most efficient solution. Welfare losses attributable to the necessary financing of fixed costs by consumer prices are minimized by applying higher prices when demand is more inelastic (less sensitive to prices) and vice versa.

The implication of economic theory for price regulation is clear in this case: policies that tend to force international prices to converge (price regulation based on comparisons between countries or parallel imports) are likely to reduce welfare in the long run. The level of R&D that can be financed would be lower with uniform prices than with Ramsey prices.[6,13]

Leaving aside those European countries where pricing is free, namely Germany and Denmark, it can be seen that among Europe's price regulation systems, regulation is most commonly based on the analysis of the cost of the products. This mechanism can be interpreted as a particular case and an imperfect approximation, and is considerably more restrictive than the traditional mechanism of rate of return regulation (RORR), which is explicitly adopted only in the UK, for products sold to the National Health Service (NHS) (excluding generics), since unlike RORR it prevents price flexibility. The system used in the UK is applied to the pharmaceutical industry as a whole rather than to the price of each product, which can be fixed freely within the limits established by the regulation system.

Economic theory on price regulation in public services with market power considers two alternatives: (RORR) and price-cap regulation (PCR). The following two sections of this chapter deal with the advantages and disadvantages of these two forms of regulation as applied to the pharmaceutical sector.[14]

RORR

RORR is a mechanism that is based on cost recovery in which the regulator determines an expected level of income on the basis of the company's total costs. These are calculated as the sum of the costs allocable to the period plus the yield of the 'fair' rate of return, which is set by the regulator as the current non-amortized value of the capital invested, including R&D costs. Prices are fixed freely by the company within the general restriction imposed on the rate of return. The problems encountered in this form of regulation, which has been traditionally been used to regulate public services, have been widely discussed in the literature, and in recent years there has been a gradual shift towards forms of regulation that incorporate incentives. Briefly, the main drawbacks to RORR are as follows:

1. Cost recovery 'removes incentives for production efficiency': every penny of additional spending (for example, on advertising and commercial promotion) increases the restriction by one penny.
2. If the 'fair' rate of return is greater than the capital cost, a bias is generated in the use of resources in favour of capital (for example, 'overinvestment in R&D') that leads to the use of an inefficient combination of resources (Averch–Johnson effect). This overinvestment can be attractive to the regulator, which attaches much value to the goals of industrial policy and employment.
3. The information requirements to establish 'justified' costs in certain items such as R&D and advertising and promotion are numerous, as a result of which the administrative costs of the regulation system can be high, given the existence of information asymmetry between regulator and regulated.
4. When the company makes some of its products for a regulated market (products with a patent in force) and some for a competitive market (for example, generic drugs), incentives exist to assign a larger proportion of the 'shared' and/or non-separable costs to the products for the regulated market and consequently to bring about an inefficient increase in the quantity of the product for the competitive market, establishing a price that is below the marginal cost. The result is that the price level of the patented products (which are introduced more recently) will be higher.

The rate of return regulation system applied in the UK since the 1960s, the Pharmaceutical Price Regulation Scheme or PPRS, limits the rate of return on capital used by laboratories in the production of medicines administered to the population through pharmacies on prescription by NHS doctors, with the exception of generics since 1986. The calculation of justified costs is based on two components: (a) costs assigned directly to NHS sales, with limits to the proportion of promotion and R&D expenses, and (b) allocation of common costs, which comprise general and administrative costs and capital costs assigned to sales to the NHS. One evaluation of the UK system of price regulation[17] suggests that: (a) it has had little effectiveness as far as the goal of influencing pharmaceutical price formation is concerned, (b) it has facilitated price rises in markets less subject to competition, and the expansion of companies into competitive submarkets subject to regulation, and (c) it has been useful as a policy for promoting UK-based pharmaceutical companies on international markets.

The scheme applied in the UK suffers from certain defects that can cause major inefficiency problems.[9,15,16,17,18] Among these problems, the following are particularly important:

- It encourages unnecessary spending (inefficiency is rewarded); in this way, incentives for all R&D investment to be really productive disappear.
- Inefficient companies can solve their problems by asking for price rises.
- Problems of arbitrary cost allocation arise owing to joint production for markets worldwide.
- Cross-subsidies occur, as the company is given incentives to expand its production activity even in low-profit productions (for example, producing brand name generics), as it can recover the authorized rate of return for the entirety of the capital invested.
- Action is taken to return the excess profit only when it is 25 per cent above the threshold set by the regulation scheme.
- It can favour large corporations with many R&D projects, providing them with greater possibilities of recovering the costs of products that fail to reach the market or do not achieve a large market share.
- Distortions occur on the capital market, as the market value of companies that operate under this regulation scheme is not an indicator for the efficient allocation of capital between companies.

The fixing of a controlled price for each product rules out flexibility in the fixing of individual prices by the company under RORR. The aim of this would appear to be to restrict the profit obtained by the company and to block strategies of transferring common costs to products on less competitive markets. Really, this is no more than a pseudo-regulation of the company's overall rate of return, since in the presence of high fixed costs, this regulation depends on the average cost, which is a function of the estimated demand in the future, about which there is uncertainty. It is not surprising that, as the market penetration of the product increases, the regulator should attempt to restrict subsequent price revisions. This reaction by the regulator creates an incentive for the company to introduce new products at higher prices, even if the therapeutic improvement they represent is only marginal. In addition, the problem of allocating common costs to each product is identical to that observed in the case of RORR, given the acute information asymmetry between the regulator and the company as regards justifiable costs. Individual price authorization does, however, seem to have been a useful instrument for protecting the interests of domestic industries.

PCR AND MIXED SYSTEMS

PCR is a form of price regulation that limits the profit maximization behaviour of the company by placing a restriction on the growth rate of a composite price index. Thus, the formula allows ample flexibility; as long as the overall restriction is respected, some prices can grow considerably more than the pre-fixed rate, while others can undergo notably less growth. This form of regulation is based on four basic features:

1. The regulator establishes the maximum price level that the regulated company can fix, with flexibility of prices below that level.
2. This price cap is established in the form of a price index for a set (or a series of subsets) of the services offered by the regulated company, excluding those offered on competitive markets (for example, generics).
3. The price index is adjusted periodically according to an adjustment factor that is pre-established and exogenous to the company during the lifetime of the regulatory contract, but can be established on the basis of the fulfilment of certain policies by the company in the previous period (for example, R&D policies, limits on spending on advertising and promotion and so on).
4. The system is revised at intervals of several years, sometimes involving a general change in the products included and the adjustment factor.

PCR shows some advantages over the traditional cost recovery of RORR, in particular the following:

1. Re-establishment of the incentive to minimize costs and to adopt cost-cutting innovations.
2. Efficient use of resources, as the inefficient bias in the combination of resources is removed.
3. It is simpler than RORR and less manipulable than individual price control, and therefore generates lower transaction costs.

The production efficiency properties of PCR are complemented by its allocation efficiency, as under certain restrictive conditions, the resulting price structure can in the long term converge with that of Ramsey prices, that is, it provides a solution to a problem of consumer surplus maximization subject to a given level of producer surplus. Furthermore, the use of the PCR system with a 'basket' of products is more efficient than fixing individual prices, as it reduces or removes the need to allocate fixed costs among different products.

Most of the problems attributed to the implementation of the PCR system lie with its implications in a dynamic environment: what products to include in the basket for regulation, how to fix the initial price of the products, how to set the value of the adjustment factor and how often to revise it and so on. In connection with this, despite the theoretical superiority of PCR over RORR, some conditions of the pharmaceutical market may affect the implementation of PCR: (a) major variations in costs, technology and demand can only be forecast with a high degree of uncertainty, (b) the regulator needs to be watchful that cost reductions are transferred to the prices paid by the user (public financing), and (c) investments in R&D, which have a long and uncertain payback period, are of great importance in the cost structure.

An evaluation of the effects of the legislative proposals in the USA to apply PCR-type restrictions to the price growth rate of the pharmaceutical sector revealed two main drawbacks:[19]

1. The behaviour of the company will consist in applying price increases to products with a faster-growing and more inelastic demand (new products) and price cuts to products with a decreasing and more elastic demand owing to increasing competition or obsolescence.
2. PCR regulation does not restrict the price of new products, so the initial price of the product introduced onto the market will be higher than in the absence of regulation. In the simulation carried out by Abbott[19] the initial price can be seen to be higher under PCR than with free pricing in the first years. The effect on welfare is very sensitive to the social and private discount rate.

Why does the price flexibility of drugs that are already on the market at the beginning of the regulatory contract represent a problem, when in other markets it is seen as an advantage? PCR is equivalent to maximizing company profits under a restriction on consumer surplus, and therefore price variations from the initial level do not involve a loss of consumer surplus, as long as average variation of each price, weighted by the quantity of that product, is nil or negative. However, in the pharmaceutical market the condition that marginal price variations under PCR cannot reduce the aggregate consumer surplus is not always fulfilled, since the agency relationship between the prescribing doctor and the patient is incomplete and the doctor has imperfect information on the marginal therapeutic value of each product. Neither does the individualized control of the growth rate of the price of each product provide an efficient solution, as it means eliminating the flexibility without providing the regulator with obvious information advantages to support its superiority; it amounts to a return to RORR and the discretionality of a product-by-product price control system.

Fixing the initial price of a product is recognized as one of the problems of implementing PCR in any sector of the economy,[20] and can lead to inefficiently high prices. The issue of the right initial price to put on a new drug in growing demand still lacks an explicit solution in the PCR framework, just as it does under RORR, and this is probably the main disadvantage of drug price regulation systems in the face of the extremely dynamic and volatile nature of the sector. The only feasible answer is to use specific mechanisms for initial price fixing that take into account additional information on the opportunity cost of each therapeutic innovation, such as that provided by the economic evaluation of pharmaceuticals.

The theoretical and practical features of PCR and the specific problems involved in its possible application to the pharmaceutical market lead to the following recommendable courses of action:

1. PCR should be removed from all products that are subject to competition, whether they be generics or therapeutic substitutes for which reasonable elasticity can be expected.
2. Initial product prices should be established ambitiously in order to maximize the incentive to improve productivity and use economic evaluation information in negotiations.
3. A reference inflation index for the pricing of products already on the market should be defined or established as a reference for price regulation.
4. Expected sales should be used to calculate the weighting of each product in the 'basket' for regulation, rather than observed sales for the year before the fixing of the regulation mechanism.
5. Given the volatile nature of the market, the regulatory periods should not be excessively long.
6. A profit-sharing mechanism should be included, when the rate of return exceeds a particular level at the end of the regulatory period. The company would be entitled to keep all the profits obtained under price flexibility if the rate of return is below a given threshold; above that level the company would keep a decreasing proportion of the profit.
7. The results of economic evaluation studies should be used as the most relevant information for establishing the initial price of products.

EFFECTS OF REGULATION SYSTEMS ON CONSUMPTION, PRICE LEVELS AND SPENDING

In this section we analyse the effects of price regulation and control systems in pharmaceutical markets on levels of consumption, the level and evolution of prices and levels of expenditure.

It has been observed in many European countries that the main cause of growth in spending on pharmaceuticals can be traced to the appearance and diffusion of new, higher-priced products. Most price regulation and control systems do not appear to have been very effective at containing growth in spending, even though they have been effective at controlling unit prices, unless combined with other measures. In other words, as is to be expected, prices appear to be lower in countries where prices are regulated individually, yet these very systems create incentives to shift consumption towards more expensive products and/or an increase in the quantity consumed.

In order to determine whether or not the growth in pharmaceutical expenditure entails an increase in the price of the resources used in health production, the important factor to determine is the significance or otherwise of the innovation and its marginal contribution to health production. The large number of new products in some markets, such as Spain, Italy and Germany that provide a very small degree of innovation may constitute an indication of increasing prices rather than an increase in value (contribution to the improvement of health status and welfare).

One study on the evolution of Spanish public pharmaceutical expenditure[21] concludes that spending on pharmaceuticals rose 264 per cent in real terms from 1980 to 1996. This figure can be broken down into a 39 per cent decrease in the relative price of medicines, a 10 per cent increase in the quantity and a variation of 442 per cent explained by a residual that reflects the effect of the introduction of new products and a shift in consumption. As we can see from these figures, we have no practical price index and no quantitative approximation to the breakdown of the increase in expenditure into price and quality.

The comparison of drug prices in different countries has commonly been used to support the need for price regulation, as it has been observed that the highest price levels are to be found in countries where pricing is free. This observation is fairly disputable for several reasons, particularly methodological ones concerning the construction of the price indexes on which the comparisons are based (see Chapter 1). Aside from these problems, which urge caution in the interpretation of comparisons, international price differences are smaller than expected. Three groups of countries can be identified in the OECD:[10]

- Countries with higher prices: USA, Germany and Switzerland.
- Countries with intermediate prices: UK, Australia and Canada.
- Countries with lower prices: Spain, Portugal, Greece and Japan.

On analysing the price variations of particular products in EU countries it has been observed that there are large differences. For example, taking the overall EU average as a value of 100 in 1993, France had a rating of 63.4, while the Netherlands stood at the upper extreme with a rating of 148.4.[22] It is interesting to note that Spain, traditionally regarded as a country with low prices, is fast approaching the European average: its rating rose from 71.6 in 1988 (taking the EU average as 100) to 93.5 in 1993.

Price differences between countries owing to regulation and control systems create incentives for parallel trade of pharmaceutical products, whereby drugs from a country with low prices are imported into other countries with higher prices and resold there (see Chapter 5).

However, pharmaceutical expenditure is not lower in countries with lower price levels and stricter price control systems; the level of consumption can be higher, and the expenditure can actually be higher than in other countries with greater price flexibility. Thus, the level of expenditure is quite high in countries such as Japan, France and Italy.

DEREGULATION OF PHARMACEUTICAL PRICES

Despite widespread application of regulation and control systems for drug prices in the OECD countries, and in view of the recommendations of economic theory, it is important to take into account the potential improvements in welfare associated with price deregulation, taking this as meaning a policy of implementing changes in regulation (re-regulation) that tend to free up prices when the conditions and market structure make it advisable to do so.

In some of the above sections of this chapter we have shown that, from a theoretical perspective: (a) price regulation lacks theoretical justification for products whose patent has expired (in this case, regulation can even hinder competition and stop prices from dropping towards the marginal cost), (b) profit control by means of individual price fixing is not feasible and induces strategic behaviour that is unfavourable to social welfare, and (c) price regulation based on comparisons with the price in other countries, which tends to smooth prices, can cause welfare losses in the long term.

By way of illustration and exploration, this final section of the chapter provides evidence of the potential effects of policies aimed at deregulation and the encouragement of competition, through the empirical analysis of two aspects that are at the centre of the debate on pharmaceutical financing in the international sphere. Both case studies offer interesting implications for the reform of the regulation and control systems in force throughout a large part of the EU. First, we analyse the responses of the pharmaceutical market to the increase in competition when the protection provided by patents is removed and prices become free. We then go on to analyse the available information on the extent to which price control systems are really guaranteeing lower drug prices.

The response of prices to the increase in the penetration of generics in the USA as of 1984 (especially in hospitals) has been an increase or a very small decrease in the prices of brand products, even when the prices of the generics are much lower (from 40 per cent lower when there is only one generic to 70 per cent lower when there are more than 10 generic competitors). This 'generic competition paradox', to quote Scherer,[23] can be explained by the combined effect of the following factors: (a) risk aversion and cost insensitivity in the prescriber (the patient's agent), (b) scant knowledge of substitution alternatives among consumers shopping in pharmacies, and (c) price discrimination mechanisms that identify two groups of consumers; one formed by those individuals who are very sensitive to price and the other by those who are most insensitive.

Frank and Salkever[24] presented a theoretical model that explained the positive correlation between the price of brand products and the entry of generics onto the market. When generics are introduced, price-sensitive consumers shift their demand towards the generics, and only those consumers who are very price-insensitive buy the brand product. As a result, demand for the brand product drops, but at the same time also becomes more inelastic, which enables the company to increase its price. The model presented by Frank and Salkever in 1992 demonstrates that in order for the price of the brand pharmaceutical to drop when the number of generics on the market increases, one of the following conditions would have to be fulfilled: (a) the entry of the generic increases the demand for the brand product, (b) the marginal cost is decreasing, or (c) generic entry makes the demand for the brand product more elastic. These authors interpret the positive partial correlation between the number of generics and the price of the brand pharmaceutical as an indicator of the impact of the entry on the demand curve of the brand product.

Empirical studies in the US market yield results that do not coincide. While some reports confirm the descriptive information (rising prices of brand products in the face of generic entry) others present contradictory results. Thus, Wiggins and Maness[25] noted that generic entry had reduced the price of anti-infective drugs. A more recent article by Frank and Salkever[26] analyses a sample of 32 drugs that underwent competition as a result of generic entry, and observes the behaviour of their prices in the period 1984–1987 in the US market. The descriptive analysis of the data offers the following evidence.

First, as time passed the relative price of the brand product rose in relation to that of the generic; or to say much the same thing, the price of the generic in relation to that of the brand product decreased as the moment of generic entry receded. And second, the relative price of the generic decreased as the number of competing companies marketing the generic increased.

Frank and Salkever[26] evaluate three types of econometric models for the prices of brand products and of generics: (a) a single-equation model with fixed effects, (b) a two-stage ordinary least squares model with fixed effects in which the number of generics is an endogenous variable, and (c) a two-stage random-effects model. The evidence provided by the econometric models leads the authors to draw the following conclusions:

1. An increase in competition between manufacturers of generic drugs does indeed cause a drop in prices. The entry of each new competitor brings about a price reduction of between 5.6 per cent and 7.2 per cent; an increase from three to six competitors results in a drop of between 17 per cent and 22 per cent.
2. The increase in competition that should occur with generic entry does not cause the brand products to drop in price.

However, the behaviour of prices when faced with an increase in consumption of generics depends to a very large degree on the type of price regulation that is imposed on each market.

Finally, the empirical evidence shows that in cross-national comparisons of drug prices, when the relative weight of generic consumption in each country is taken into consideration, the conclusions are different from those of previous estimates. Danzon and Chao[27–29] compared price levels in Canada, Germany, France, Italy, Japan and the USA using the relative weights of each group of products within the consumption registered for several countries. The conclusion they reached was precisely that the competition created by the presence of generics in countries with free prices or with very flexible regulation systems (without individual price regulation), such as the USA, Germany and Canada, is very effective for reducing prices, whereas this phenomenon is almost inexistent in countries that have rigid price control systems, such as Italy, France and Japan.

This empirical result would appear to indicate that the prices of products that are marketed under the protection of a patent are very likely to be higher in countries with free pricing, but that the price level in these same countries is no higher than in those that regulate prices strictly, as a result of the large market share acquired by generics and the notable price reduction brought about by their introduction onto the market. The box below contains a summary of Danzon and Chao's research.[27–29]

In general, several studies have shown that generics achieve a larger market share in countries with more flexible price regulation systems:[30,31] 39 per cent of the sales value for 1996–7 in Germany, 22 per cent in the UK, 13 per cent in the Netherlands and only 3 per cent in Italy and 2 per cent in France. These figures reveal that the level of competition when the patent has expired is considerably lower in markets with strict price regulation systems; prices are much more stable over time in these countries, and the price variation between different products containing the same active ingredient is also seen to be smaller.[31]

PUBLIC CONTROL OF PHARMACEUTICAL PRICES DOES NOT GUARANTEE LOWER PRICES WHEN THE PATENT EXPIRES

Patricia M. Danzon and Li-Wei Chao, *Prices, Competition and Regulation in Pharmaceuticals: A Cross-national Comparison*, Office of Health Economics, June 2000, 84 pages.
Patricia M. Danzon and Li-Wei Chao, 'Cross-national price differences for pharmaceuticals: how large and why?' *Journal of Health Economics*, 2000, 10, 159–95.
Patricia M. Danzon and Li-Wei Chao, 'Does regulation drive out competition in pharmaceutical markets?' *Journal of Law and Economics*, 2000, XLIII, October: 311–357.

Objective The objective of this study is to construct pharmaceutical price indexes in order to be able to make cross-national comparisons and analyse the causes of the differences between countries.

Method The authors use information on all non-hospital sales of pharmaceutical products in 1992 in a sample of countries consisting of the USA, Canada, Germany, France, Italy, Japan and the UK. The database was provided by Intercontinental Medical Systems (IMS). The empirical analysis is based on the calculation of the Paasche and Laspeyres price indexes and the ratio between them. The descriptive analysis is completed with the econometric analysis (quasi-hedonic model) of the determining factors of the variation in the relative prices of each active ingredient in each country taking the USA as the point of comparison.

Results Using the quantities of each active ingredient consumed (brand pharmaceuticals and generics) in the USA as weighting factors, the differences in international prices are found to be smaller than those observed in previous studies, and prices in a market without price regulation (the USA) are not always higher than in the other countries. Comparisons between price indexes for each country appear to be strongly influenced by the choice of relative weights of consumption (those of the same country or those of a different one). The results of the study indicate that the competition created by the entry of generic pharmaceuticals into the market causes prices to fall significantly in countries without price regulation (the USA) or with a type of regulation that allows flexibility when fixing the price of each product (the UK, Germany and Canada). In contrast, the competition created by generics is ineffective or even counter-productive in countries with very strict price regulation (France, Italy and Japan). In the case of the USA, when the number of generics in a market doubles, the price falls by 56.7 per cent on average, whereas in France, Italy and Japan, for example, no reduction at all is observed in the average price, and even slight rises are registered.

Conclusions When weighted samples are used that are representative of consumption in each country, the differences in the pharmaceutical price indexes are much smaller than those observed until now. Strict price regulation is related to lower prices for older and more universally distributed compounds. However, generic competition is responsible for notable price reductions in non-regulated markets.

Sources of funding: a grant awarded by Pfizer to the University of Pennsylvania and a Public Health Service grant from the AHCPR for the second author.

Correspondence to: Patricia M. Danzon, Health Care Management Department, The Wharton School, University of Pennsylvania.

E-mail: danzon@wharton.upenn.edu.

COMMENTARY

The implications of the differences in pharmaceutical prices between countries can be far-reaching for any health system with public funding. Let us focus our attention on two aspects. The first of these concerns the capacity of price regulation systems to guarantee low prices without causing excessive harm to incentives to innovate. The second concerns the widespread practice of using observed prices in other countries as a reference for the pricing authorization of new pharmaceuticals.

Very strict price control systems can give rise to higher prices at the time of introduction of a new product and the weakening of potential price reductions on expiry of a product's patent (the case for 88 per cent of products in the USA). These observations support the idea that it does not appear to be at all efficient to continue with the system of product-by-product price intervention currently in force in Spain. A regulation system that gives the company flexibility of pricing and excludes products that are subject to competition would be far more recommendable.[1]

There are economic and social reasons to hold that prices need not be identical between countries (they are not for other goods), and therefore the tendency to use observed prices in other countries to regulate domestic prices is open to question.[32] Moreover, the fact that they are identical at the time of introduction onto the market does not prevent them from developing differently over time, which undermines the effectiveness of the mechanism.

Source: Puig-Junoy J. (2001), 'Por una politica del medicamento integrada y de calidad', *Gestión Clínica y Sanitaria*, **3** (1), 35.

REFERENCES

1. Puig-Junoy, J. (1998), 'Regulación y competencia de precios en el mercado farmacéutico', Papeles de Economía Española, 67, pp. 96–122.
2. Calfee, J.E. (2000), *Prices, Markets, and the Pharmaceutical Revolution*, Washington: AEI Press.

3. Green, D.G. (1997), *Editor's introduction: is price regulation necessary?*, in G.D. Green (ed.) et al., *Should Pharmaceutical Prices be Regulated?*, London: IEA Health and Welfare Unit, pp. 1–9.

4. Fisher, S., I. Cockburn, Z. Griliches and J. Hausman (1997), 'Characteristics of demand for pharmaceutical products: an examination of four cephalosporins', *Rand Journal of Economics*, 28, pp. 426–46.

5. Abbott III, T.A. (1995), 'Regulating pharmaceutical prices', in T.A. Abbott III (ed.), *Health Care Policy and Regulation*, Boston: Kluwer Academic Publishers, pp. 105–34.

6. Danzon, P.M. (1997), *Pharmaceutical Price Regulation: National Policies versus Global Interests*, Washington: AEI Press.

7. Schweitzer, S.O. (1997), *Pharmaceutical Economics and Policy*, New York: Oxford University Press.

8. Kaufer, E. (1990), 'The regulation of new product development in the drug industry', in G. Majone (ed.), *Deregulation or Re-regulation? Regulatory Reform in Europe and the United States*, London: Pinter Publishers.

9. Mossialos, E. (1998), 'Pharmaceutical pricing, financing and cost containment in the European Union Member States', in R. Leidl (ed.), *Health Care and its Financing in the Single European Market*, Amsterdam: IOS Press.

10. Jacobzone, S. (2000), 'Pharmaceutical policies in OECD countries: reconciling social and industrial goals', *labour market and social policy occasional paper no 40*, Paris: OECD.

11. Lobato, P., F. Lobo and J. Rovira (1997), *La industria farmacéutica en España tras la unificación del mercado europeo*, Madrid: Farmaindustria.

12. López, Bastida J. (1997), 'El mercado farmacéutico español: una panorámica', in *Gestión sanitaria: Innovaciones y desafíos*, Barcelona: Masson/Grupo MSD, p. 105–24.

13. Danzon, P.M. (1997), *Trade and Price Differentials for Pharmaceuticals: Policy Options*, London: Office of Health Economics.

14. Puig-Junoy, J. (1996), *Incentivos y eficiencia en la regulación de los precios máximos: propiedades teóricas y prácticas*, Bilbao: Fundación BBV.

15. Borrell, J.-R. (1999), 'Pharmaceutical price regulation: a study on the impact of the rate-of-return regulation in the UK', *PharmacoEconomics*, 15 (3), pp. 291–303.

16. Scherer, F.M. (2000), 'The pharmaceutical industry', in *Handbook of Health Economics*, vol. 1, Amsterdam: North Holland, pp. 1295–336.

17. Burstall, M.L. (1997), 'How do they do it elsewhere in Europe?', in G.D. Green (ed.) et al., *Should Pharmaceutical Prices be Regulated?*, London: IEA Health and Welfare Unit.

18. Rapp, R.T. and Lloyd, A. (1994), ' "Civilized" pharmaceutical price regulation: can the U.S. have it too?', NERA working paper no 24, Washington.

19. Abbott III, T.A. (1994), 'Price regulation in the pharmaceutical industry: prescription or placebo?', *Journal of Health Economics*, 14, pp. 551–65.

20. Liston, C. (1993),'Price-cap versus rate-of-return regulation', *Journal of Regulatory Economics*, 5, 25–48.

21. López, Bastida J. and E. Mossialos (2000), 'Pharmaceutical expenditure in Spain: cost and control', *International Journal of Health Services*, 30 (3), 597–616.

22. IOO (1995), *Beoordeling ABDA-Prijsvergelijking Geneesmiddelen*, The Hague: IOO.

23. Scherer, F.M. (1993), 'Pricing, profits, and technological progress in the pharmaceutical industry', *Journal of Economic Perspectives*, **7** (3), 97–115.
24. Frank, R.G. and D.S. Salkever (1992), 'Pricing patent loss and the market for pharmaceuticals', *Southern Economic Journal*, **59** (2), 165–79.
25. Wiggins, S.N. and R. Maness (1994), 'Price competition in pharmaceutical markets', unpublished document, Texas A&M University.
26. Frank, R.G. and D.S. Salkever (1997), 'Generic entry and the pricing of pharmaceuticals', *Journal of Economics & Management Strategy*, 6, 75–90.
27. Danzon, P.M. and L. Chao (2000), *Prices, Competition and Regulation in Pharmaceuticals: a Cross-national Comparison*, London: Office of Health Economics.
28. Danzon, P.M. and L. Chao (2000), 'Cross-national price differences for pharmaceuticals: how large and why?', *Journal of Health Economics*, 10, 159–95.
29. Danzon, P.M. and L. Chao (2000), 'Does regulation drive out competition in pharmaceutical markets?', *Journal of Law and Economics*, **XLIII**, 311–57.
30. Garattini, L. and F. Tediosi (2000), 'A comparative analysis of generics markets in five European countries', *Health Policy*, 51, 149–62.
31. Gambardella, A., L. Orsenigo and F. Pammolli (2000), 'Global competitiveness in pharmaceuticals: a European perspective', report prepared for the Directorate General of Enterprise of the European Commission.
32. Berndt, E.R. (2000), 'International comparisons of pharmaceutical prices: what do we know, and what does it mean?', *Journal of Health Economics*, 19, 283–7.

4. Regulation and competition in pharmaceutical markets

J.R. Borrell Arqué, A. Costas Comesaña and R. Nonell Torres

INTRODUCTION

The objective of this chapter is to analyse the extent to which pharmaceuticals withstand competition from therapeutic substitutes and generics in the UK and Spain. Our hypothesis is that substitute drugs compete in markets, but that the type of competition they face depends on the specific regulations in force in each of the countries studied with regard to entry, price and prescription.

In this chapter we assume that pharmaceuticals are strongly differentiated products that compete in a space with multidimensional characteristics, one of them being price. According to Danzon,[1] 'aggressive competitive entry of differentiated therapeutic substitutes implies that the industry is best characterized as monopolistically competitive, with possible pockets of oligopoly early in the life of a new therapeutic class'. Danzon[1] also states that research and development (R&D) costs are fixed and common costs in the activity of offering pharmaceuticals to any number of consumers anywhere in the world. Patents force competitors to bear the costs of research, development and the authorization of new products before a generic substitute is launched onto the market. When patents expire generic competitors can enter the market, bearing only the authorization costs incurred by demonstrating the substitute's bio-equivalence to the innovative product, which is already on the market.

This chapter provides evidence on competition between rival drugs in the UK and Spain, and shows the number of pharmaceuticals on the market, the position of dominance occupied by products in relation to their substitutes, and the prescription concentration at various levels of therapeutic and generic differentiation.

European pharmaceutical markets are strongly regulated as regards the introduction of new products onto the market (through authorization and patents) and also as regards prices and consumption (medical prescription and public financing). However, the way in which entry, prices and consumption of pharmaceuticals are regulated varies enormously from country to country.

In the wake of the third round table on the completion of the single market in pharmaceuticals in Frankfurt in December 1998, there is a broad consensus in the European Union (EU) on the need to reform regulation in national pharmaceutical markets. The core element of this consensus between the participants in the round tables is that competition is already sufficient in two types of pharmaceutical markets: both the general case of drugs whose patents have expired and the particular case of over-the-counter (OTC) drugs (drugs that do not require a medical prescription and are advertised directly to the patients, known in Spain as *especialidades publicitarias* or 'advertising products'). In these two drug markets, competition renders price regulation unnecessary.

Although the regulation of Europe's pharmaceutical markets is gradually converging, competition is at present very different in each of the Member States. This work shows that the various national regulations make for markets that differ greatly as regards the type of competition to be found between substitute drugs.

HOW TO EVALUATE COMPETITION BETWEEN PHARMACEUTICALS

In order to make an empirical evaluation of how substitute pharmaceuticals compete in the UK and Spain, we analyse the number of substitutes, how they dominate the market and the prescription concentration at different levels of therapeutic and generic differentiation.

According to Shepherd,[2] 'The minimum conditions for effective competition are reasonably clear, both from theory and business experience'. Shepherd[2] states that any of the following conditions is sufficient to ensure that competition is effective: first, at least five comparable competitors; second, no single company with a dominant position (the share of the market leader should be no greater than 40 per cent, and there should be no substitute product in the close vicinity); and third, freedom of entry into the market and the various market segments.

In this chapter we follow the criteria laid down by Shepherd[2] to show that the existence of dominant positions and closed oligopolies in environments without full freedom of entry can easily lead to a lack of effective competition in markets. We begin by studying the number of active ingredients, pharmaceutical products and pharmaceutical presentations that compete on different therapeutically and generically defined markets. We are especially interested in determining the situation when there are fewer than five substitute drugs competing in a given market.

For those readers who are not accustomed to the jargon of pharmaceutical markets, at this point we give an example to illustrate the nomenclature of pharmaceutical products. A pharmaceutical presentation in the UK called 'Amix® 500 mg capsules' is one of the versions of the brand product Amix®, which contains the active ingredient amoxycilin. In Spain, the pharmaceutical presentation 'Clamoxyl® 500 mg 12 cápsulas' is one version of the brand product Clamoxyl®, which likewise contains the therapeutic active ingredient amoxycilin. In both countries, generic products are currently available that commercialize the therapeutic active ingredient amoxycilin under its generic name, which cannot be included in the register of commercial names and brands.

Second, we analyse the position of the leading products in the different therapeutic and generic drug markets. Our aim is to evaluate the extent to which the leaders achieve dominant positions in each market. Positions of dominance are shown in terms of the market share of the most frequently prescribed active ingredient, product or presentation in its therapeutic group of active ingredients, products or presentations, called ψ_g, in which $g = 1, 2, ..., G$ are mutually exclusive groups.

The expression below shows the habitual concentration ratio of a product (cr_1) where q_j is the number of times a product is prescribed. We are interested in evaluating when the leader's position of dominance crosses the threshold of the 40 per cent market share.

$$cr_1 = max\ s_{j/g} = max\left(\frac{q_j}{\sum\limits_{j \in \psi_g} q_j}\right) \tag{3.1}$$

Third, we study the degree of prescription concentration in each market. We show the prescription concentration using the Herfindahl–Hirschman index (H). The statistic H is the sum of the squares of the market shares of each product j included in group g of active ingredients, products or presentations Ψ_g, as defined above. The following expression gives the definition of the Herfindahl–Hirschman index:

$$H_g = \sum_j \left(\frac{q_j}{\sum\limits_{j \in \psi g} q_j}\right)^2 \tag{3.2}$$

where $\qquad\qquad 0 < H_g < 1 \tag{3.3}$

The H index is an indicator of market concentration used by antitrust authorities, chiefly to evaluate the impact of mergers and takeovers on market structure. When a market has only one company, that is, when that company has a market share of 100 per cent ($s_j = 1$), the H index is equal to 1 per cent or 100 per cent.

According to the 1992 Merger Guidelines published by the US Department of Justice and the Federal Trade Commission, markets fall into one of three categories after a merger or takeover. When the H index is lower than 10 per cent, the market is said to be 'unconcentrated' and the merger can go ahead without further delay. When the H index stands between 10 per cent and 18 per cent, the market is described as being 'moderately concentrated', and objections are only raised to those mergers that cause the H index to increase by more than 1 per cent from the situation previous to the merger. When the H index steps over the 18 per cent mark after the merger, the market qualifies as 'concentrated' and therefore all mergers that cause the index to rise more than 0.5 per cent are challenged. Kwoka and White[3] show that the 10 per cent and 18 per cent cutoff points translate empirically into concentration ratios of around 50 per cent and 70 per cent respectively for the four main competitors (cr_4).

Our empirical evaluation of competition between pharmaceuticals was based on information on prescription drug consumption by non-hospital patients in the National Health Service (NHS) in England in 1996 and the *Sistema Nacional de Salud* or SNS (National Health System) in Spain in 1997. The authors wish to thank Statistics Division 1E of the UK Department of Health and the Directorate-General of Pharmacy and Health Products of the Spanish Ministry of Health and Consumer Affairs for supplying us with these data. As can be seen from Table 4.1, public consumption of pharmaceuticals

Table 4.1   Retail sales of pharmaceutical products

	England, 1996		Spain, 1997	
	Million £ (EFP)	%	Million £ (EFP)	%
Sales of OTC products	642	14.00	223	6.03
Sales of non-OTC products without public financing	175	3.82	645	17.46
Publicly financed sales	3771	82.18	2829	76.51
Total retail sales	4589	100.00	3697	100.00

Notes: EFP: ex-factory price (excluding pharmacists' markups, wholesalers' markups and VAT); PPP exchange rate: 192.5 pts/£.

Source: Authors' calculations on the basis of data provided by IMS.[4–9]

outside hospitals accounts for most of the retail sales of pharmaceutical products both in England (82.19 per cent) and in Spain (76.51 per cent).

The information in the Prescription Cost Analysis System and the *Base de Datos de Especialidades Farmacéuticas* (Pharmaceutical Product Database) is compiled according to accounting criteria. We processed the information and created two structured databases in order to obtain the statistics that will show us the competition and the structure of the pharmaceutical markets of each of the countries studied.

The British information is only for the English NHS, as this information and that corresponding to Scotland, Wales and Northern Ireland are not incorporated in the same database. In the English case we obtained information for pharmaceutical products prescribed more than 50 times in 1996. In order to make homogeneous comparisons, we excluded products prescribed fewer than 50 times in Spain in 1997.

The most useful information for our purposes is the following. First, we are very interested in knowing the therapeutic class within which each product is classified. The therapeutic class is defined in accordance with the British National Formulary in England, and the *Clasificación Terapéutica de Medicamentos* (Therapeutic Drug Classification) in Spain. In both cases, four codes identify, in hierarchical fashion, the four levels of exhaustive and mutually exclusive groups. We use the terminology of the British National Formulary to designate each of the four levels of the classifications: products are classified into a small number of therapeutic chapters, a larger number of therapeutic sections into which each chapter is subdivided, and an even larger number of paragraphs and subparagraphs into which each section is in turn subdivided.

Second, it is of great use for our analysis to have information on the name of the active ingredient (or ingredients) each product contains. In the English system a maximum of three active ingredients can be distinguished in those products that contain a combination of chemical entities. In order to ensure the homogeneous nature of the comparisons between countries, we considered all combinations of more than three active ingredients as belonging to a single group called 'combination', in both the English and the Spanish data.

Third, information on the brand or generic name under which each product is marketed is useful for our study. In the English information we cannot distinguish the various generic products that offer the same active ingredients. The data for all the competitors that offer these products are grouped together.

Fourth, we are interested in information on the various presentations of each product. The presentations differ in pharmaceutical form (tablets, capsules, injectables, creams and so on), the concentration of the therapeutic active ingredient (usually specified in milligrams) and the number of tablets, vials, or units in general, provided in each package. The Spanish data enable us to identify the number of units per package for all the observations. The

English data, however, does not provide information on the number of units in each package, as doctors usually prescribe the number of units necessary to complete the treatment, and pharmacists dispense the units in accordance with the prescribed dosage. Finally, it is essential to have access to information on the number of packages prescribed for each presentation in each country.

The databases we use in this study do not allow us to identify which companies market each product. This information constraint makes it impossible to compare competition between laboratories, and we are forced to restrict our analysis to competition between drugs. Hence, this work does not analyse the strategic behaviour of firms that market a series of pharmaceuticals in each of the therapeutic or generic markets.

Table 4.2 shows the number of groups within which pharmaceutical presentations are classified at different levels of therapeutic differentiation. The classifications are made up of 15 and 14 main therapeutic chapters in England and Spain respectively. At this level, products are grouped according to their therapeutic effect in terms of the main anatomical systems: gastrointestinal system, cardiovascular system, respiratory system and so on.

Below these broad groups, medicinal products are placed in anatomico-therapeutic subgroups which we will call therapeutic sections (101 in the English system and 79 in the Spanish). For example, in the English classification the chapter dealing with the cardiovascular system has therapeutic sections for anti-arrhythmic drugs, antihypertensive drugs and anticoagulants and protamine, among others.

Finally, on the maximum level of detail in the Spanish classification, we find 228 groups of presentations, which we call subparagraphs, corresponding to the 258 groups in the English system that we call paragraphs. For the most detailed level of analysis we use the information at paragraph level in the English case (258 groups) and at subparagraph level in the Spanish case (228 groups). In this way, comparisons between the groups of the different national therapeutic classifications will be more homogeneous.

Table 4.2   Therapeutic classifications

	England, 1996	Spain, 1997
Chapters	15	14
Sections	101	79
Paragraphs	258	175
Subparagraphs	362	228

Source: Authors' calculations on the basis of the databases.

THERAPEUTIC AND GENERIC COMPETITION IN ENGLAND AND SPAIN

Therapeutic Competition

Table 4.3 shows the number of active ingredients, pharmaceutical products and pharmaceutical presentations contained in our databases. It reveals that more active ingredients are marketed in Spain than in England. However, there are more products and presentations in England than in Spain. The data suggest that there are more therapeutic competitors in Spain, as there are more products containing different therapeutic substances. In contrast, there are more generic competitors in England, as there are more products that contain the same therapeutic substance and are marketed either under competing brand names or under generic names.

Table 4.4 shows the market share of the most frequently prescribed chemical substance in England and Spain and the *H* index for prescription concentration in public health care.

The market share of the most frequently prescribed active ingredient is very small both in England and in Spain, and the prescription concentration at the level of therapeutic substances is also very low. These data paint a picture of fierce competition in markets of drugs containing different active ingredients. However, we need to study the market structure and therapeutic competition at a lower level of therapeutic aggregation in order to be able to evaluate the extent to which pharmaceuticals enjoy dominant positions in their respective groups of therapeutic substitutes.

Table 4.3 Number of active ingredients, pharmaceutical products and pharmaceutical presentations

	England, 1996	Spain, 1997
Presentations[a]	6181	5609
Products[a]	3691	3095
Active ingredients[b]	1444	1771

Notes:
a. In the English system it is not possible to distinguish between generic presentations and products marketed by different laboratories.
b. We do not distinguish between combinations of more than three active ingredients.

Source: Authors' calculations on the basis of the databases.

*Table 4.4   Therapeutic competition in the pharmaceutical market as a
whole (%)*

	England, 1996	Spain, 1997
Market share of the most prescribed ingredient	3.44	3.24
H index of the active ingredients	0.78	0.51

Source: Authors' calculations on the basis of the databases.

Table 4.5 provides some descriptive statistics on the number of active
ingredients per therapeutic chapter, section and paragraph/subparagraph in
England and Spain.

In England there are fewer therapeutic substances available per chapter,
section and paragraph/subparagraph. These data confirm that the number of
therapeutic competitors is greater in Spain than in England.

Table 4.5 also shows that the median of the number of active ingredients
is always lower than the average number of active ingredients per chapter,
section or paragraph/subparagraph, both in England and in Spain. For example, the weighted average in terms of the number of packages prescribed
stands at 11 different substances in England, whereas the median is 4 different substances per therapeutic paragraph. Therefore, in most of the therapeutic paragraphs the number of substitute substances is small. However, there
are a few high-turnover markets in which the number of competitors is
greater.

Table 4.6 provides some descriptive statistics on the market share of the
most frequently prescribed substance at the level of chapters, sections and
therapeutic paragraphs/subparagraphs.

For the most prescribed substances in each therapeutic chapter, positions of
dominance are uncommon. Both the median and the weighted average are
below 25 per cent. However, Table 4.6 shows that a small group of active
ingredients enjoy dominant positions in most of the therapeutic sections and
paragraphs/subparagraphs, particularly in England (arithmetic mean of market
shares over 55 per cent), but also in Spain (arithmetic mean of market shares
over 34 per cent).

The market share of the most frequently prescribed active ingredients is
larger in England. For example, the weighted average of the market share of
the most prescribed substance at therapeutic section level stands at 41 per cent
in England, yet only 23 per cent in Spain.

Table 4.7 provides some statistics on the prescription concentration of various substances at chapter, section and paragraph/subparagraph level.

Table 4.5   Therapeutic competition: number of active ingredients

	Minimum	Median	Arithmetic mean	Weighted average	Maximum	Observations
Spain, 1997						
Per chapter	13	125	135	181	246	14
Per section	1	15	22	52	124	79
Per subparagraph	1	5	8	18	42	228
England, 1996						
Per chapter	37	88	103	134	216	14
Per section	1	13	14	29	82	101
Per paragraph	1	4	6	11	26	258

Notes: Weighted average calculated on the basis of the number of packages prescribed. In the figures for England, Chapters 14 and 15 are treated as one chapter.

Source: Authors' calculations on the basis of the databases.

Table 4.6 Therapeutic competition: market share of the most prescribed active ingredient (%)

	Minimum	Weighted average	Median	Arithmetic mean	Maximum	Observations
Spain, 1997						
Per chapter	6	11	12	13	49	14
Per section	8	23	34	43	100	79
Per subparagraph	13	42	60	63	100	228
England, 1996						
Per chapter	9	18	21	23	43	14
Per section	17	41	55	58	100	101
Per paragraph	22	56	76	74	100	258

Notes: Weighted average calculated on the basis of the number of packages prescribed. In the figures for England, Chapters 14 and 15 are treated as one chapter.

Source: Authors' calculations on the basis of the databases.

Table 4.7   Therapeutic competition: H index of prescription concentration between various therapeutic substances (%)

	Minimum	Weighted average	Median	Arithmetic mean	Maximum	Observations
Spain, 1997						
Per chapter	2	4	4	5	30	14
Per section	4	13	20	33	100	79
Per subparagraph	7	30	48	54	100	228
England, 1996						
Per chapter	4	7	8	11	24	14
Per section	10	27	38	46	100	101
Per paragraph	15	43	62	65	100	258

Notes: Weighted average calculated on the basis of the number of packages prescribed. In the figures for England, Chapters 14 and 15 are treated as one chapter.

Source: Authors' calculations on the basis of the databases.

The prescription concentration is very low at therapeutic chapter level. The median and weighted averages are lower than 10 per cent. However, the markets are highly concentrated in most sections and paragraphs/subparagraphs, particularly in England, but also in Spain. The medians and weighted averages are above 18 per cent, with the exception of the weighted average of the concentration at therapeutic section level in Spain, which stands at 13 per cent.

Table 4.7 also shows that the concentration is higher in England than in Spain. For example, the weighted average of the concentration index at paragraph/subparagraph level is 43 per cent in England, as opposed to 30 per cent in Spain.

Finally, the weighted averages of the concentration indices are lower than the medians of these indices. For example, the median of the concentration indices at paragraph level is 62 per cent in England, whereas the weighted average is 43 per cent. Therefore, prescription is more concentrated in the majority of therapeutic markets than in a small number of high-turnover markets.

Generic Competition

Having shown that a small group of therapeutic substances enjoy positions of dominance at section and paragraph/subparagraph level, especially in England, we now go on to analyse competition between products containing the same active ingredients, that is, generic competition.

Table 4.8 shows the extent of generic competition. In Spain, only 6.21 per cent of active ingredients have commercial versions using generic names. The market share of pharmaceutical products that use generic names amounts to only 2.34 per cent of the total number of packages consumed in the non-hospital sector of the SNS. Only 14.44 per cent of products are marketed using the generic name of the substance they contain, or have an equivalent competitor on the market that uses a commercial brand. Products sold under the generic name of their component have only been authorized as 'generic pharmaceutical products' (*especialidades farmacéuticas genéricas* or EFGs) since the end of 1997, by means of a special administrative process that simply evaluates their bio-equivalence to innovative products already on the market. In our database most of the products with generic names were approved prior to the creation of the EFGs, as if they contained new chemical substances.

In contrast, in England 35.04 per cent of active ingredients have versions on the market that bear generic names. The market share of products with generic names reaches 46.22 per cent of prescriptions made out in the non-hospital sector of the NHS. In England, doctors can choose between brand name products and generic equivalents in 72.09 per cent of prescription decisions.

Table 4.8 Generic competition (%)

	1 Generics	2 Brand products with generic competitors	1+2 Generic competition	3 Brand products without generic competitors	1+2+3 Total
Spain, 1997					
Number of packages prescribed	2.34	13.32	15.66	84.34	100.00
Number of products	5.20	9.24	14.44	85.56	100.00
Number of active ingredients			6.27	93.73	100.00
England, 1996					
Number of packages prescribed	46.22	25.87	72.09	27.09	100.00
Number of products	16.23	35.08	51.31	48.69	100.00
Number of active ingredients			35.04	64.96	100.00

Source: Authors' calculations on the basis of the databases.

Table 4.9   Length of time substances have been on the market (%)

	8 years or less	Over 8 years	Total
Spain, 1997			
Number of packages prescribed	11.27	88.23	100.00
Number of products	10.44	89.56	100.00
Number of active ingredients	10.33	89.67	100.00
England, 1996			
Number of packages prescribed	5.57	94.43	100.00
Number of products	4.55	95.45	100.00
Number of active ingredients	7.20	92.80	100.00

Source: Authors' calculations on the basis of the databases.

Furthermore, 51.04 per cent of products on the market are generic or have a generic competitor. In recent years the NHS has encouraged a policy of generic prescription, not only when there is a generic version of the relevant active ingredient but even before the generic version reaches the market.

Table 4.9 shows the number of new active ingredients (substances marketed for the first time during the last eight years) in England and Spain in terms of number of packages prescribed, number of products and number of substances. We chose the period of eight years from first-time marketing of a new substance because it is highly likely that the innovators of the therapeutic use of the substance will be protected by patents for this length of time, if we assume that 12 of the 20 years of patent length have elapsed before the new chemical entity is introduced onto the market.

The percentage of new chemical entities is higher in Spain than it is in England. Only 7.20 per cent of the total number of substances on the market were authorized for the first time during the last eight years in England, whereas in Spain these new entities amount to 10.33 per cent of the total number of substances in our database. Moreover, the new substances in Spain have a market share that more than doubles (11.27 per cent) those of the new substances in England (5.57 per cent).

Table 4.10 provides some descriptive statistics on the number of products that contain the same composition in England and Spain. The table shows these statistics for all the substances in our database, for the set of substances for which no version is marketed under a generic name, and finally for the set of new substances marketed for the first time during the last eight years.

The median and the weighted average of the number of products containing

Table 4.10 Generic competition: number of products per active ingredient

	Minimum	Median	Arithmetic mean	Weighted average	Maximum	Observations
Spain, 1997						
Per active ingredient	1	1	2	5	33	1771
Per active ingredient with no generic version	1	1	1	4	33	1661
Per new active ingredient	1	1	2	2	10	183
England, 1996						
Per active ingredient	1	2	3	14	49	1444
Per active ingredient with no generic version	1	2	2	7	49	938
Per new active ingredient	1	2	2	10	20	104

Note: Weighted average calculated on the basis of the number of packages prescribed. It is not possible to distinguish between generic products marketed by different laboratories.

Source: Authors' calculations on the basis of the databases.

the same therapeutic substance are higher in England. In fact, the number of products per active ingredient in England is greater than Table 4.10 indicates, as we cannot distinguish between the various different products that are sold under generic names.

In order to analyse competition between products containing the same therapeutic substances and at the same time overcome the problem of not being able to distinguish the different generic products in England, we have also calculated the statistics for the set of chemical entities that have no generic version on the market. The results show that the median and the weighted average of the number of products per therapeutic substance are greater in England. Again, this result suggests that generic competition is keener in England.

Table 4.10 also shows the statistics for the number of products per active ingredient introduced for the first time over the last eight years. Once again, the results show that the median and the weighted average of the number of products per therapeutic substance are greater in England. Considering that substances are very likely to be protected by patent for the first eight years on the market, these data suggest that the licensing of products by more than one or two laboratories is more common practice in England than in Spain. In England, patent holders prefer to recover their investment in R&D not only by marketing their own products but also by granting licences to competing laboratories. In contrast, in Spain patent holders prefer only one or two companies to market their products.

Finally, Table 4.10 reveals that the medians are lower than the averages of the number of products per therapeutic substance. Therefore, most therapeutic substances are available in the form of a single product in Spain, whereas in England they are available as two or more products. In England a large number of high-turnover therapeutic substances are sold in the form of between seven and 14 different products, while in Spain this is the case for only two to five products.

Table 4.11 provides some descriptive statistics on the market shares of the most commonly prescribed products that compete offering the same therapeutic substances in England and Spain.

Table 4.11 shows that the statistics on the market share of the most commonly prescribed product among those that compete offering the same therapeutic substance are very similar in England and Spain. However, as we mentioned above, we cannot distinguish the market shares of the different generic versions. Therefore, in Spain the most prescribed products among those that contain the same active ingredients enjoy clear positions of dominance, whereas in England all we can conclude is that the most frequently prescribed products enjoy clear positions of dominance among their generic competitors in cases of new therapeutic substances and in cases in which commercial versions bearing generic names have not yet reached the market.

Table 4.11 Generic competition: market share of the most prescribed product (%)

	Minimum	Weighted average	Arithmetic mean	Median	Maximum	Observations
Spain, 1997						
Per active ingredient	20	76	91	100	100	1771
Per active ingredient with no generic version	20	80	92	100	100	1661
Per new active ingredient	35	84	83	100	100	183
England, 1996						
Per active ingredient	15	75	87	100	100	1444
Per active ingredient with no generic version	19	80	91	100	100	938
Per new active ingredient	38	81	94	100	100	104

Note: Weighted average calculated on the basis of the number of packages prescribed. It is not possible to distinguish between generic products marketed by different laboratories.

Source: Authors' calculations on the basis of the databases.

Nevertheless, in England dominant positions at therapeutic substance level appear to subside when generic versions enter the market. If we could distinguish the market shares of each generic version, the statistics showing dominance at therapeutic substance level would diminish, especially in the case of certain therapeutic substances for which turnover is high. The data do not enable us to measure the impact of generic entry on the market share of the most prescribed product.

Table 4.12 provides some descriptive statistics on the prescription concentration of products containing the same therapeutic substance.

The concentration indices are slightly lower in England. Bearing in mind again that we cannot distinguish the sales of each generic version containing the same therapeutic substance, we can conclude that prescription is not so concentrated in one or a few products containing the same therapeutic substance in England.

Varieties Per Product

Finally, Table 4.13 shows the number of different presentations of the same product in terms of pharmaceutical form, concentration of the therapeutic substance and size of package. The differences between countries are very small. Nevertheless, in England there appears to be a larger number of varieties per product. The weighted average of different preparations stands at two in Spain as opposed to three in England. However, these differences are not significant in terms of prescription concentration.

NATIONAL REGULATION AND COMPETITION

The empirical evidence presented above enables us to draw two main conclusions: first, competition in pharmaceutical markets is effective between therapeutically differentiated products whereas a small number of products enjoy positions of dominance over their closest therapeutic and generic rivals; and second, competition in pharmaceutical markets depends enormously on national regulations.

National regulations shape the type and degree of competition to which pharmaceuticals are subject. One aspect is that therapeutic competition is more intense in Spain, regardless of the level of therapeutic differentiation. Another is that the evolution of generic competition over time differs substantially from one country to the other. In England, generic competition is more acute the longer the therapeutic substances have been on the market. Initially, rivalry increases because brand products other than the innovator gain market share as time passes. Later on, rivalry increases when the patent of the therapeutic

Table 4.12   Generic competition: H index of product prescription concentration (%)

	Minimum	Weighted average	Arithmetic mean	Median	Maximum	Observations
Spain, 1997						
Per active ingredient	9	69	88	100	100	1771
Per active ingredient with no generic version	9	73	90	100	100	1661
Per new active ingredient	33	80	78	100	100	183
England, 1996						
Per active ingredient	8	67	83	100	100	1444
Per active ingredient with no generic version	12	73	88	100	100	938
Per new active ingredient	30	73	92	100	100	104

Note: Weighted average calculated on the basis of the number of packages prescribed. It is not possible to distinguish between generic products marketed by different laboratories.

Source: Authors' calculations on the basis of the databases.

Table 4.13 *Prescription of different preparations per product*

	Minimum	Median	Arithmetic mean	Weighted average	Maximum	Observations
Number of preparations per product						
Spain, 1997	1	1	2	2	12	3095
England, 1996	1	1	2	3	19	3691

	Minimum	Weighted average	Arithmetic mean	Median	Maximum	Observations
Market share of the most prescribed preparation of the same product (%)						
Spain, 1997	23	78	87	100	100	3095
England, 1996	23	78	89	100	100	3691
H index of prescription concentration of the different presentations of the same product (%)						
Spain, 1997	17	71	82	100	100	3095
England, 1996	16	72	86	100	100	3691

Source: Authors' calculations on the basis of the databases.

substance expires and generic versions are introduced onto the market, gradually gaining market share. In contrast, in Spain generic competition undergoes no substantial change with market age of the product. The English case shows how generic competition can be promoted by the authorities when the patent that protected the innovator of the therapeutic substance expires.

Differences in the rivalry between pharmaceuticals on the market are related to the principles that guide national regulations. In the UK, the principles that have guided pharmaceutical policy are anchored in considerations of industrial policy. The main aims of regulation in the UK have been to promote innovation and exports. To this end, the authorization process for new therapeutic substances has been specially difficult to overcome, and the patent system has historically been very thorough in protecting innovation. The pharmaceutical public spending containment policy has not questioned the principle of freedom of prices. The control of the public pharmaceutical bill has been entrusted to the policy of restricting the profits of the pharmaceutical firms involved in sales of brand name drugs to the NHS, the policy of encouraging generic prescription, and the policy of raising public awareness of drug prices.

In Spain, on the other hand, the regulatory framework has given more priority to curbing the pharmaceutical spending of the SNS and providing patients with low-cost medicines outside the SNS. The various governments have imposed widespread reductions on all prescription drug prices in public and private health care alike. At the same time, in this climate of price restriction via direct regulation, governments have failed to encourage generic competition. In Spain, laboratories have been able to offset the pressure on prices by means of larger and more stable market shares for their products in the face of generic substitutes.

We now conclude this work by showing how differences in regulation can account for such substantial differences in competition between one country and the other. We focus our attention on three aspects: first, we discuss the differences in market entry regulations, then we go on to describe the differences in price regulations, and finally, we show the differences that exist in demand-side policies within the respective public health systems.

With regard to entry regulations, the differences are eloquent. Thomas[10] showed that 66.4 per cent of the therapeutic substances authorized in the UK between 1965 and 1985 were marketed in more than six of the largest markets worldwide. Thomas[10] notes that not only is the UK more open to authorizing 'worldwide products' but furthermore it is more reluctant to authorize so-called 'local products'. The Medicine Control Agency has traditionally been highly rigorous in its evaluation of new active ingredients.

For their part, the Spanish health authorities have historically been less demanding in the authorization process for new therapeutic substances.

Laboratories are known to apply for the authorization of new active ingredients in order to ensure that the prices of new products are higher than those of products already on the market. Once marketed, products are subject to such strict price regulation that the authorities barely allow adjustment even for general inflation. We have calculated that only 30.05 per cent of the new chemical entities authorized for the first time in Spain between 1990 and 1997 were actually classified as therapeutic improvements at the time of their introduction onto the market. For this evaluation we used the definitions and data on therapeutic improvement released each year by the Ministry of Health and Consumer Affairs in their publication *Información Terapéutica del Sistema Nacional de Salud.*

The differences in authorization regulations for new products go some way towards explaining the greater therapeutic rivalry in Spain. However, we need to complete the picture with a review of the differences in the patent system in order to understand why generic competition is greater in the UK.

In the UK the patent system was designed and reformed with a view to providing ample protection and promotion for innovation. In 1978 the protection period was extended to 20 years. In Spain only those chemical substances discovered after 1992 can be fully protected by means of product patents. Therefore, if 8–12 years tend to elapse between the discovery of new chemical entities with therapeutic potential and the authorization of the corresponding pharmaceutical product containing the new therapeutic substance, it is only of the period 2000–2002 that the first active ingredients to be fully protected by the new product patents have been appearing on the market. In Spain, non-innovative laboratories could market 'copies' of products discovered and developed by other (usually foreign) laboratories if innovative laboratories failed to offer them licences at a 'good price'. Therefore, entry regulations are stricter and more complete in the UK, owing to differences both in the system of authorization of new products and in patent law.

Likewise, the differences in price regulation are essential aspects to be taken into account in order to be able to understand the different patterns of generic competition to be found in the markets. In the UK, laboratories are free to fix the price of their drugs. However, the agreement reached between government and industry, known as the Pharmaceutical Price Regulation Scheme (PPRS), imposes limits on the rate of return that can be obtained by laboratories from sales of their brand products to the NHS. Generic products are subject to a reimbursement mechanism that provides an incentive for pharmacists to dispense generic versions as if in a reference pricing system.[11] The PPRS works as a mechanism for promoting innovation and exports.[12,13] Wholesale distributors and retailers both operate under the principle of freedom of prices in drug sales. However, pharmacists and the NHS agree upon

Table 4.14   Average price per item prescribed in the public health sector

	England, 1996		Spain, 1997
	£	pts[a]	pts
Average ex-factory price	8.26	1590	579
Average wholesalers' markup	0.33	63	72
Average pharmacists' markup	1.40	270	256
Average VAT	0.00	0	37
Average retail price	9.99	1924	944

Note: a.   PPP exchange rate in 1996: 192.55 pts/£.

Source: Authors' calculations on the basis of data provided by OECD[9] and Towse.[15]

the dispensing margin in the public health sector, taking into account the discounts offered by wholesalers to pharmacists.

In contrast to this, the main objective of price regulation in Spain is to contain the pharmaceutical bill of the SNS.[14] The Directorate-General of Pharmacy fixes the ex-factory price of each and every one of the presentations of the pharmaceuticals included in public health care. This authorized price is the maximum ruling price in both the public health sector and direct sales to the public in pharmacies. Laboratories can only make price increases above the maximum price fixed for each presentation when the government authorizes a general price revision. The markups of distributing wholesalers and pharmacists are also fixed by the authorities as a percentage over the ex-factory price.

Table 4.14 shows that the keener therapeutic competition in Spain and the more intense and broader price regulation enforced have restricted ex-factory prices enormously. However, the remuneration of wholesale distributors and pharmacists is very similar in the two countries.

Finally, in addition to the differences in entry and price regulations, the way the public pharmaceutical bill is controlled also differs between the UK and Spain. Since 1990 the NHS has gone to great lengths to promote generic prescription, primary care has been reformed to induce doctors to prescribe with an eye to pharmaceutical health care costs, even with economic incentives to this end, and the policy of excluding drugs from public health care has been employed. Table 4.15 shows that the number of packages prescribed per patient in the English public health sector is far less than the number of packages prescribed per patient in Spain.

In conclusion, we can say that pharmaceuticals compete more moderately or more keenly in the space of prices and characteristics at different levels of

Table 4.15 Number of items prescribed per patient

	England, 1996	Spain, 1997
Population attended (millions)[a]	48.980	39.347
Number of packages (millions)[b]	468.900	564.038
Packages per patient[a,b]	9.573	14.335

Source: a. DH[7] and INE[16]; b. databases.

therapeutic and generic differentiation. Nevertheless, a small group of drugs enjoy positions of dominance over their closest substitutes. At present, therapeutic competition between products containing different substances is stronger in Spain. However, changes in the patent system and in the authorization process for new products in Spain will make therapeutic competition increasingly less intense. On the other hand, generic competition between products containing the same therapeutic substance is keener in England.

Spanish markets have historically been subject to very weak entry regulation and very strong price regulation. The authorities have placed their trust in price regulation rather than competition between generic substitutes to keep prices low. Historically, the authorities have allowed patients to obtain the health benefits of innovations made abroad without making them pay a substantial part of the innovation costs by means of a strict patent system. Price regulation and the past laxness of the authorization process for new products have brought with them the undesired side effect of providing an incentive for the introduction of 'local products'. Finally, the authorities have preferred price regulation over demand management policies in the public health sector.

Today, the Spanish government can no longer count on lax entry regulations to obtain the benefits of pharmaceutical innovation at low cost, as its patent and authorization systems have converged with those of the rest of Europe. Moreover, Spain's European partners are insisting more strongly than ever that it should depend less on price regulation, in order to stop parallel imports from Spain to countries with higher prices. Therefore, the government will be forced to make the necessary reforms to enable competition, rather than the less precise, more arbitrary and less costly option of regulation, to impose discipline in drug prices and control of public pharmaceutical expenditure.

ACKNOWLEDGEMENTS

We thank the members of the research group in public policies and economic regulation of the University of Barcelona and the participants in the 3rd

International Conference of the European Network on Industrial Policy, held in Dublin in December 1999, for their comments.

REFERENCES

1. Danzon, P.M. (1997), 'Discrimination for pharmaceuticals: welfare effects in the US and EU', *International Journal of the Economics of Business*, **4** (3), 301–21.
2. Shepherd, W.G. (1997), 'Dim prospects: effective competition in telecommunications, railroads, and electricity', *The Antitrust Bulletin*, **42** (1), 151–75.
3. Kwoka, J.E. and White, L.W. (1994), *The Antitrust Revolution: the Role of Economics*, New York: HarperCollins.
4. Farmaindustria (1998), *La industria farmacéutica en cifras*, Madrid: Asociación de Empresarios de la Industria Farmacéutica.
5. Geursen, R. (1998), 'Globalización del mercado farmacéutico mundial: concentración global en la industria farmacéutica', *Industria Farmacéutica*, March/April, 105–12.
6. Asociación Española de Especialidades Farmacéuticas (1994), 'El mercado de las EFP: prolemas y oportunidades', *El Farmacéutico*, April, 37–8.
7. Department of Health (1998), 'Statistics of prescriptions dispensed in the community: England 1987 to 1997', *Statistical Bulletin*, issue no 24.
8. INSALUD (1998), *Indicadores de la prestación farmacéutica*, Madrid: Instituto Nacional de la Salud.
9. Organisation for Economic Co-operation and Development (OECD) (1998), *National Accounts, Main Aggregates, 1960–1997, vol I*, Paris: OECD.
10. Thomas, L.G. (1997), 'Regulation and firm size: FDA impacts on innovation', *RAND Journal of Economics*, **21** (4), 497–517.
11. Griffin, J.P. (1996), 'An historical survey of UK Government measures to control NHS medicines expenditure from 1948 to 1996', *PharmacoEconomics*, **10** (3), 210–24.
12. Sargent, J.A. (1987), 'The politics of the pharmaceutical price regulation scheme', in W. Streek and P.C. Schmitter (eds), *Private Interest Government: Beyond Market and State*, London: Sage.
13. Borrell, J.R. (1999), 'Pharmaceutical price regulation: a study on the impact of the rate-of-return regulation in the UK', *PharmacoEconomics*, **15** (3), 291–303.
14. Nonell, R. and J.R. Borrell (2001), 'Public demand for medicines, price regulation, and government – industry relationships in Spain', *Environment and Planning C: Government and Policy 2001*, **19** (1), 119–34.
15. Towse, A. (1996), 'The UK pharmaceutical market: an overview', *PharmacoEconomics*, 10 (supplement 2), 14–25.
16. Instituto Nacional de Estadística (INE) (1998), *Anuario Estadístico de España 1997*, Madrid.

5. Mechanisms to encourage price competition in the pharmaceutical market and their effects on efficiency and welfare

J. Rovira Forns and J. Darbà Coll

INTRODUCTION

Mainstream economics presupposes that the market is, in conditions of perfect competition, an automatic mechanism for resource allocation that leads to allocative efficiency, that is, allows the maximization of consumers' welfare with available resources. On this basis, liberal economists tend to defend that public powers should abstain from intervening in or regulating the market, assuming that the result of any intervention will distort resource assignation and cause efficiency and welfare losses for society. Nevertheless, even those economists who are most staunchly in favour of the free market acknowledge that there are situations in which *laissez-faire*, the inhibition of the public powers, is not the best course of action.

The first of these situations consists of what is known as market failures; in other words, cases in which the market does not give an efficient response: public goods, externalities, information asymmetry and so on. In these cases, there is widespread consensus in the discipline that public intervention is necessary to reach an efficient solution. However, this does not mean that just any sort of intervention is justified, as there may be problems or failures in the public regulation, causing the result to be worse than if there had been no intervention. As the saying goes, in terms that are curiously relevant to the matter in hand, sometimes the remedy is worse than the disease.

Another case warranting public intervention is when in reality the conditions for perfect competition are not fulfilled, for example, when there are situations of monopoly or oligopoly, product differentiation (monopolistic competition) or other factors preventing or restricting competition. Public intervention in this case might be in the direction of restoring or promoting this competition.

Finally, intervention may be justified by the non-acceptance of some of the premises of conventional analysis: for example, if we postulate the existence of merit goods, that is, if we reject the pertinence of the normative principle of consumer sovereignty and accept the imposition of preferences by a technical or political elite.

In the following section of this chapter we analyse the various types of market structure that occur in the case of pharmaceuticals, and we review the different factors that can limit the functioning of price competition in this market on both the supply side and the demand side. Finally, we analyse possible forms of intervention, in particular mechanisms to encourage price competition in pharmaceutical markets, and discuss the extent to which they might improve efficiency and social welfare.

CHARACTERISTICS OF PHARMACEUTICAL MARKETS

Market Delimitation

Delimiting a pharmaceutical market is no easy task. For the purposes of this analysis, which focuses on the role of price competition, the market should be delimited in such a way that it includes homogeneous or substitute drugs. According to the criterion of substitutability, markets should be defined by the diagnosis or indication for which one or more drugs are prescribed, but homogeneity and substitutability as categories are not dichotomic but of degree, and there is no single objective way of delimiting pharmaceutical markets. Furthermore, this type of information is far from easy to obtain in practice. Anatomico-therapeutic classifications, on which information is readily available, provide an imperfect approximation.

Types of Pharmaceuticals and Market Structure

Pharmaceutical markets are probably among the most regulated in developed economies. Furthermore, the demand side has some characteristics that are very different from those of the conventional market model, in which demand reflects consumers' aggregate preferences with regard to a set of units for consumption, and is subject to their budget constraint. The demand for a pharmaceutical is the result of a series of decisions, including those related to the collective financing of the product, the habitual prescribing by a doctor, and the following of the prescription by the patient. Heterogeneous units, usually with little or no vertical coordination, take these decisions. Furthermore, to talk sweepingly of the characteristics of the pharmaceutical market, as if it constituted a homogeneous entity, would be an unacceptable oversimplification. As regards the analysis of competition, which is the main objective of this chapter, we have to consider at least the following differentiating characteristics of medicinal products:

1. *Over-the-counter (OTC) drugs and prescription or ethical drugs*   The market in over-the-counter drugs is much closer to that of other consumer goods and the conventional model of demand than to that of prescription drugs, as in the former the doctor is not usually involved and the consumer decides freely which product he or she wishes to consume. However, the doctor may on occasions prescribe OTC drugs, and sometimes prescription drugs are reclassified as OTC drugs.

2. *Innovative and non-innovative drugs*   We will define an innovative drug as one that can be patented, even though its introduction may not amount to an important therapeutic improvement over those that are already on the market. Granting a patent is tantamount to guaranteeing the patent holder exclusive production and marketing rights for a particular length of time. These exclusive rights do not always mean a temporary monopoly in the economic sense, as the market may include substitutes of the patented product.

3. *Brand-name pharmaceuticals and generics*   The brand name or trade name of a drug enables it to be differentiated from substitute products that may be indistinguishable from a chemical, pharmacological and therapeutic point of view. Product differentiation, together with the limited price sensitivity on the demand side, means that competition is seen mainly in terms of quality (real or presumed) and the cultivation of prescriber loyalty by means of incentives. In contrast, generics compete basically in terms of price, as they are prescribed through the International Non-proprietary Name (INN).

4. *Hospital and non-hospital drugs*   The market in hospital drugs is sharply differentiated from that of non-hospital drugs. Pharmaceuticals as used in hospitals can be regarded as an input or a factor of production rather than a consumer good: not only do the patients not decide to consume them, but often they are even unaware of what and how much they have consumed. Furthermore, hospital pharmacy services mean that patients are better informed and have more bargaining power than any individual doctor or patient. The fact that hospitals receive an overall budget out of which they have to pay their pharmaceutical bill makes them more price-sensitive than other units of demand such as doctors in health care centres or patients, as the former do not bear the entirety of the economic consequences of their decisions, and the latter only pay part of the cost of the drug. Thus, the hospital market behaves more competitively than the non-hospital market.

Often a particular market – antihypertensive drugs, for example – can include products of different types, such as generics and brand products, innovative and non-innovative drugs, and hospital and non-hospital ones, which further complicates their analysis.[1]

SUPPLY FACTORS THAT RESTRICT COMPETITION

Patents

Patents grant their holders exclusive rights to produce and market certain products, and as such constitute a barrier to entry that ensure the owner a greater or lesser degree of monopoly power. The specific features of a country's patent system determine the degree of protection of the holder of the right, and hence also the degree of monopoly power. Product patents usually provide more protection than process patents. However, it is important to take into account other factors such as patent length, the possibility of establishing compulsory licensing and the cost of the patent itself, all of which affect the resulting degree of monopoly power. In addition, it is important to remember that a patent does not always generate a situation of monopoly; such would be the case, for example, of the patent for a new molecule with similar therapeutic effects to those of other active ingredients already on the market.

The abolition of drug patents – or the modification of the patent system towards a less protective option – would undoubtedly bring about an increase in competition and a lowering of prices. When a patent expires, it is common to see several manufacturers begin to offer the same drug at lower prices than the original, thus forcing the innovator's price down.[2] However, the abolition of patents would have a negative effect on companies' incentives to invest in research and development (R&D), which would result in a drop in the rate of innovation. The conventional argument in favour of patents states that without patents there would be far less research, as any company that did research would see how their 'competitors' (who would have no R&D expenses to cover) copied their successful innovations at lower prices and with higher rates of return. In view of this, it is necessary to strike a balance between conflicting objectives, for example by granting patents but controlling the prices of patented products that are in a situation of monopoly.[3]

Brands

Patent expiry does not spell the replacement of the possible monopoly with a situation of competition, for a number of reasons. One of these is the factor of the brand names or trade names with which laboratories identify their products.

Brands have a logical justification: they make it possible to associate a product with a firm, thus 'rewarding' the quality, prestige and other desirable consequences of the firms' behaviour. By purchasing, and perhaps even being willing to pay more for, a drug with a particular brand name, the consumer is not behaving irrationally, nor is the result necessarily inefficient: the brand name enables buyers to reduce their uncertainty about the quality of the product, as they associate it with the firm that owns the brand. The demander – patient or prescriber – can value and be willing to pay for the greater confidence inspired by a firm that, for example, has reliable research facilities that can respond to the appearance of previously unidentified adverse effects or provide the doctor with assistance in the event of doubt as to the suitability of using a certain drug in a given situation.

However, brands can introduce elements of inefficiency. Advertising and other forms of commercial promotion may induce demanders to prefer using a particular brand that holds no objective advantage over other brands of the same product. It has been argued in some contexts that the additional charge paid by the consumer in a market with differentiated products is the cost of variety and of the right to choose. This argument would not appear to be very relevant to the pharmaceutical market, where the patient usually neither pays nor chooses. Spending on advertising, aside from the information the prescriber needs on the characteristics of a product in order to ensure that it is properly used, is an expense that is ultimately laid on the doorstep of the consumer or the taxpayer, without any benefit being generated in return. The fact that neither the prescriber nor the patient suffer the economic consequences (or at least not all of them) of their decisions may induce them to choose a more expensive brand without any evidence of higher quality, for example because they irrationally consider that a higher price necessarily means higher quality, or simply because it is the latest product to have appeared on the market. In a context of low-price sensitivity on the demand side, it is easy to understand that companies seek to compete not price-wise but in real or perceived quality. Finally, the use of trade names constitutes an unnecessary source of confusion for the prescriber.

Thus, brands allow product differentiation, which, according to market theory and empirical evidence, results in a higher price than would be the case with perfect competition. Yet whereas patents provide rewards and incentives for those companies that assume the economic effort and the risk involved in research, brands benefit any company that has the wherewithal to develop effective marketing strategies and give doctors incentives to prescribe its products, regardless of their therapeutic value and the possible research orientation of the firm.

In this context, policies tending to promote generics basically seek to eliminate or reduce product differentiation and encourage price competition.

Registration and Marketing Authorization

At present, in all countries the marketing of pharmaceuticals is subject to prior government authorization based on the evaluation of the effectiveness, safety and quality of the new product. These requirements are set following both health and economic criteria, since a company may be interested in exaggerating the effectiveness and concealing or understating the risks of a new product in the face of the profits it stands to gain from its commercialization. The difficulties the consumer comes up against in the attempt to obtain and value the necessary information justify the establishment of public control over marketing, pending a government decision based on a technical evaluation of the product. However, the establishment and progressive increase of requirements prior to marketing generates additional costs and raises barriers to entry into pharmaceutical markets, and this reduces competition and makes for pharmaceutical price rises.

In recent years in some developed countries, the requisite of presenting economic evaluation (that is, pharmacoeconomic) studies of new drugs has been introduced alongside the existing one of clinical trials. These studies have to provide proof of their efficiency (or cost-effectiveness) as a condition for the public financing of the new product. These studies improve information and market transparency and may help to make competition keener, but like the earlier requirements regarding effectiveness and safety, they constitute an additional cost factor and as such raise further barriers to entry.

In conclusion, we could say that entry requirements are justified inasmuch as they are necessary to guarantee the effectiveness or efficiency of pharmaceuticals. However, establishing or maintaining unnecessary requirements to this end is tantamount to establishing costs that constitute barriers to market entry which some companies, especially smaller ones, will be unable to clear. Ultimately, these barriers also weaken competition and the consequent possibility of prices being forced down.

DEMAND FACTORS THAT RESTRICT COMPETITION

Absence of Incentives

The main factor on the demand side is probably lack of incentive; in other words, the fact that economic responsibility plays no part in the decisions taken by prescribers and consumers of pharmaceuticals. When consumers bear the consequences of their decision to buy (the usual case in a non-subsidized market) they have an incentive to compare products' benefits with their price, which is normally the main element of the cost for the consumer. When this relationship is broken or weakened by public subsidization, the consumer will tend to be guided exclusively by the expected or perceived benefits of the product and will always try to obtain that which he or she associates with the greatest benefit, regardless of the price.

Attempts to raise awareness of, or moderate, the supposed tendency towards users' overconsumption by introducing cost sharing run a real risk of damaging equity criteria, as it is difficult to modulate cost sharing and at the same time take into account each individual's economic capacity. Furthermore, it does not seem logical to attempt to influence the behaviour of a patient who does not habitually make decisions regarding drug consumption, and who can be assumed to be ignorant of the clinical and therapeutic aspects of a treatment. It would appear to be more logical to try to provide the doctor with information and incentives, as after all it is the doctor who controls the prescription.

The improvement of competition in pharmaceutical markets can, then, be an effective strategy to improve efficiency if it meets the characteristics of the pharmaceutical market. Possible strategies should take the following points into consideration:

1. Price competition could be encouraged, and at the same time the quality of the product maintained, by providing users and doctors with more information and introducing incentives for the latter, along the lines of prospective budgets or per capita payments. The reference pricing system, in conjunction with a determined policy of promoting generics, may be the most appropriate way to create incentives for efficient behaviour in users, and should have no negative affect on access and the equity of the health system.

2. The reduction of the part played by brands and trade names, or even their abolition in favour of generic names, is a strategy that seems to encourage competition without causing side effects from the point of view of social interests.

3. The abolition or weakening of patent protection would also promote competition, but probably at the cost of reducing the efforts made by industry in R&D and the resulting future probabilities of discovering new drugs that would permit or improve the treatment of diseases. It is diffi-cult to judge whether the present volume and distribution of pharmaceu-tical R&D is optimal. There is reason to believe that some of the research that is conducted has a questionable social return. For example, this partly affects research into 'me-too' drugs, whereby a company attempts to capi-talize on an existing market by developing a patentable molecule even though it is unlikely to provide any advantage, therapeutically speaking, over existing molecules. However, the abolition of patents would result in

Table 5.1   Factors affecting price competition on the supply side and the demand side

Supply side	Demand side
Patents	Absence of incentives
Brands	
Registration and marketing authorization	

a lower level of R&D than is now the case, perhaps lower than optimal socially. It can also be argued that research into 'me-too' drugs is not entirely useless from a social point of view, as it lessens the monopoly power of the original innovator and generates competition, thus forcing prices down. The issue is complex, as it intertwines health policy objectives with industrial policy ones, and neither can we ignore the matter of international relations, an aspect we will develop in the following section of this chapter.

Table 5.1 sets out the factors that affect price competition on the demand side and the supply side that we have analysed above.

Empirical studies examine the possible advantages of price competition in countries in which producers enjoy a high degree of freedom as regards pricing. Specifically, Reekie[4] analyses the evolution of the average prices of the five products that have the highest sales figures in various therapeutic subgroups and at the same time have several substitute drugs (competitors), in the USA, the UK, Denmark, the Netherlands, Germany and South Africa. The study reveals a drop in the average price year after year, after adjusting for inflation, as a result of competition.

THE INTERNATIONAL PHARMACEUTICAL MARKET

The innovative pharmaceutical industry is one of the clearest exponents of the familiar process of the globalization of the economy. The reasons for this are obvious: first, companies need to recover the huge investment in R&D that is necessary to get an innovative medicinal product with added therapeutic value onto the market. Second, the cost of transporting pharmaceuticals is usually low in comparison with the economic value of the product, which facilitates the geographical extension of markets. Finally, the company does not even need to transport goods, as it can limit itself to selling technology, especially if the innovation is protected by a system of patents, and this facilitates international expansion even more.

Innovation displays the typical characteristics of a public good: there is no rivalry in consumption and – in the absence of a patent system – it is difficult to exclude economic units who are unwilling to pay for the good.

Many countries, especially those that did not have a strong innovative industry, for a long time indulged in what is known as free-riding: by not accepting the patent – or accepting only a weak patent, such as a process patent – they enabled domestic industry to copy innovative products developed in other countries, thus generating employment and wealth at home and breaking or weakening the possible monopoly power of the innovative companies, which are usually multinationals. This, in conjunction with a strong price control policy, allowed them to enjoy relatively low prices in comparison with those of other countries. In general, the countries of southern Europe constituted a clear example of this strategy, until integration into the European Union (EU) forced them to accept a unified model of patent system, specifically the product patent for pharmaceuticals.

This same process is under way on a world scale, as a consequence of the General Agreement on Tarrifs and Trade – trade-related aspects of intellectual property (GATT-TRIP) agreements and their application through the World Trade Organization (WTO). This process is generating a single world market, with a clear trend towards the unification or at least convergence of prices internationally.[5,6] However, until a relatively few years ago the tradition was – and still is today, to some extent – a notable country-to-country variation in prices of similar or even identical drugs.

Why do prices vary from country to country? The variation in drug prices between countries has chiefly been attributed to the existence of a segmented national market, that is, independent domestic markets isolated from one another, and also the important part played by governments in fixing drug prices. Governments finance a large part of the pharmaceutical expenditure, and price control is assumed to help keep this spending on drugs within reasonable limits. It is often argued that the absence of an efficient mechanism for financing by patients, who usually do not pay 100 per cent of the price of the drugs, together with the prescription habits of doctors, also justify price intervention by the authorities.

The methods used to control drug prices range from direct control over the price of the product, by means of a system of authorized prices, to control of the overall profits of pharmaceutical companies, including indirect mechanisms based on the funding or reimbursement of the drugs (reference pricing), enforced price cuts and freezes, and the creation of positive and negative lists (the exclusion of certain drugs from public financing). A detailed description of how the various Organisation for Economic Co-operation and Development (OECD) countries control prices can be found in Mossialos.[7,8]

From the above we can see that there are different degrees of intervention in drug prices depending on the pharmaceutical legislation of the country concerned and the political and budgetary opportunities of the government in power at any given moment. This discretionality of the intervention in the pharmaceutical market leads to price differentials, primarily in patented innovative products. These differences in prices did not cause great concern or problems to companies before the abolition of national barriers, and hence they accepted the existence of different price levels for their products in different countries and adapted their business strategies to the situation as best they could. However, with the removal of tariff barriers and the trend towards a single market, these historically determined price differences have given rise to what is known as parallel trade.[9,10]

Within the EU, the parallel importer needs to obtain a licence in order to carry out this activity. Licences are granted subject to fulfilment of four conditions: (a) the product originates from a Member State, (b) it has already been given marketing authorization in the importing country, (c) it has no therapeutic differences from the product already available there, and (d) it is manufactured by the same company or group of companies in the country of origin and the importing country, or is manufactured under licence from the producer.

Government intervention is not the only source of price variation between countries. Fluctuations in the exchange rate, price discrimination by the producer and indeed each country's health care system all contribute to perpetuate and extend these differences.

For the moment, then, it is not appropriate to talk of a world pharmaceutical market as such, as there are fragmented domestic markets corresponding to each country's geographical boundaries, each characterized by its own system of price regulation and intervention.

Simplifying, we could say that countries can be grouped into high-price and low-price countries. As we discuss below, low-price countries usually contribute less to the recovery of the R&D costs incurred by the company prior to the marketing of the product, since in these countries the price is fixed just above the marginal cost of production.[11] In addition, parallel trade forces prices down to the level of the countries with the lowest prices among those in which the product is sold. If this situation were to become widespread, in the long term pharmaceutical companies would not allocate sufficient resources to develop new molecules and new drugs, and society at large would suffer. Nevertheless, this scenario is unlikely, as parallel trade mainly affects old pharmaceuticals for which the producers accepted substantial price differences between countries from the start. Nowadays multinational companies tend to fix a single price in all countries, and are not prepared to market their products in a given country below a certain price level with regard to the price in other countries, even if that means depriving certain patients and consumers of access to the latest innovative drugs available on the market. This problem is particularly acute in Third World countries, which could benefit from these drugs but are denied access to them because of the low standard of living in those countries.

PRICE DISCRIMINATION, RAMSEY PRICING AND EQUITY PRICING

A distinctive characteristic of the innovative pharmaceutical industry is the high sunk (that is, unrecoverable) costs it has to meet. These sunk costs are related to the investment made in R&D prior to actually manufacturing the product, which the company expects to recover by charging a selling price that is higher than the marginal cost of production. If this were not the case, the company would not be prepared to continue researching and marketing new products.

In the case of on-patent drugs, the patent holder is likely to enjoy a situation of monopoly. According to the discriminating monopolist model, if markets can be segmented – there is no resale between markets, so products destined for one particular market are not sold in a different one, that is there is no parallel trade – and the demand elasticity is different in each market, it will be more profitable for the manufacturer to charge a different price in each market rather than a single international price. Under certain assumptions, price discrimination by a monopolist might also lead to more efficient and equitable solution than the single price alternative.

A similar model is provided by what is called Ramsey pricing, after the economist Frank Ramsey.[12,13] This author showed that if the above conditions for market segmentation are fulfilled, social welfare is maximized in a particular market when the profit margin that is added to the marginal cost of production in order to determine the ex-factory price is inversely proportional to the price elasticity of demand. In other words, the price is always fixed above the marginal cost in order to recover the sunk costs, but this margin is inversely proportional to the sensitivity of demand in that market. Formally, this can be expressed as follows:

$$(p_i - CMg) / p_i = (1/\varepsilon_i) \cdot [\lambda / (1 + \lambda)] \qquad (4.1)$$

where p_i is the price in market i, CMg the marginal cost of production, ε_i the elasticity of demand in country i and λ a parameter that is constant in all the various countries/national markets and reflects the R&D figure that the company wishes to recover by marketing the product. Note that when λ is equal to zero the price is equal to the marginal cost.

Below we present a numerical illustration of Ramsey's argument. It consists in comparing the results of establishing a uniform price with those of applying Ramsey prices, and observing how the consumer surplus and the producer surplus are altered. The exercise requires the introduction of specific assumptions with regard to the demand function for pharmaceuticals in the markets considered, which for the sake of simplicity we limit to two, although the conclusions can be generalized for n markets.

We will suppose that the sunk costs that the company is seeking to recover amount to 500 monetary units and that the marginal cost of the product is 5 monetary units. The demand functions are $q_1 = 50 - p_1$ for market 1, and $q_2 = 50 - 2p_2$ for market 2. It is plain to see that when the price is zero, the same quantity is consumed on both markets. However, demand is more price-sensitive (that is, elastic) in market 2 than in market 1.

The results regarding the retail price of the product, the quantity sold in each market, the consumer surplus (CS), the producer surplus (entrepreneur's profit) and the social surplus (the sum of the previous two surpluses) as a consequence of establishing either a single price or discriminatory prices are shown in Table 5.2 and Figure 5.1.

Comparing the two situations, we find that the social surplus is greater when the producers practise price discrimination than when they establish a uniform price for both markets. The same happens with the level of production and the total consumer surplus. Note that the overall profit is the same in both systems, so the producer should have no preference for one or another type of pricing (they recover the sunk cost of 500 monetary units in both

Table 5.2 Comparison of the results of the hypothetical application of a single price or Ramsey prices in a two-country model

	Single price $p_1 = p_2 = 13$	Ramsey prices $p_1 = 15; p_2 = 9$
Q1	37	35
Q2	24	32
Total *Q*	61	67
CS1	684	612
CS2	144	256
Total *CS*	828	868
Profit 1	300	365
Profit 2	200	135
Total profit	500	500
Social surplus	1328	1368

Single price

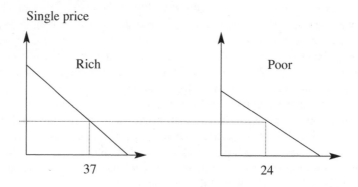

Price discrimination: Ramsey prices

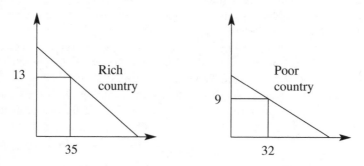

Figure 5.1 Result of establishing a single price and Ramsey prices

cases). In our example, the only figure that would drop with price discrimination is the consumer surplus in market 1.

The main difference between price discrimination and Ramsey pricing is that the former model results in the highest potential profit for the monopolist, whereas Ramsey pricing, as a prescriptive tool for regulating a public monopoly, only aims at recovering the sunk cost of the investment.

The fact of establishing a single international price for a patented product may be the result of a decision by a drug multinational to market an innovative product at a particular price, without considering the possibility of doing so below that price. In the context of the EU, and also in the global economy, two additional factors contribute to price uniformity between markets (or to their convergence within a very narrow band).[14,15] These two factors are: (a) the threat of large volumes of parallel imports that are likely to continue in future, or to be more exact, the pricing strategies used by pharmaceutical companies to combat them, which works for a very small price differential between markets, and (b) price fixing by national health authorities on the basis of the existing price in another market, or other markets, which are taken as a reference. Either national regulation or practice often establish that the domestic price of a drug cannot be higher than that found in a particular market (what is known as the 'average price'). This practice is very wide-spread in the EU; Germany, the UK, France and Denmark are regarded as the only countries that do not fix drug prices on the basis of those of other countries. The rest all use the average price, either directly or indirectly.[16]

In recent times, the acquired immune deficiency syndrome (AIDS) epidemic has brought under the spotlight the issue of intellectual property rights and on-patent drug pricing and its effects on accessibility to drugs in developing countries. Some patent holders have in principle agreed to sell antiretroviral drugs to developing countries at discounted (and income-related) prices under certain conditions that guarantee that the products will not be diverted to high-price markets. Moreover, the negotiations on patent rights in the context of the TRIPS agreement, by allowing developing countries to issue compulsory licensing for certain essential drugs, might result in a two-tiered international market, in which developed countries will pay a high price for new drugs while on patent, while developing countries might enjoy lower prices for the same products as a result of the possibility of circumventing patent protection and making generic competition work.

POLICY OPTIONS IN THE INTERNATIONAL PHARMACEUTICAL MARKET

Those who defend international free trade do so on the basis that it increases economic efficiency. The most commonly used arguments are:

1. The profits resulting from specialization in the manufacture of products in which a company has a comparative advantage lead to an increase in welfare.
2. A larger market means keener competition between products, which leads to lower prices and the disappearance of inefficient producers.
3. The consumer has more products to choose from.
4. Competition between producers leads to the reduction of prices to just above the marginal cost of production, resulting in the maximization of social welfare.

Of course, these arguments are not universally accepted. Many experts consider, for example, that free trade without any sort of control is to the relative disadvantage of less developed countries. But the inappropriateness of a free market policy is particularly evident in the case of innovative drugs, which comprises a specific series of conditions. First of all, innovative drugs possess characteristics of a global public good. Moreover, high sunk costs are involved in their production, and finally, there is a problem of international equity or solidarity. As we have tried to argue above, the most appropriate option in this complex situation is the existence of a certain price differential between markets, to maximize the surplus obtainable by the company for the recovery of R&D costs and to facilitate access to these drugs for the populations of countries with less purchasing power. The relevance of the Ramsey pricing model is not that it provides the best solution to the problem of international drug pricing, but that it shows that the establishment of different prices can be a beneficial option both for companies and for consumers at large. In such a controlled market as that of pharmaceuticals it can be difficult to estimate the elasticity of demand, and even if it were possible, it is not clear that for normative purposes it would constitute the most suitable pricing criterion for each country.

Recent proposals by the World Health Organization (WHO) and other stakeholders point to the concept of equity pricing. The rationale of these proposals is that countries should be expected to contribute to the recovery of the research costs of global drugs according to their wealth. This could be implemented by setting a price structure whereby the surplus paid by each country over the marginal cost of production – that is, its contribution to the recovery of the investment in R&D – would be proportional to some sort of wealth indicator such as the gross domestic product (GDP). After all, this is the criterion that is already used in the funding of various international bodies to calculate the corresponding quota for each country.

The party that might feel disadvantaged in an agreement of this sort is the population of richer countries, who may wonder why they have to pay more than what consumers in poorer countries pay for the same drug. The logical answer is that with price discrimination richer countries would be paying less towards the company's recovery of its investment in R&D than with the system whereby a single price is fixed and poorer countries have absolutely no access to the drug. This is an issue that should be dealt with through some system of internal redistribution in the country, such as the establishment of a national health system financed according to individuals' ability to pay.

An equitable international drug price structure could also be attained by setting differential licence fees and allowing generic competition to work within each price segment of the international market.

Other proposals question the efficiency of the present system of intellectual property rights as an incentive to innovation and point to a more radical change in the way R&D on pharmaceuticals is organized: these proposals include open-source research, public funding of R&D on global drugs and neglected diseases, international R&D agreements, non-exclusive market rights and so on.

None of the solutions mentioned in the above lines will be forthcoming from any 'invisible hand', nor can it be decided by one state as a corrective measure against market failures, because national authorities lack the capacity to impose regulations beyond their national borders. The way forward should be along the lines of an international agreement between countries, promoted and guaranteed by international bodies such as the WHO and the World Trade Organization (WTO).

The solutions presented in this chapter may seem unrealizable at present. However, there is evidence that some initiatives are being taken in this direction. Although these initiatives are faced with a host of difficulties, there can be no doubt that it will be necessary to develop novel and imaginative solutions if we are to avoid the intolerable situation of a large part of the world's population being denied the benefits of technological innovation in health care, without this even representing an advantage for the population of the more developed countries.

REFERENCES

1. Schweitzer, S. (1997), *Pharmaceutical Economics and Policy*, New York: Oxford University Press.
2. Bogner, W. (1996), *Drugs to Market*, Oxford, Tarrytown, NY, Pergamon.
3. Grabowski, H. and J. Vernon (2000), 'The distribution of sales revenues from pharmaceutical innovation', *PharmacoEconomics*, 18 (supplement 1), 21–32.
4. Reekie, W. (1996), *Medicine Prices and Innovations: an International Survey*, London: Institute of Economic Affairs.
5. International Federation of Pharmaceutical Manufacturers Associations (IFPMA) (1995), *GATT, TRIPs and the Pharmaceutical Industry: a Review*, Geneva: IFPMA.
6. Correa, C. (1997), *The Uruguay Round and Drugs*, Washington: World Health Organization.
7. Mossialos, E., C. Ranos and B. Abel-Smith (1994), *Cost Containment, Pricing and Financing of Pharmaceuticals in the European Union: the Policy-makers' View*, London: LSE Health and Pharmetrica.
8. Mossialos, E. (1998), 'Pharmaceutical pricing, financing and cost containment in the European Union Member States', in R. Leidl (ed.), *Health Care and its Financing in the Single European Market*, Amsterdam: IOS Press, pp. 85–115.
9. Darbà, J. and J. Rovira (1998), 'Parallel imports of pharmaceuticals in the European Union', *PharmacoEconomics*, 14 (supplement 1), 129–36.
10. Danzon, P. (1997), *Trade and Price Differentials for Pharmaceuticals: Policy Options*, London: Office of Health Economics.
11. Ballance, R., J. Pogan and H. Forstner (1992), *The World's Pharmaceutical Industries: an International Perspective on Innovation, Competition and Policy*, Aldershot, UK and Brookfield, US: Edward Elgar.

12. Ramsey, F. (1927), 'A contribution to the theory of taxation', *Economic Journal*, 37, 47–61.
13. Eatwell, J., M. Milgate and P. Newman (1988), *The New Palgrave: a Dictionary of Economics*, London: Macmillan.
14. Simon, H. (1987), *Parallel Imports*, London: Collins Professional Books.
15. Simon, H. and E. Kucker (1992), 'The European pricing time bomb and how to cope with it', *European Management Journal*, **10** (2), 136–45.
16. Commission of the European Communities (1997), *Panorama of EU industry*, Brussels: Commission of the European Communities.

PART II

6. Reference pricing as a pharmaceutical reimbursement mechanism

G. López-Casasnovas and J. Puig-Junoy

INTRODUCTION

The concern voiced in Spain regarding the rationalization of pharmaceutical consumption has a logical foundation in both the trend and the level of drug expenditure borne by the Spanish public health system in comparison with those of the countries in its immediate vicinity. Spain undoubtedly constitutes an atypical case in the context of the European Union (EU) as regards the proportion of national health spending accounted for by pharmaceutical expenditure. According to the Organization for Economic Co-operation and Development (OECD) Health Data File, in 1997 public spending on pharmaceuticals in Spain amounted to 19.5 per cent of total public health expenditure, the highest proportion in any EU country except Portugal. This figure is notably higher than the average for EU countries, which stands at around 11.9 per cent. In per capita terms too, public pharmaceutical spending has begun to show values that are higher than the average for EU countries (129 ecus on average in EU countries as a whole in 1996 as opposed to 152 ecus per capita in Spain), in contrast to the figures for the rest of public health expenditure, which are lower than the European average. Spain's public per capita spending on pharmaceuticals is clearly greater, in the EU context, than that of countries with a higher per capita income, such as the Netherlands, Belgium and the UK.

Since 1990, responsibility for containing the public pharmaceutical bill in Spain has fallen to a variety of instruments, none of which has proved particularly effective at cost containment, as can be seen from Table 6.1. These instruments have included stricter control over the National Health Service (NHS) (*Sistema Nacional de Salud* or SNS) budget for pharmaceuticals, modifications to the co-payment rates for certain drugs for chronic diseases, the exclusion of certain drugs from public financing (negative lists) and agreements with laboratories and pharmacies.[1]

The Agreement of the Parliamentary Subcommittee to advance in the consolidation of the National Health System, of 30 September 1997, set out to

Table 6.1   Evolution of public health expenditure in Spain (1989–2001) (%)

Year	Public pharmaceutical spending/GDP	Public health spending (excluding pharmaceuticals)/GDP	Public pharmaceutical spending/total public health spending
1990	0.9	4.5	12.8
1991	0.9	4.6	13.1
1992	1.0	4.8	13.3
1993	1.0	4.9	13.0
1994	1.0	4.8	13.4
1995	1.1	4.6	13.7
1996	1.1	4.7	14.2
1997	1.1	4.7	15.1
1998	1.1	4.3	15.2
1999	1.2	4.2	15.6
2000	1.2	4.1	15.7
2001	1.2	4.2	15.7

Source: OECD Health Data (2003).

develop new formulas for the rationalization of pharmaceutical services as a cost containment measure. The three measures chosen to this end were as follows: (a) the separation of the registration of medicines and their public financing, in order to enable selective financing, (b) the promotion of 'generic drugs' and the application of 'reference pricing' (RP) as a public sector payment system, and (c) improvement of consumer information for both patients and prescribers, with the possibility of establishing pharmaceutical budgets in each health care unit.

   This was not the first attempt to introduce a policy on generics and reference pricing in Spain, as legislative measures were adopted at the end of 1996, with the concept of the generic (*especialidad farmacéutica genérica* or EFG) being included in the Pharmaceuticals Act (Law 13/96, concomitant to the 1997 budget), with a view to a future limitation of public financing on the basis of price competition, which involves the existence of generics. An EFG is defined as a product with the same pharmaceutical form and the same quantitative and qualitative composition in medicinal substances as a reference product, the profile of which with regard to effectiveness and safety is sufficiently established by its continued clinical use.

   The Parliamentary Subcommittee's proposal to create a generic market and apply reference prices to the public financing of medicines seeks, at least in theory, to encourage price competition in the highly regulated pharmaceutical market, with the aim of helping to moderate the growth of public health spending due to the purchase of drugs. The Spanish Ministry of Health and Consumer Affairs introduced a reference pricing system for the public financing of several groups of drugs in December 2000.

However, it must be stressed that pharmaceutical expenditure is just another input in health production policies, and its complementariness or substitutability with other inputs, and cross-effects in general, make it necessary to take an overall approach to any rationalization process. In pharmaceutical policy in particular, it is impossible to ignore the deficits caused by distribution costs, the absence of real competition in the dispensing market and the perverse effects of the present system of remuneration for pharmacists.

The purpose of this chapter is to present the main economic characteristics of reference pricing (RP) as a system for the public funding of pharmaceuticals financed by the public sector. The following sections deal with the definition and objectives of RP and analyse the features of the various reference pricing systems that are applied internationally. This is followed by a look at the justification for RP from the economic point of view. We then go on to analyse the impact of RP policies, especially with regard to expenditure, consumption and drug prices. In the final section we discuss what can be expected from the application of RP to the Spanish health system.

DEFINITION, OBJECTIVES AND BACKGROUND OF REFERENCE PRICING

Definition

What does the application of RP mean in the pharmaceutical market? Policies establishing reference prices as a strategy to contain pharmaceutical expenditure by encouraging competition through prices consist in defining a maximum level of reimbursement for the public financing of prescription drugs, the difference between this level and the retail price of the chosen product being charged to the patient.[2-4] The maximum reimbursable amount or reference price is determined in relation to a group of alternative drugs, considered to be comparable or equivalent. In this respect, the system is a policy for promoting competition through prices, and works by channelling public funding towards the lowest-price products. Since its introduction in Germany in 1989, reference pricing systems have been applied in the Netherlands, Sweden, Denmark, New Zealand, Poland, Slovenia, British Columbia (Canada), Norway, Italy and Australia.

What type of markets has RP been applied to? The first countries to introduce RP systems share, in varying degrees, three characteristics. First of all, in many of them drug pricing was free (the case in Germany, Denmark and New Zealand) and unit prices were high. Second, generic drugs accounted for a fairly large market share at the time of RP introduction: for example, 16.1 per cent of prescription drug sales in pharmacies in Germany, 22 per cent in Denmark and 12.6 per cent in the Netherlands. And third, they were countries in which the public sector is the main buyer of pharmaceuticals: 71.4 per cent of sales in Germany, 64.2 per cent in the Netherlands, 79.2 per cent in Norway, 71.2 per cent in Sweden, 50.5 per cent in Denmark and 58.8 per cent in New Zealand. Table 6.2 shows the comparative situation of pharmaceutical expenditure in Europe in 1997 on the basis of several indicators.

Objectives

As a system of public financing, the most immediate goal of RP is to control public pharmaceutical expenditure, independently of the trend in total pharmaceutical expenditure. It is based on the assumption that the moderation of public spending should be achieved through the reduction of the price paid for products submitted to RP in view of the greater cost they may entail for users who choose a product with a higher price than the RP.

Two mid-term objectives are closely related to the principal goal of RP. The first of them has to do with encouraging price competition, as it provides an incentive for companies to bring their prices close to the reference level. This is precisely one of the reasons why the European Commission[5] recommends RP. The second mid-term objective concerns incentives, as it takes into account the cost-effectiveness ratio of prescription drugs by increasing the financial responsibility of patients, which in turn may influence prescriber decisions. It is important to note that, unlike in traditional co-payment, under this system the patient's share of the cost of the product is 'avoidable' if the patient and/or doctor select a product with a price that does not exceed the reference price.

Background

Although this measure was first introduced in Germany in 1989, constraints on public drug spending and the creation of incentives for cheaper alternatives are not new to cost containment policies, especially in public health systems. Several forms of public financing of pharmaceuticals based on comparison (yardstick competition) have been used in some countries by public and private insurers. Public financing mechanisms that pursue a similar strategy to that of RP include the 'maximum allowable cost' (MAC) applied by the

Table 6.2   National expenditure on health care and pharmaceuticals in Europe (1997)

Countries	Health expenditure (% GDP)	Pharmaceutical expenditure (% GDP)	Pharmaceutical expenditure (% health spending)	Pharmaceutical expenditure ($ per capita)
Austria	7.9	1.1	10	260
Belgium	7.6	1.4	13	267
Bulgaria	n/a	n/a	35	25
Czech Rep.	n/a	n/a	28	94
Denmark	7.7	0.7	12	215
Estonia	n/a	n/a	28	20
Finland	7.3	1.1	11	192
France	9.9	1.7	17	435
Germany	10.4	1.3	11	269
Greece	7.1	1.8	25	118
Hungary	n/a	n/a	30	63
Ireland	7	0.7	10	111
Italy	7.6	1.4	14	209
Latvia	n/a	n/a	25	19
Lithuania	n/a	n/a	25	19
Luxembourg	7.1	0.8	12	260
Netherlands	8.5	0.9	13	272
Poland	n/a	n/a	19	36
Portugal	8.2	2.2	18	127
Rumania	n/a	n/a	23	10
Slovakia	n/a	n/a	17	23
Slovenia	n/a	n/a	13	52
Spain	7.4	1.5	16	193
Sweden	8.6	1.1	16	315
Switzerland	10.2	0.8	11	396
UK	6.7	1.2	10	143

Source: International Pharma News, OECD (1998), EPISCOM.

Medicaid programme in the USA, differential co-payment for cheaper drugs, also applied in the USA, and the system based on the lowest-cost alternative in British Columbia (Canada).

CHARACTERISTICS OF REFERENCE PRICING SYSTEMS

Basic Features

First, public financing systems based on reference prices show the following five basic features:[6]

1. Products are classified into subgroups of 'equivalent' drugs (with 'similar' therapeutic effects).
2. The RP is the maximum and only reimbursement for all the drugs in the same subgroup (the insurer limits the assumed risk).
3. The RP is fixed on the basis of some point (minimum, average and so on) in the distribution of observed market prices.
4. Pharmaceutical companies have freedom of pricing for products under RP.
5. If the retail price fixed by the producer is higher than the RP, the patient pays the difference (variable and avoidable co-payment).

It is very important to pay attention to the details of how the system is applied in order to be able to predict the impact of RP implementation. Problems and perverse incentives appear in the details of the system, and it is very easy for a good idea in theory to turn into a sour reality.[7] Table 6.3 shows the basic characteristics of the application of RP in various countries.

Basic Arithmetic

Let RP be the reference price, CP the price paid by the consumer, EFP the selling price fixed by the laboratory, and k the co-payment rate. In this context, we can analyse two situations:

Case 1:   If $LP_1 < RP$, then CP is fixed at kLP_1

Case 2:   If $LP_2 > RP$, then CP is fixed at $LP_2 - RP + kRP$

The subsidy implicit rate in each case will be

$$T_1 = (1 - k) \text{ and } T_2 = (LP_2 - CP) / LP_2 = RP (1 - k) / LP_2$$

Table 6.3   Some international experiences in the application of RP

Country and year of introduction	Application criteria
Australia (1998)	Coverage: six therapeutic groups, especially coronary diseases and ulcers (pharmacological equivalence) RP: the lowest in each group Reviewal: every four months
British Columbia (1995)	Coverage: products with different active ingredients within the same therapeutic group RP: generally the lowest in each group Reviewal: ad hoc
Denmark (1993)	Coverage: products whose patent has expired and that have generics with the same active ingredient RP: the average of the two lowest in each group
Germany (1989)	Coverage: active ingredients with identical chemical composition (group 1); active ingredients with allied or related composition and comparable pharmacological and therapeutic action (group 2); active ingredients with different chemical composition and comparable therapeutic action (group 3) RP: generally the lowest on the market; the statistical median based on a regression model for the various forms of presentation Reviewal: the list of products included is reviewed every three months and the system is reviewed once a year
Netherlands (1991)	Coverage: products that are interchangeable in terms of mechanism of action and use, therapeutic and side effects and use for treating the same age group RP: the average of the same group Reviewal: the list of products included is reviewed monthly and the system is reviewed twice a year
New Zealand (1993)	Coverage: products in the same subgroup, defined as products with identical or similar therapeutic effects RP: the lowest Reviewal: the list of products included is reviewed monthly and the system can be reviewed whenever a product is added to the list for RP
Sweden (1993)	Coverage: products whose patent has expired and generic equivalents (identical presentation, active ingredient and quality) RP: the lowest price plus 10% Reviewal: the list of products included is reviewed every three months and the system is reviewed once every two years

Source: Own data, from J. Puig-Junoy[8] and G. López-Casasnovas and J. Puig-Junoy.[6]

Given that $LP_1 < LP_2$ and $LP_2 > RP$, the relationship between T_1 and T_2 will depend on k and RP. That is, the percentage of subsidy per product is greater the smaller the difference between RP and LP_2, and the smaller the co-payment k.

From the point of view of welfare economics, the mechanism whereby reference prices operate effectively replaces an *ad valorem* subsidy with another based on a fixed percentage, regardless of the size of EFP. In effect, whereas previously the volume of the public subsidy depended on the retail price, now under RP there is a ceiling at $(1 - k)RP$. As occurs in cases in which the substitution effect is reinforced (in favour of one drug and against another, a 'brand-name pharmaceutical'), the stronger distortion in consumer sover-eignty that is introduced must be offset – in principle, to a larger extent – by the greater social efficiency in the resulting allocation. Hence the crucial importance of guaranteeing the identical effectiveness of the substitute drug in the RP system.

Public Financing System or Price Regulation System?

RP entails a limit to public funding rather than the regulation of the retail price of a drug. Producers are free to fix the retail price above the RP if they think the patient will be willing to pay the difference. However, as Drummond et al.[9] note, pricing and public financing are conceptually related: financing deci-sions (inclusion or exclusion) depend on price, but changes in prices or the initial price level of a new product also depend on financing. In practice, the influence of RP on pricing can be important if companies are forced to fix prices that are equivalent to the reference level. In this case the RP acts as a price cap.

The influence of RP on selling prices depends on the monopsony power of the buyer, the price elasticity of the product and the cross-price elasticity for substitute products, and also the coverage of products under RP. The situation most likely to result in equivalence between RP and price-cap regulation is when there is a majority buyer, the number of products under RP is very large and demand is very elastic. In general, the RP system attains its objectives best when the pharmaceutical bill has a close relationship with price pressure and when price differentials in the market for equivalent products are high, which has clear links with the presence of generics.

The differences found in the application of different RP systems cloud the differences between a public financing system and a price-cap regulation system. An RP becomes a price cap when the decision either to include a drug within public financing or to exclude it depends on its price. The use of RP in New Zealand and Italy is a good illustration of this situation. Italy introduced a very restrictive RP system in 1996. In this case, the maximum financing level determines the maximum price, as patients have to pay 100 per cent of EFP if EFP > RP.[10] Strictly speaking, then, the Italian case is not an RP system, as it only finances the cheapest product in each group of drugs: companies are forced to reduce their prices unless they want to see their products excluded from public financing. In New Zealand, the RP system is applied in such a way that in order for a product to be included within public financing its price must be lower than the current RP in the corresponding subgroup.[11]

Table 6.4   The Kinked Demand model

THE KINKED DEMAND MODEL

Let D1 be the demand for a drug before the application of reference pricing (RP) in a health system without any pharmaceutical co-payment. For the sake of simplicity, let us assume that the marginal cost is constant (CMg). We suppose that the adoption of a RP system is passed, establishing that the patient must pay the difference between the retail price of the product and the RP. When RPs are introduced, the maximum level of public financing (the RP) is fixed at RP for a given product. Thus, when the ex-factory price (EFP) coincides with the RP the marginal cost for the patient is zero. However, when EFP > RP, then the marginal cost increases for the patient and also for the doctor, who has to justify the choice of that drug to the patient. Therefore, after the introduction of RP, demand for the product will be more elastic for prices above RP.

Conversely, when RP < EFP, the marginal cost for the patient is likewise zero, so the totality of the saving (the distance between RP and EFP) becomes less cost for the insurer, and therefore demand will be more inelastic after the introduction of RP. In this case, the patient's and the doctor's demand is indifferent to a price rise, as long as it does not exceed RP. D2 represents demand after the introduction of RP under the assumption that doctors have perfect information on EFP and RP prices, and shows a kink at RP. Note that in a pure kinked demand model it will never be optimal to fix a price below RP. Thus, those companies that market products whose EFP was lower than RP prior to the introduction of RP may now have an incentive to raise EFP to the level of RP.

Any effort made by doctors to obtain and update information on product prices (EFP and RP) also has a cost. Under the more realistic assumption of uncertainty about prices, doctors can cut the cost of obtaining information by adopting the assumption that brand products always have an EFP higher than RP; in this case, they would always tend to choose a generic with a price lower than RP (or a particular drug which they know to be cheap) in order to avoid the co-payment resulting from the price differential and the consequent justification of this choice to the patient. In this situation, demand for prices above RP, and even for prices slightly lower than RP, will become more elastic (demand curve D3), see Figure 6.1 below.

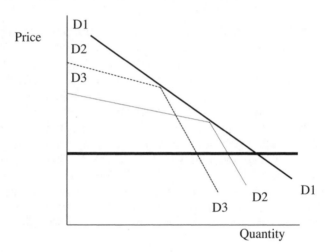

Figure 6.1   The Kinked Demand model

Source: (*) Adapted from Danzon and Liu.[22]

Avoidable Co-payment

Unlike negative and positive lists, RP does not restrict the list of available medicines for the prescriber and the patient. If the doctor prescribes a product with a price higher than RP, the patient pays the difference; but there is no additional co-payment if EFP is equal to or lower than RP.

This public financing system respects freedom of choice, subject to one's willingness to bear the additional cost. It aims to raise patients' awareness of cost, thus encouraging the rational use of 'equivalent' or similar products. In the context of a public decision-maker with the objective of maximizing health (for example, the number of quality-adjusted life-years or QALYs), the limit to unitary financing can be interpreted as the equivalent to applying a decision rule based on the maximum price that the insurer is prepared to pay for one additional unit of 'health'. However, the equivalence of RP with a social decision rule depends on the degree of suitability of the effectivity measure implicit in the equivalence between products. At the same time, avoidable co-payment can become unavoidable if drugs classified in the same subgroup are not perfectly 'interchangeable' for a particular patient, and in this case the co-payment would depend on the price strategies of the company marketing each product.[12]

The Concept of Equivalence

The RP systems currently in force differ in practice, first in accordance with the size of the market covered. This in turn depends on the equivalence criterion chosen to classify drugs, and also on the inclusion or otherwise of patented drugs.

There are three levels of equivalence for classifying products, each submitted to an identical maximum level of public financing: chemical equivalence, pharmacological equivalence and therapeutic equivalence. The first level entails establishing groups for the same active ingredient, which at the same time include both generics and brand-name pharmaceuticals whose patent has expired. This is the system applied in Sweden, Denmark, Norway and Spain. It encompasses bio-equivalent products with 'identical qualitative or quantitative composition, pharmaceutical form, dose, administration method and presentation'.

There are two more levels of equivalence that make it possible to enlarge the market share of products subject to this control. The second level of application groups together in the same category drugs with active ingredients that are comparable from a pharmacological and therapeutic viewpoint, for example, angiotensin converter enzyme inhibitors; this is the level considered in Australia and British Columbia. Finally, the third level contains products with the same therapeutic function, for example, all antihypertensive drugs. Thus, the second and third levels can include or exclude drugs protected by patents. Germany applies the third level of equivalence but since the beginning of 1996 has excluded products under patent, whereas patented products are included in the reference pricing systems of New Zealand and the Netherlands.

The extension of the RP system to equivalence levels 2 and 3 is far from free of controversy. A host of problems arise as a result of the heterogeneity of the effects of the drugs at the level of each patient, making the system very complicated to apply. The physiological responses of individual patients to each drug may vary due to differences in quality, absorption, indications, side effects, chemical preparation, form of application, frequency of undesired effects, contraindications and so on.[13] This means that countries that do not limit the scope of RP are forced to make many individualized exceptions, causing disputes between professionals and the insuring entity and major transaction costs. The exact magnitude of these costs depends on how the exception is formulated, the period in which it is passed, the responsibilities incurred in the interim 'administrative silence', the degree of informed consent required between prescriber, patient and dispenser, and other factors.

What effects can be expected from the inclusion of heterogeneous medicines in the same subgroup? The problems associated with the heterogeneity or rough equivalence of drugs with the same RP fall into three groups.[6] First, if the product is not equivalent for a particular patient, co-payment becomes unavoidable and generates equity problems. Second, selecting the product with EFP equal to RP may lead to reduced effectiveness and negative side effects for patients wishing to avoid co-payment. This may give rise to an increase in spending on complementary health services. And third, the adoption of a single price for roughly equivalent products distorts competition in the market and may discriminate against certain companies.

The application of RPs to completely equivalent pharmaceuticals (perfect substitutes) whose patent has expired (for example, generic drugs) is a mechanism that potentially increases the efficiency of health expenditure. However, the extension of the scope of RP by applying the levels of pharmacological and therapeutic equivalence (levels 2 and 3) presents, in short, two main disadvantages that impose serious limitations on the efficiency of the measure. First, the classification of two products, A and B, in the same subgroup with the same maximum level of public financing but different retail prices poses problems when the patient has imperfect information: patients are not well acquainted with differences in effectiveness and side effects, unless doctors take time to explain them to them, for which they have little incentive. Second, the administrative costs of the exceptions, together with the costs for additional health care use as a result of the change in medicament and the time used by doctors to explain the situation to their patients may cancel out the potential gains of the system.

The Treatment of Drugs under Patent

When the RP system was introduced in Germany it included patented products, although they were exempted in January 1996. In other countries such as Denmark and Sweden, the system only covers products whose patents have expired and generics. The inclusion of drugs with extant patents in the RP system reduces the efficiency of the patent system and may cause dynamic efficiency losses that are much larger than the gains forthcoming from RP (loss of incentive to conduct research and development (R&D)): if new patented products are grouped together with generics and a common level of public financing is established, the RP can be too high for the generic and too low for the new product. The international literature highlights the negative incentives for pharmaceutical innovation when the RP system includes drugs under patent (which is possible in the event of applying the second and third levels of product equivalence as described above).[3] The pharmaceutical companies argue that this practice reduces incentives to develop incremental improvements or additional indications in drugs that are already on the market and subject to the system, and to develop new drugs that would be included in one of the groups subject to RP. Instead, firms have incentives to develop new products that are not subject to the RP system.

The social welfare effects of these negative incentives for innovation depend on the degree of information one possesses when selecting a pharmaceutical. Under the assumption of perfect information, if the patient has little willingness to pay for an incremental improvement, the disincentive to spend should not cause significant welfare losses. However, when there is imperfect information and little willingness to pay, the risk of negative effects on welfare can be quite high. This is particularly true when there are potential differences in the effects of the drugs, for example between those classified in the same subgroup, as occurs with equivalence levels 2 and 3.

If products under patent are exempted from the RP system, do the negative effects on the R&D of the pharmaceutical sector disappear? The exclusion of medicines with a current patent may reduce the economic erosion of the rights granted by the patent, and also the disincentive to invest in R&D. But negative effects on innovation are not totally eradicated, as: (a) RP increases the uncertainty on the expected return on the investment, (b) incentives for innovation will be damaged due to the fact that the R&D process is a joint production process, since the overall return is reduced when RP is applied, and (c) the exclusion of patented products has proved to be only partial in some cases (for example, not excluding drugs under a process patent).

JUSTIFICATION FOR RP

What distinguishes the pharmaceutical market and justifies the need to fix maximum limits to public financing such as those involved in RP systems? The pharmaceutical sector differs from other sectors in very important respects,[14,15] including an imperfect agency relationship, imperfect information, moral hazard and joint, sunk and fixed costs.

Imperfect Agency Relationship

The prescribing doctor acts as an agent for both the patient and the insurer. There is information asymmetry between patient and doctor as regards the effectiveness and the quality of the product. Moreover, it has been shown that in many cases the existence of certain prescription-related costs incumbent on doctors renders them imperfect agents for their patients. An example of these costs would be those incurred in the process of obtaining objective information on the availability, effectiveness and price differentials of pharmaceutical products. There is empirical evidence to the effect that doctors have little information on drug prices.[16] Doctors make less of an effort to obtain information than would be desirable ideally from the principals' viewpoint, as doctors receive no income for this effort.[17] However, there are two sides to the agency problem: the doctor is also the prescribing agent for the public or private insurer. The insurer would like all doctors to prescribe cost-effectively, evaluating the prescription according to its cost and its therapeutic benefit. If doctors are more concerned about patients' welfare than about the cost of the prescription, the imperfections in the agency relationship may give rise to overprescription and lack of price sensitivity.

Imperfect Information

The pharmaceutical market is large and complex, new products being introduced at a very brisk pace, and it is difficult for doctors to judge which is the best possible alternative without some sort of help. One example of these information problems is the fact that doctors make their decisions on the basis of effectiveness and attach little importance to price. Caves et al.[18] state that doctors lack information on comparative effectiveness and the risk of substitute pharmaceutical products.

Moral Hazard

The consumer does not usually have to pay the whole of the price of the drug prescribed by the doctor. Even in the case of a perfect agency relationship between prescriber and patient, drug consumption may not be optimal because of the existence of moral hazard. This means that the insured patient has no incentive to induce the doctor to make the effort to seek information on lower-cost treatments. Even if the doctor had complete information, because of moral hazard the patient would tend not to demand the socially optimal quantity of prescribed drugs. Consequently, the patient may receive an excess of prescriptions and/or the drugs prescribed may be too expensive in relation to the social optimum.[17]

Joint, Sunk and Fixed Costs

The structure of the pharmaceutical sector differs from that of other industries in the important part played by joint costs. Thus, the costs that can be attributed to a particular product in a particular country may represent a very small fraction of the total costs.[19] The existence of joint, sunk and fixed costs gives rise to two types of imperfections in this market.[3] First, pricing based on the marginal cost is not always efficient. A competitive market does not allow the recovery of R&D costs, a fact that most countries use to justify the patents they grant to pharmaceutical innovations. Second, a monopsonist has incentives to take advantage of joint, sunk and fixed costs. If the regulator or the insurer acting as a monopsonistic buyer of pharmaceuticals draws prices towards the marginal cost, the supply of new products in the long term will not be optimal.[3] This is due to the fact that the supply of new products is critically dependent on R&D spending.

In short, the imperfections of the pharmaceutical market cause: (a) less price sensitivity on the demand side, (b) a certain amount of market power on the supply side, and (c) demand curves that do not reflect the true social benefit. Demand for pharmaceuticals is greater and less price-elastic than it should be. The reason for this is that consumers have little price sensitivity, especially under insurance coverage.

On the supply side, patents allow the innovating company considerable discretion in pricing their new products. However, new products may be complements or substitutes of those of rival companies. In reality, pharmaceutical firms operate in oligopolistic markets characterized by a limited number of competitors (especially in submarkets such as that of cardiovascular products, for example), differentiated products and competitive innovation strategies.

Furthermore, the agency relationship and imperfect information, added to the problems on the supply side, give rise to prices above the marginal cost even when the patent has expired. The expected result of the introduction of generic drugs should be a rise in competition and falling prices for brand products. In the long run it seems reasonable to assume that the price of generics should drop to the marginal cost. In reality this does not appear to be the case, and we find what Scherer[14] called the 'generic competition paradox' (see Chapter 3): the average price of brand products tends to increase when generics enter the market. Evidence suggests a high degree of brand loyalty for innovative products, as a result of which brand products are capable of retaining a large market share in the face of lower-cost generics after the patent has expired. Frank and Salkever[20] conclude that 'increased competition from generics is not accompanied by lower prices for brand-name drugs. We found no evidence of brand-name price reductions being associated with entry by generic producers. In fact, the evidence we did uncover is consistent with small price rises being tied to expanded competition'.

To sum up, the factors that enable the supply side to fix prices above the marginal cost are: (a) the imperfect agency relationship between the doctor (the agent) and the insurer (the principal); the prescriber may prefer the brand product, about which he or she has acquired knowledge and experience during the patent period (risk aversion), (b) the patient, and sometimes also the doctor, may have imperfect information on the quality of cheaper alternatives, and (c) the lack of incentives to change prescription habits (moral hazard).

Public spending containment policies aimed at curtailing the pricing power of companies after patent expiry seem to require incentives for prescribers and distributors to replace more expensive brand-name pharmaceuticals with cheaper generics. In this context, RP could be justified as a way of helping to reduce the welfare losses generated by choosing more expensive drugs when suitable and cheaper alternatives are available.

IMPACT OF RP

RP has been introduced in countries where the monopsony power is considerable yet not by any means the only instrument used to influence the pharmaceutical market. In most countries, RP has been accompanied by a wide range of reforms affecting both the demand side and the supply side. Given this situation, it is very difficult to attribute the changes observed in pharmaceutical expenditure and prices solely to the strategy of RP. Studies that compare expenditure, consumption and prices before and after the introduction of RP, which constitute most of the empirical literature on this mechanism, do not allow us to separate the influence of RP from that of other economic and social factors on the behaviour of the dependent variable.[6]

The main drawback of RP is that cost containment is not always achieved, and when it is, it is fleeting. The reasons for the limited effect (small, short-term savings) of RP on cost containment are: (a) as we have seen, it is applied to a limited proportion of the market, which is generally not that which leads the growth in expenditure, (b) companies react by recovering the losses incurred on the products covered by the system through price increases in non-covered products, and (c) the system seeks to control prices yet does not influence either the increase in the number of drugs prescribed or the structure of this consumption.

From the empirical point of view, the main conclusions to be drawn regarding the effect of RP on expenditure, consumption and prices in the pharmaceutical market are as follows:

1. RP produces a short-term reduction in the expenditure financed by the insurer. The overall impact depends on the extension of the products included in the system. The short-term saving requires changes in the behaviour of prescribers (a change to cheaper drugs), lower prices, changes in the extension of the RP system and an increase in the cost borne by patients. In Germany, the net effect on insurer expenditure in 1993 in comparison with 1992 was a reduction of 19.5 per cent. In Denmark, the first year of application resulted in a lower growth in spending than in the previous six years.

2. Experience shows that RP does not generate major long-term savings. After the initial impact, growth in spending reappears, partly owing to new and more expensive drugs. In Germany, the proportion of prescription drugs protected by a patent rose from 11.7 per cent in 1991 to 20 per cent in 1996. There is an increase in prescriptions, prices and the consumption of products not covered by the RP system. This creates the need to introduce additional measures to control the growth in spending once again.

3. The price of products included in the RP system tends to diminish. Most countries register initial price reductions. In Sweden the price of products affected by RP dropped to the level of RP, with very few exceptions. In Germany too, most companies have opted to bring down their prices to RP. The first year was marked by an immediate reduction in prices of 13 per cent, and subsequent years showed reductions ranging from 2 per cent to 10 per cent. Giuliani et al.[21] have observed that the price per defined daily dose (DDD) fell in Germany after the adoption of the RP system, but that this reduction in unit cost was compensated by a rise in expenditure on those products not covered by RP.

   Danzon and Liu[22] show that the short-term effect of RP is to produce a kink in the demand curve at the point corresponding to the RP, assuming that all doctors have perfect information on prices. The kinked demand model put forward by these authors to explain the behaviour of prices subject to RP predicts that it will never be optimal to fix a price below RP, the optimal pricing response being EFP = RP (see box above).

   In general, it can be seen that there is no incentive to price below RP: the price of some generics in Germany has risen to RP, which was established as a statistical median of observed prices.

4. The price and the market share of products not covered by RP undergo a notable rise. Generally, companies have raised prices of products not subject to RP. In Germany, prices of drugs included in RP dropped 1.5 per cent between 1991 and 1992, whereas the price of excluded drugs rose 4.1 per cent. In some cases, companies prefer to see their products excluded from public financing in order to be able to increase prices, as has occurred in Sweden, Italy and New Zealand.

EXPECTED EFFECTS IN SPAIN

The application of the RP system in Spain (passed in June 1999; effective as of 1 December 2000) will have, at best, a fairly limited effect on public pharmaceutical spending. The health authorities have estimated that the saving will amount to €60 million in 2001, on the basis that generic drugs are on average 30 per cent cheaper than brand-name pharmaceuticals. In addition, the effect that the system will have on price competition is dubious to say the least, and may bring about a moderate increase in the presence of generics on the market and the growth of market shares.

Generic products still play a very minor role in the Spanish pharmaceutical market: in 1995 they amounted to only 1.3 per cent of total sales, although this percentage may increase considerably given the growth in marketing authorizations for generics. In fact, the 51 active ingredients for which generic authorizations have been granted to date account for a pharmaceutical expenditure of less than €600 million. The effectiveness of the proposed system depends, therefore, on the thoroughness of the policy of authorization and registration of generics.

However, RP achieves its greatest effectiveness on expenditure in health care environments in which the problem with pharmaceutical spending is high unit prices. This is not the case in Spain. The price index for pharmaceutical products in Spain has followed a downward trend, indicating an average price rise below general inflation.[1] On the contrary, the main driving force behind the growth in expenditure is to be found in the growth factor that reflects higher consumption.

The average price levels of products whose patent is expiring or has expired are low in Spain, and far lower than those of the countries with the highest levels. The price differential of brand products and generics is probably smaller than that observed in other countries. The main cause of the growth in spending in Spain is the high price of recently introduced products,[23] Spain being one of the EU countries where these products attain the largest market. The introduction of RP will give the industry incentives to exert pressure precisely on these products, in order to offset the drop in prices affected by this mechanism.

These concerns aside, the Spanish RP system applied until December 2003 established that the reference price is fixed 'according to the average, weighted by sales, of the retail prices of the minimum number of lowest-price products necessary to reach a 20 per cent market share in units'. It guarantees that the difference between the RP and the highest price will be at least 10 per cent and at most 50 per cent; it also guarantees that the RP will be no lower than that of the cheapest generic. Considering price levels in Spain, price differentials between brand-name pharmaceuticals and generics are unlikely to be as large as in other countries. Furthermore, the introduction of this system poses problems when the market share of generics is notably small.

First, the drop in prices of brand-name pharmaceuticals (the industry has estimated that the scheme will mean an average price cut of 10 per cent for covered brand products) will hinder the potential growth of the market share of generics, although this drop represents an undeniable achievement for the RP system in itself.

Second, it has been observed in other countries that the price diminishes as the number of generics for any given active ingredient increases, tending to approach the marginal cost. When there is only one generic, or very few, the reference price can actually become a barrier to falling prices. With one or very few generics on the market, their price may still be considerably higher than the marginal cost. However, the system reduces incentives for new entrants to fix their prices below the RP, as any saving would end up in the public sector. Paradoxically, the result of RP may be to hold back the growth of generics and to build a barrier to the price competition that is supposed to bring the price of unpatented drugs down towards the level of the marginal cost.

And third, with the system chosen to determine the reference level it seems reasonable to expect some products with prices below the RP to increase it to this level.

In general, however, this initial analysis is open to doubt, in view of the high degree of intervention in Spanish drug prices and the fact that authorized prices are regarded as maximum prices, although this is not always sufficiently stressed. These two factors complicate any forecast of the possible outcome of the competition induced by RP in the Spanish pharmaceutical market.

Finally, it should be noted that substitution without conformity enables the pharmacist to replace the drug prescribed by the doctor with another of his or her choice out of those approved by the Department of Health as bio-equivalent. In some countries, however, doctors are allowed to determine the substitutability. In Spain this will only be possible if the doctor justifies his or her opposition to the substitution on the grounds of allergy or intolerance. Generally, the gap between prescription and financial consequences works against the assumption of full responsibility by doctors in their patients' contingencies. Furthermore, although it is established that the pharmacist 'will' proceed to replace the prescribed drug with a generic (why only when there is a generic?) when the former exceeds the RP, the remuneration system for pharmacies, based on a margin/percentage of the price, provides little incentive to do so.

Do the above comments disqualify the government's efforts to redress the growth of health spending? We think not, although to our mind it would be wise to keep a broader perspective of the role of pharmaceuticals in our health system and not take for granted that these partial measures are sufficient to solve underlying problems.

ACKNOWLEDGEMENTS

This chapter was first published in Spanish with the title 'Análisis económico de los precios de referencia como sistema de financiación pública de medicamentos' in Información Comercial Española 2000; 785: 103–118. The authors wish to thank Información Comercial Española for releasing the copyright of this work.

REFERENCES

1. Nonell, R. and J.R. Borrell (1998), 'Mercado de medicamentos en España: diseño institucional de la regulación y de la provisión pública', *Papeles de Economía Española*, 76, 113–31.
2. Zammit-Lucia, J. and R. Dasgupta (1995), 'Reference pricing: the European experience', *Health Policy Review*, St. Mary's Hospital Medical School paper no 10, London.
3. Danzon, P.M. (1997), *Pharmaceutical Price Regulation: National Policies versus Global Interests*, Washington, DC: AEI Press.
4. Dickson, M. and H. Redwood (1998), 'Pharmaceutical reference prices: how do they work in practice?', *PharmacoEconomics*, **14** (5), 471–79.
5. European Commission (1998), *Commission Communication on the Single Market in Pharmaceuticals*, 25 November, Brussels: Directorate General III – Industry.
6. López-Casanovas, G. and J. Puig-Junoy (2000), 'Review of the literature on reference pricing', Health Policy, 54, 87–123.
7. Danzon, P. (1998), 'Reference pricing: theory and evidence', paper presented at the conference on the Effects of Reference Pricing of Medicines, 14–16 December, Universitat Pompeu Fabra, Barcelona.
8. Puig-Junoy, J. (1998), 'Regulación y competencia de precios en el mercado farmacéutico', *Papeles de Economía Española*, 76, 106–12.
9. Drummond, M., B. Jönsson and F. Rutten (1997), 'The role of economics evaluation in the pricing and reimbursement of medicines', *Health Policy*, 40, 199–215.
10. Fattore, G. and C. Jommi (1998), 'The new pharmaceutical policy in Italy', *Health Policy*, **46** (1) 21–44.
11. Woodfield, A., J. Fountain and P. Borren (1997), *Money & Medicines: an Economic Analysis of Reference Pricing and Related Public-sector Cost-containment Systems for Pharmaceuticals with Special Reference to New Zealand*, New Zealand: Merck Sharp & Dome.
12. De Vos, C.M. (1996), 'The 1996 pricing and reimbursement policy in the Netherlands', *PharmacoEconomics*, 10 (supplement 2), 75–80.

13. Maassen, B.M. (1998), 'Reimbursement of medicinal products: the German reference price system – law, administrative practice and economics', *Cuadernos de Derecho Europeo Farmacéutico*, 8, 69–100.
14. Scherer, F.M. (1993), 'Pricing, profits, and technological progress in the pharmaceutical industry', *Journal of Economic Perspectives*, 7 (3), 97–115.
15. Scherer, F.M. (1996), *Industry, Structure, Strategy, and Public Policy*, New York: HarperCollins College Publishers.
16. Kolassa, E.M. (1995), 'Physicians' perceptions of prescription drug prices: their accuracy and effect on the prescribing decision', *Journal of Research and Pharmaceutical Economics*, 6 (1), 23–37.
17. Hellerstein, J.K. (1998), 'The importance of the physician in the generic versus trade-name prescription decision', *Rand Journal of Economics*, 29 (1), 108–36.
18. Caves, R.E., M.D. Whinston and M.A. Hurwitz (1991), 'Patent expiration, entry, and competition in the US pharmaceutical industry', *Brooking Papers on Economic Activity*, 1991, 1–66.
19. Danzon, P.M. (1996), 'The uses and abuses of international price comparisons', in R.B. Helms (ed.), *Competitive Strategies in the Pharmaceutical Industry*, Washington: AEI Press, pp. 85–106.
20. Frank, R.G. and D.S. Salkever. (1997), 'Generic entry and the pricing of pharmaceuticals', *Journal of Economics & Management Strategy*, 6 (1), 75–90.
21. Giuliani, G., G. Selke and L. Garattini (1998), 'The German experience in reference pricing', *Health Policy*, 44, 73–85.
22. Danzon, P. and H. Liu (1997), 'Reference pricing and physician drug budgets: the German experience in controlling pharmaceutical expenditures', Wharton School working paper, Philadelphia, PA.
23. López, Bastida J. and E. Mossialos (1997), 'Spanish drug policy at the crossroads', *The Lancet*, 350, 679–80.

7. Insurance in public financing of pharmaceuticals

B. González López-Valcárcel

INTRODUCTION

This chapter focuses on the issue of co-payment, which occurs in insurance environments when insurer and insured share the payment of the price of the medicine. Using this as our central axis, we begin by addressing certain conceptual aspects, including the various forms, formulas and personal extension of co-payment, in the first section, and in the second section we go on to make a comparison between co-payment in insurance markets and in compulsory public insurance systems.

In the third section we analyse expected effects from a microeconomic perspective, and we discuss to what extent the neoclassical microeconomic theory of demand is applicable to the case of pharmaceuticals. We explore the effects of co-payment on consumption and expenditure, and how it is shared between user and insurer, but also the possible effects on the health of individuals and populations. Equity considerations are inevitably raised in this analysis. The elements on which the analysis hinges in this section are: price and income elasticities of demand for pharmaceuticals; the role of the doctor as an inducer of demand; consumer sovereignty; discontinuities in demand functions; and other notable exceptions to the classical marginalist theory of demand. These exceptions require special microeconometric models and methods.

The following section deals with international experiences with co-payment, both from the regulatory viewpoint (comparative legislation) and on the basis of empirical evidence on elasticities and effects experienced in the wake of reforms that have been implemented or resulting from 'quasi-natural' experiments.

In a short final synthesis, we briefly discuss the political implications of the various different regulation schemes and the present heterogeneity of Europe as regards co-payment practices.

CONCEPT AND FORMS OF PHARMACEUTICAL COST SHARING

The participation of the user of health services in general and pharmaceuticals in particular is given three names in the literature, referring to each of its three functions: co-payment, cost sharing and *ticket modérateur*. The term 'co-payment' originates from the sphere of insurance. The co-insurance rate, or co-payment rate, in a free market is decided by the insuree as one of the parameters of the scheme. The expression 'cost sharing' refers to the portion of co-responsibility the patient is required to have in the management of the process. It refers also to the logic of sharing the financial burden between the two parties, the insurer and the insured. Finally, when we talk of *ticket modérateur* we are pointing to the overconsumption (abuse) that inevitably accompanies the moral hazard because of the existence of a third-party payer. This abuse results in loss of efficiency and welfare; therefore, some cost must be imposed on patients in order to moderate their consumption of pharmaceuticals.

The insurance of pharmaceutical services does not differ essentially from that of other health services. Therefore, the mechanisms for sharing the risk and the financial burden between the parties involved are the same as those applied to the rest of the objects of insurance.

We define the co-insurance rate or co-payment rate as the (fixed) percentage of the sum that insurees are required to pay out of their own pocket at the moment of purchase. For example, in Spain it is 40 per cent for the employed and for the great majority of listed pharmaceuticals. Some authors use the term 'co-payment' to mean the fixed sum per package that is paid by the user, independently of the price.

Another mechanism designed to distribute the financial burden of pharmaceuticals is the deductible (D), the sum of money that patients are required to pay out of their own pocket before the effective insurance coverage is activated. In other words, patients must in all cases pay the first D monetary units. Above that figure, the insurer begins to assume the financial burden of the drug. In addition, maximum or minimum amounts are sometimes fixed to limit the risk of one of the parties.

One way of discouraging excessive consumption, without cost sharing, is through pre-payment. The user advances the money, paying the provider, and is reimbursed at a later date after reclaiming.

CO-PAYMENT IN INSURANCE MARKETS AND COMPULSORY PUBLIC INSURANCE SYSTEMS

We start by considering the (free) health insurance market. An actuarially fair insurance premium is one that equals the expected value of its yield in health and in sickness. In this context of the free market, the main reason for contracting an insurance policy is risk aversion. If the marginal utility of wealth or income were constant, the individual would have no preference between not taking out insurance and paying the actuarially fair insurance premium. These actuarially fair premiums vary greatly from person to person, according to their health status and forecasted future needs. Thus, when we live under a veil of uncertainty it is risk aversion that justifies the need for insurance.

Voluntary insurance would be the market solution to uncertainty for risk-averse individuals. In this context, the user chooses the optimum co-insurance rate. Theory offers some analytical results on optimal health insurance contract designs.[1] The consumer decides the extent of the coverage and the optimum co-insurance rate, and ultimately the price to be paid for the premium. In competitive markets, with actuarially fair premiums, the optimum co-insurance rate varies between individuals and depends on the risk of falling sick and the price elasticity of demand.

It is important to note that in the case of pharmaceuticals there are situations in which there is no veil of uncertainty, and uncertainty is one of the mainstays that justify voluntary insurance as a market solution. And these situations are becoming increasingly frequent. The chronically ill have to take drugs on a lifelong basis. These drugs for the chronically ill represent a growing percentage of the pharmaceutical expenditure in advanced societies.

However, these results are not applicable to compulsory public insurance, nor to National Health Systems. The most notable differences between drug co-payment in an insurance market and in a National Health System or compulsory public insurance environment lie in their voluntariness or otherwise (users' ability to choose their coverage) and the ultimate financing of the services (risk-adjusted premiums as opposed to taxes or social insurance contributions adjusted according to economic capacity). Hence, in compulsory public insurance systems, co-payment regulation is used not only as a health policy instrument but also as one of redistribution of income.

Why must the cost of pharmaceuticals be shared between the two parties? There are two main reasons: to gain efficiency and to raise money. Efficiency will be gained if the welfare loss associated with excess consumption and moral hazard is reduced. Therefore, the larger the increase in the co-payment rate, the greater the gain in efficiency, yet this solution enters into conflict with equity. The co-payment rate no longer belongs to the sphere of consumer decision-making, but forms part of health policy in the broad sense. Seen in this light and in this context, the regulation of drug co-payment is used not only to reduce the welfare losses associated with moral hazard, as occurs in any insurance environment, but also to redistribute income (from the rich to the poor, by discriminating between the employed and pensioners, for example, from the healthy to the sick, and from the rest of society to the chronically ill). It is used, then, to improve not only efficiency but also – and above all – equity.

As instruments of health policy and redistribution of income, formulas for financing pharmaceutical retail tend to discriminate positively in favour of certain types of patients or medicines, by means of eligibility rules of greater or lesser complexity. There are two basic forms of discrimination: patient-based and drug-based. For example, exempting pensioners from co-payment is positive discrimination in favour of this social group, who are assumed to be at a disadvantage as regards their purchasing power. Subsidization is also common for drugs used to treat illnesses that render their victims particularly vulnerable (for example, antiretroviral drugs against AIDS) or which society is particularly interested in having under clinical control, due to the externalities in costs that they generate (for example, psychotropic drugs for treating certain mental illnesses). Society considers unmedicated mental patients to be a potential danger.

EXPECTED EFFECTS OF CO-PAYMENT: MICROECONOMIC ASPECTS

Introduction

In this section we examine the possible effects of drug co-payment. We analyse how it affects consumption, prices and pharmaceutical expenditure, and also how this expenditure is shared by the insurer and the patient. We study the differences and similarities between the expected effects of several forms of co-payment. By way of general reference, we present the classification devised by Murillo and Carles[2] to describe the effects of co-payment on financing, use and equity of health services (Table 7.1).

Insurance Coverage of Pharmaceuticals, Use, Moral Hazard and Efficiency. Effects of Co-payment

There is some controversy in the theoretical literature about the relationship between health insurance and efficiency. Puig-Junoy[3] has conducted an excellent review of this issue. The scope of the welfare loss associated with health insurance has also been the object of empirical research with econometric procedures.

Figure 7.1 shows the situation for an individual consumer with a particular health status. If pharmaceuticals were conventional goods and coverage were complete, that is, without co-payment, the user would purchase the quantity Q_{max}, in other words, carry on consuming until the next package no longer

Table 7.1   Effects of cost sharing on financing, use and equity

Financing	Costs will be transferred from the insurer to the user
	There will be an increase in administrative costs
	There will be an increase in private coverage for the amount of the co-payment
	Variation will depend on the interdependence between the demand and the supply of health care
Use	Variation will depend on price elasticity
	The use of unnecessary services will not decrease
	There is a substitution effect towards higher-cost services
	There is a decrease in preventive services
	Use decreases among low-income users
Equity	It has no effect on high-income groups

Source: Murillo and Carles.[2]

provided any marginal utility. The demand function for this case is totally price-inelastic and is represented by the vertical line that rises from Q_{max} in Figure 7.1.

At the opposite extreme, if the user is not insured (100 per cent co-payment) the demand function is represented by the line that slopes furthest to the left. The consumer reacts by varying his or her consumption more intensely in the face of price changes, since he or she foots the whole bill. There are an infinite number of intermediate situations, corresponding to an infinite number of possible co-payment rates. By way of illustration, Figure 7.1 shows the demand corresponding to 50 per cent co-payment: the effective price for the consumer is half of that shown on the y-axis, because he or she only has to foot half the bill. The demand is that which corresponds to the price $P_0/2$, that is, the quantity Q_1. If we join the two points Q_{max} and C, we are drawing the demand function for a co-payment of 50 per cent. In general, if we impose a co-payment rate (c) that is proportional to the price (P), starting from an initial situation of total coverage (no co-payment), the demand function slopes leftwards and the point of maximum consumption remains steady $(0,Q_{max})$.

Let us assume that the marginal cost ('market' price) is P_0. Uninsured patients consume the quantity Q_0, which is the efficient quantity in that the marginal benefit and the marginal cost are equal. If coverage is complete, patients will consume Q_{max} units, with a total expenditure equal to $P_0 \cdot Q_{max}$, which exceeds the efficient level of expenditure by $P_0 \cdot (Q_{max} - Q_0)$ monetary units. The benefit of consuming Q_0 units is represented by the triangle Q_0AQ_{max} in the figure, and by difference the shaded area (triangle ABQ_{max}) is the welfare loss attributable to the moral hazard (ex post).

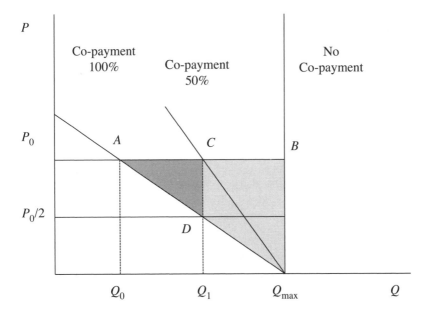

Figure 7.1   Demand functions, co-payment levels and welfare loss

The moral hazard associated with health insurance is twofold: that which occurs ex ante, which consists in failing to prevent health problems because he or she knows that he or she is protected in the event of falling ill, and ex-post moral hazard, which is what occurs when rational consumers consume quantities that are greater than the optimum once they fall ill, because the marginal cost for the co-insured patient is lower than the marginal cost of production.

Following a similar reasoning, the reader can see that when pharmaceuticals are subsidized to the extent that patients pay only half the price, the welfare loss is as shown by the hatched triangle *ACD* in Figure 7.1.

This welfare loss implies inefficiency. Moral hazard gives rise to an inefficient reallocation of consumption, channelling it towards pharmaceuticals and away from other goods and services, both health care and others, which are not covered by insurance. Preventive services – sport, nutrition – become underused.

If we consider the aggregate supply and demand functions, in a conventional market we would find the situation described in Figure 7.2.

The market supply function grows with respect to prices. Therefore, if the co-payment rate is raised from level (2) to level (1) the point of equilibrium shifts from *B* to *A*. Not only does consumption drop, from Q_1 to Q_0, but so does the price, from P_1 to P_0. This reaction, which has been detected

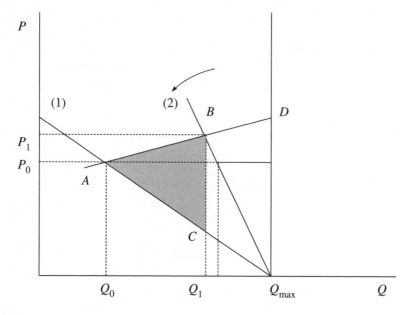

Notes:
(1) Demand function for a market without insurance, 100% co-payment.
(2) Demand function for a market with a fixed percentage partial co-payment.

Figure 7.2   The pharmaceutical market: co-payment levels and welfare loss

and quantified in the American market,[4] may not occur in the European environment, where prices are subject to strict public regulation and control, as explained in detail elsewhere in this book. In Figure 7.2, the collective welfare loss attributable to the 'dead weight' of overconsumption of pharmaceuticals is represented by the triangle ABC. Again, it is caused by poor distribution of society's resources between pharmaceuticals and other goods.

Effects of Deductibles and Maximum Limits

Let us return to Figure 7.1. When a deductible (D) is fixed, one of two things can happen: either it is more than the amount the patient would spend if he or she were not insured, given the market price (P_0), or it is less. If the deductible is greater than this expenditure ($P_0 \cdot Q_0$), then the relevant demand function for the patient is that of 100 per cent co-payment, that is, in practice it is as if it he or she were not insured. However, if the deductible does not exceed this figure, then the relevant demand function becomes that which corresponds to the current co-payment rate, which in the example shown in Figure 7.1 stands at 50 per cent. In other words, in practice and as far as the quantity consumed is concerned, it is as if there were no deductible. Thus, deductibles make for discontinuities in the demand function for pharmaceuticals, which will be a broken line with 'jumps' from one demand function to the next. However, what the deductible does affect is the share in the financial burden that falls to each of the two parties. The patient's effective co-payment rate will be higher than c in both cases.

If an upper limit is imposed on the amount to be paid by the user, the effect is similar. If the limit does not exceed the amount spent by the patient, given the price of the medicine and the co-payment rate, it is as if no limit had been imposed: the effective co-payment rate is the nominal rate (c). In the opposite case, patients 'jump' to consuming the quantity Q_{max}, as if they were totally insured, without co-payment. In this case too, the contribution made by each party to foot the bill is affected.

In the 1970s and 1980s in the USA, the need for health cost containment and the alarming empirical estimates on the extent of moral hazard advised an increase in the co-payment rate for health services. Thus, Feldstein[5] estimated that if the co-insurance rate were raised from 33 per cent to 67 per cent, the costs incurred due to welfare loss would fall much more than the benefits derived from reducing the risk. Subsequently, Feldman and Dowd,[6] using data from the Rand experiment in the 1980s, reached similar conclusions.

Recently, Nyman[7] took a fresh look at the traditional approach presented in Figures 7.1 and 7.2, which dates back to Pauly.[8] Nyman argues that Pauly overestimated the welfare loss attributable to insurance, because he unduly included the income effect on consumption, whereas it should have been subtracted to leave the price effect. The income effect to be subtracted is due to the income transfer from the healthy to the sick. The pure price effect of insurance is 'the change in consumption of medical care that would occur if a consumer who is already ill were to purchase a contract from an "insurer" to reduce the price of medical care in return for an actuarially fair premium'. In order to calculate the extent of the welfare loss of the insurance – which Nyman understands as the transaction cost of the insurance itself – it would be necessary to apply the classical Slutsky equation, but in practice it has yet to be quantified.

Moral Hazard, Pharmaceutical Consumption and Elasticities

The phenomenon of moral hazard, and the consequent welfare loss, occurs when the demand of the insured party shows price elasticity, and the greater the elasticity the greater the moral hazard. Recall that the price elasticity of demand is defined as follows:

$$E_p = \frac{dQ/Q}{dP/P}$$

If we say, for example, that it stands at −0.2, we mean that if the price rises by 1 per cent, the quantity demanded will decrease by 0.2 per cent. In fact, the price elasticity of demand measures the potential for moral hazard.[9] In Figure 7.1, the slope of the demand function for 100 per cent co-payment is what ultimately determines the shaded area, which as we already know, corresponds to the welfare loss of total coverage pharmaceutical insurance.

In addition to this, however, as the reader can see from Figures 7.1 and 7.2, the price elasticity of demand increases as the co-payment rate increases.

Clearly, if the co-payment rate (c) is proportional to the price (P), the elasticity of demand with respect to the price paid ($P^* = c \cdot P$) coincides with the elasticity with respect to the co-payment rate c:

$$E_{p^*} = \frac{dQ/Q}{dP^*/P^*} = \frac{dQ/Q}{dc/c} = E_c \qquad (7.1)$$

Furthermore, the price elasticities of demand for pharmaceuticals are likely to differ depending on individuals' income. If low-income households have a more price-elastic demand, an increase in co-payment will cause them to make a proportionally larger reduction in their pharmaceutical consumption than high-income households. The same thing could happen if we make the comparison in terms of levels of health. We are faced with equity problems, to which we will return below.

In order to evaluate the practical effects of co-payment it is essential to have access to quantifications of elasticities. The fourth section of this chapter deals with this. It is far from straightforward to obtain reliable estimates of the elasticities of demand for pharmaceuticals with respect to co-payment and price. Distinctions must be made between active ingredients, brands and generics, and between 'essential' and 'non-essential' drugs, and substitution elasticities must be taken into account.

How the Financial Burden is Shared between User and Insurer when the Co-payment Rate Varies

If the co-payment rate is raised from c to $c + \lambda c$ and the price (P) remains constant, the quantity consumed will decrease by λQ units and therefore the total expenditure will fall by $P \cdot \lambda Q$ monetary units. Figure 7.3 depicts this

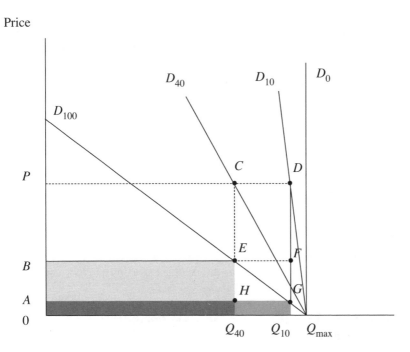

Price

Figure 7.3   Effects of raising the co-payment from 10 per cent to 40 per cent: distribution of the pharmaceutical expenditure between patient and insurer

situation, for an initial co-payment rate of 10 per cent ($c = 0.1$), which is then raised to 40 per cent ($c + \lambda c = 0.4$). This would be the case if in Spain drugs for chronic diseases were put on a par with the rest. The intensity of the drop in consumption (λQ) depends on the elasticity of demand with respect to the price paid (and to the co-payment).

How the pharmaceutical expenditure is shared between the two parties (the patient and the insurer) depends on the initial co-payment rate (c), the size of the increase (λc) and the drop in the quantity (λQ), which in turn depends on the elasticity of demand. Before the rise, the patient bore expenditure equal to cPQ. This is shown in Figure 7.3 as the rectangle $0AGQ_{10}$. After the rise in the co-payment, the patient spends ($c + \lambda c$) $P (Q + \lambda Q)$. In the figure, this is represented by the rectangle $0BEQ_{40}$.

The difference in the expenditure borne by the patient is, therefore:

$$\lambda c\, PQ + cP\lambda Q + P\, \lambda c\, \lambda Q \qquad (7.2)$$

The first addend is positive, and measures the direct effect of the rise of the co-payment rate. It expresses the effect of the normative change in the distribution of the financial burden between the two parties, before the user's reaction of restraint in the use of the pharmaceutical is taken into consideration. The other two addends are negative, and quantify the decrease in expenditure caused by the drop in consumption as a reaction to the rise in the price paid. The balance can have either sign, depending on the elasticity of demand and the size of the increase in the co-payment. In the example shown in Figure 7.3, despite a considerable decrease in the quantity consumed, the patient will end up paying more for the drug than before.

However, both the expenditure borne by the insurer and the total expenditure will decrease. In our graphic example, the decrease in total pharmaceutical expenditure is shown by the rectangle $Q_{40} CDQ_{10}$. The insurer, whose initial expenditure was the area of the rectangle $APDG$, now only spends $BPCE$. Therefore, a saving is generated that is equal to the sum of three areas in the figure: the rectangle $ABEH$, due to the normative rise in the co-payment rate; the rectangle $ECDF$, due to the decrease in consumption; and the area $HEFG$, due to the interaction of these two factors.

To what Extent can this Theory be Applied to the Demand for Pharmaceuticals?

In the above sections we have supposed that pharmaceuticals are conventional goods and that their market shows no essential differences from any other normal market. The effects of co-payment that we have studied will occur if a number of conditions are fulfilled, including the condition that the rational and perfectly informed consumer is an independent generator of demand. The phenomenon of induced demand and incomplete agency relationships, together with uncertainty as to the effectiveness of alternative treatments and doses, can cloud these theoretical results. In this section we analyse to what extent the pharmaceutical market fulfils or fails to fulfil these conditions.

The pharmaceutical market is special for a number of reasons involving demand, supply and the particular interaction between them.

Substitution Effects and Cross-elasticities. Patient–doctor Interaction

First, a distinction must be drawn between prescribed drugs and *self-prescribed drugs*, a distinction which is important for two reasons. The first has to do with consumer sovereignty. Only the demand for self-prescribed drugs expresses the patient's freely decided willingness to pay. In the other case, it is prescribing doctors who initiate the demand, and they may not be perfect agents for their patients, either because they are subject to certain explicit constraints, as occurs in the US Health Maintenance Organizations (HMO),[10] or because they impose limits on their own prescribing practices in order to achieve drug expenditure control targets, as happens in some primary care teams in Spain, or because they share the financial risks of the prescription, assuming part of the cost or having a fixed budget to share out between all their patients. The pharmaceutical industry itself may even intervene in the market by offering veiled economic incentives to doctors for their prescriptions.

Second, the cost for the user of a prescribed medicine subject to co-payment does not only involve the monetary component, but also includes the opportunity cost of the waiting and travelling time to get the prescription. As a result, estimated elasticities of prescribed drugs may be biased, whereas this is not an issue with self-prescribed drugs.

Drug co-payment induces (or may induce) major cross-effects in the demands for other health services, starting with the demand for medical visits. These cross-effects can have any or both signs. There are reports, for example, of the substitution of present consumption by future consumption, by putting off the beginning of the treatment and increasing the likelihood of spending more in the future. It has also been argued and empirically illustrated that pharmaceutical co-payment may lead to greater net expenditure because it increases the demand for other health services. This effect has been quantified for mental health services.[11] Furthermore, Soumerai et al.[12] estimate that the lack of suitable pharmacological treatment is responsible for 23 per cent of admissions in geriatric centres and 10 per cent of hospital admissions among the elderly in the USA. A recent exhaustive review of these issues, for Spain and other countries, can be found in Lobato et al.[13]

From a practical point of view, the price elasticity of demand for prescription drugs can be increased by providing incentives for the prescribing doctor rather than for the patient.[14] The idea of using multiple instruments to achieve cost containment and the efficient allocation of health resources is not new, and is employed extensively. Increasingly, the US HMOs are turning to the simultaneous use of 'suspenders' (co-payment by the patient) and the 'belt' (management constraints imposed on the prescribing doctors) to contain costs, a strategy that can be justified with theoretical arguments, particularly in cases of great diversity of levels of disease severity and inelastic demands. Between 1992 and 1995, the percentage of US HMO plans that required pharmaceutical co-payment grew from 64 per cent to 96 per cent.[15]

Uncertainty, Rationality, Iatrogenia

Uncertainty regarding treatment effectiveness, and more generally, lack of information and asymmetry in the distribution of this information, are a source of problems. There is abundant empirical evidence to show that the quality of pharmaceutical prescription could be greatly improved.[16] We are dealing with a type of goods for which more can often mean less: more consumption (or unsuitable consumption) produces iatrogenia, illness and disutility. The figures on the frequency and the cost of morbidity owing to errors in pharmacological treatment are a cause for concern.[13] Lobato et al.[13] estimate that morbidity related to pharmacological treatment generated direct costs for the Spanish public health system of nearly 10 per cent of public spending on health care. These errors include and combine, in addition to inevitable side effects produced by medication, poor quality of doctors' prescriptions and patients' failure to follow the treatment. Thus, some studies suggest that almost half of Spain's hypertensive patients fail to observe the prescribed medication guidelines,[17] and also find very high percentages among patients with diabetes, asthma and other chronic diseases. This belies the rationality of the pharmaceutical consumer, which is one of the prerequisites that lend validity to the arguments on the welfare loss associated with co-payment.

Discontinuities and Discrete Choices. The Need to Differentiate Between Pharmaceuticals for Acute and Chronic Diseases

There are few examples of pharmaceuticals – vitamins would be one – whose individual demand can be regarded as continual. In most cases, the patient's choice consists, if the process is acute, in following or not following the prescribed treatment, but the patient does not decide the quantity of drug that he or she will consume. The dose is a technical matter. Thus, in most acute processes, we are dealing with a discrete choice on an individual level, which will give rise to aggregate demand functions of a continual type, since when the price changes the number of patients entering or leaving the market likewise changes. Consuming below (or above) the correct dose produces disutility. For example, taking half the prescribed antibiotic treatment for an illness is iatrogenic; it causes harm to the patient, creating resistance to the antibiotics. Without curing the present infection, it makes the patient less sensitive to the treatment of future infections.

In the case of chronic processes, the patient can, at any time, take the decision to stop the treatment, as a reaction to changes in price or other variables. Whereas the econometric technique for analysing the demand for pharmaceuticals for acute processes is that of discrete choice models, here we will apply duration or survival models. In addition, the technology of drugs for chronic diseases can have non-constant returns to scale. For example, the consumption of anxiolytics raises the tolerance and reduces the effect, resulting in an increase in the necessary dose.

OBSERVED EFFECTS: INTERNATIONAL EXPERIENCES WITH CO-PAYMENT

Comparative Review of Co-payment Regulation in Europe

All the health systems of the European Union (EU), except that of the Netherlands, require purchasers of prescription drugs to make some form of co-payment. Mossialos and Le Grand[18] provide a detailed description of the co-payment regulations currently in force in Europe.

There are three types of countries: those that fix percentages of co-payment, those that impose fixed co-payments independently of the price, and those that combine the two systems.

Belgium, Denmark, Greece, Spain, France, Luxembourg and Portugal belong to the first group. Percentages of co-payment vary depending on the characteristics of the patient and/or the drug. The gradients between the minimum and the maximum percentages are in most cases very wide, and range from the total absence of co-payment to 100 per cent in some cases (Denmark, Greece, Italy). Within this first group of countries, Spain and Luxembourg have the lowest maximum percentages (40 per cent).

The second group includes those countries that opt to establish co-payments with a fixed monetary value: Germany, Sweden, Ireland, the UK and Austria. The amount payable per package can be identical for all prescriptions (UK, Austria), or it can depend on the size of the package (Germany). In Sweden, patients pay a fixed sum in kronor for the first prescription, and a smaller sum for each subsequent prescription.

The third group has opted for a mixed system combining fixed sums and percentages of the price. Thus, in Italy patients have to pay a particular sum in lire for type *A* and type *B* products, while type *C* products have a 100 per cent co-payment. Finland employs a linear formula consisting of a fixed minimum amount to which 50 per cent of the price is added.

In some cases maximum payable amounts are fixed. Those countries that have introduced reference pricing (RP) require the user to meet the additional cost over the RP (Germany, Spain).

In Spain, pensioners are exempted from co-payment, there is a general rate of 40 per cent for the rest of the population, and an exception is made for certain low-contribution therapeutic groups (10 per cent) for treating chronic processes, with a maximum sum fixed in 1993 at 400 pesetas and revised yearly according to the consumer price index. Also in 1993, a large number of pharmaceuticals were excluded from the list of drugs eligible for public financing, and this negative list has grown over the years.

The overall percentage of user participation in pharmaceutical expenditure is very low in Spain and has gradually decreased, from 15 per cent in 1985 to

8.5 per cent in 1997.[19] There is, then, a very small contribution, moreover subject to extremely high administrative and control costs.

To sum up, in Europe we have an enormous variety of types and formulas of co-payment, which have developed gradually over time and allow us to draw some conclusions with regard to their effectiveness. In practice, the percentage of pharmaceutical expenditure borne by patients varies greatly for different countries and therapeutic groups.[20]

Empirical Evidence of the Effects of Co-payment and Elasticities in the Light of European and American Experience

There are a considerable number of empirical estimates of the elasticity of demand for pharmaceuticals. Unfortunately, most of them deal with the USA, and their results cannot be completely extrapolated to the health systems of Europe.

Zweifel and Manning[21] divide these empirical studies on the sensitivity of the demand for health services to co-payment into three groups, according to their design: random trials (methodologically correct experimental designs, the factual paradigm for which is the study conducted by the Rand Corporation); natural experiments (measuring and analysing the consumption of groups of patients before and after a change in co-payment) and observational studies (either with aggregate temporal data or with transverse individual data on patients subjected to different co-payments).

Studies using data from insurance markets come up against the problem of self-selection of risk. This is because the estimation of the elasticity of demand for pharmaceuticals to the co-payment rate or the deductibles that is obtained by considering the quantity demanded as a dependent variable and the co-payment rate as an explanatory variable is biased; the co-payment rate is not only a cause but also an effect. Technically, the insurance scheme is said to be endogenous. Healthier individuals, who expect to make less use of health services, choose insurance schemes with higher co-payment rates and larger deductibles, in order to pay lower premiums. Thus, the empirical evidence of high correlation between high co-payment rates and low drug consumption makes for systematic overestimation of the elasticity of demand, because it is partly a consequence of the choice of insurance scheme.

The experiment conducted by the Rand Corporation in the late 1970s, designed as a large-scale experiment in order to overcome this methodological difficulty, is already a classic in the field of health economics.[22] It consisted in allocating 16 different 3–5-year health insurance schemes at random to a broad sample of people distributed geographically in six different areas of the USA. The co-payment rates varied from 0 per cent to 95 per cent, depending on the scheme and the services provided. The data supplied by the experiment made it possible to study the behaviour of the demand for services as a function of the insurance scheme and the co-payment rate. It was estimated that per capita pharmaceutical expenditure is 60 per cent higher for insurees without co-payment than for those that assume a 95 per cent rate. On the subject of estimates of the price elasticity of pharmaceuticals, the study concludes that they depend on the co-payment rate, but in any event they are low, ranging from –0.1 to –0.2.[23]

Several empirical studies attempt to estimate elasticities, differentiating between drugs on the basis of their effectiveness, or dividing them into 'essential' and 'non-essential', but the results are disparate. According to some, 'essential' drugs are less sensitive to co-payment than 'discretionary' ones; others reach the opposite conclusion. The details can be consulted in Puig-Junoy.[3]

More recently, large databases have been used to estimate the effect of drug co-payment in the USA under different insurance schemes.[10] The conclusion reached is that there is a significant interaction effect between the behaviour of demand and prescriber incentives. Thus, larger prescription drug co-payments are associated with lower expenditure when the doctor does not share the financial risk of the cost of the drugs (that is, practises in an independent practice association) but this effect is barely perceived in managed care models in which the doctor has incentives for cost containment.

Perhaps the most serious drawback with the studies discussed above is the doubt, suspicion or conviction that what happens in the USA cannot be extrapolated to Europe.

Estimates based on European data are more scarce, and present other problems. In universal public insurance systems, in which financing is not based on premiums, there is no interpersonal (intra-group) variability in the drug co-payment rates, or if there is it is very small. Therefore, temporal data are used to quantify the reactions of demand to normative changes in co-payment rates. The problem here is that such changes have occurred on very few occasions, and concurrently with other sources of variation in demand.

These considerations highlight the methodological difficulties in estimating elasticities of demand for pharmaceuticals and partly account for the extremely high variability of the results.

Those studies that focus on the UK, where co-payment takes the form of a fixed sum, also lead to the conclusion that the number of prescribed drugs is sensitive to increases in co-payment. Elasticities for that country have been quantified in the interval –0.22 to –0.50, according to the review by Hitiris.[24] The price elasticity in the UK between 1971 and 1982 was, according to a study by Lavers,[25] in the region of –0.15 to –0.20.

In Spain the price elasticity of demand for pharmaceuticals is low, according to available estimates. Puig-Junoy[26] has estimated that the figure stands around –0.14, using aggregate temporal data for the early 1980s. The same study quantifies the elasticity of expenditure with relation to co-payment as being in the region of –0.22. Other authors obtain lower estimates. Nonell and Borrell[19] quote a figure of –0.08 for the period 1965 to 1994.

Yet the goal of the quantification is far more ambitious than this. The aim is to estimate elasticities of demand for pharmaceuticals, differentiating between the short and the long term, and distinguishing between types and therapeutic groups, and also between brand products and generics. Furthermore, it is crucial to differentiate between levels of income and other socioeconomic variables. This aspect is very important for its repercussions on the equity of the designs of co-payment regulation. There is some empirical evidence, albeit not conclusive due to the method used, to suggest that in Sweden drug price elasticity varies greatly with age, income and health status. More vulnerable groups (low income, poorer health) have a more price-sensitive demand.[27]

Empirical estimates, employing methods with a varying degree of sophistication and applied to different environments, tend to conclude that pharmaceuticals have a moderate to low-price elasticity. There is practically no substitution elasticity between therapeutic groups. The price elasticity of brand products seems to be gradually decreasing as the generic market becomes properly consolidated. Recent estimates appear to indicate that demand for brand-name pharmaceuticals is sensitive to the price of the generics.[28]

In the USA in the 1990s, a debate arose on the advisability of extending public Medicare coverage to include pharmaceuticals. The studies that evaluate the consequences of this policy run into tens. One excellent review of the state of affairs is that by Stuart et al.[29] The Rand Corporation made another contribution, this time a database on the health status of the population over 65 years of age. With these data, and a technically impeccable econometric model, Lillars et al.[30] conclude that the coverage of prescription drugs significantly increases the probability of their use, but not the total spending on drugs of those that take them, and that a hypothetical coverage of pharmaceuticals by Medicare would alleviate the financial problems of many people. Stuart and Grana[31] estimate that elderly people with drug coverage within Medicare are 6–17 per cent more likely to take drugs, and the 'relative risk' of consumption is greater for the insured in ten out of the 22 health problems studied, particularly the more serious ones; and also that there is a strong differential in drug use in terms of levels of income.

Hillman et al.[10] have estimated appreciable effects of drug co-payment on health expenditure in US insurance schemes, partly because patients who attend surgeries consume less, but also because drug co-payment dissuades patients from attending surgeries. The recent report by Stuart et al.[29] evaluates the effects of drug coverage within the US Medicare programme, comparing levels of consumption, spending and health among beneficiaries and non-beneficiaries of coverage. The conclusions are striking. Users with coverage obtain one-third more prescriptions than those without cover; lack of prescription drug coverage creates equity problems, hindering access to health precisely for the least favoured groups, with the worst health, lowest income and most advanced age.[32]

SYNTHESIS, CONCLUSIONS AND POLITICAL ASPECTS

In the process of production, distribution and consumption of medicines, a large number of agents are involved. The pharmaceutical sector is very complex, strictly regulated and sensitive to the international environment, particularly as regards technology and prices. Health insurance schemes, be they private or public, cover pharmaceutical services in many different ways, seeking a balance between the various forces involved. Instruments aimed at the consumer, among which figure those based on co-payment, may have a certain capacity to contain pharmaceutical spending, as can be gathered from the simulations conducted for the entirety of the Dutch pharmaceutical sector by Canton and Westerhout,[33] although the price elasticities assumed in that paper are higher than is usually estimated (–3 and –5.7 for the brand product and the alternative respectively).

However, the extensive and varied experience undergone in Europe and its trend towards greater participation by the user in the financing of pharmaceuticals does not seem to have made any substantial contribution to cost containment. Practically all European countries use drug co-payment with the implicit objective of making the user jointly responsible for the cost, but not as an essential source of revenue for the public health care system, nor has it proved to be a political instrument with the ability to contain costs or substantially improve efficiency.

Imposing indiscriminate co-payments may generate serious inequities in financing and consumption, to the detriment of low-income households, the elderly and the chronically ill. Hence the attempts to demand differentiated rates for these population groups. Furthermore, drug co-payment will reduce demand insofar as the doctor is a perfect agent for the patient, but in practice prescribing doctors also appear to be subject to pressure, from other institutional incentives. The standardization of prescriptions and guidelines for prescription and rational drug use, incentives included in management contracts and programme contracts to encourage health centres to keep within budget limits, or to reach certain quotas of generic products, are familiar examples of influences that are unrelated to demand yet affect it. Each country has to find its optimal combination of this range of instruments, learning from its own and other countries' experience.

Co-payment as a problem of political decision-making entails a contradiction that is difficult to face: the tension between efficiency and equity. If a high co-payment is imposed moral hazard and unnecessary consumption are reduced, thus freeing up resources for demands of other goods with a greater marginal utility. Theoretically, then, a high co-payment contributes to an improvement in efficiency. But if the elasticity with respect to the price paid (and to the co-payment) of the poor is far greater than that of the rich, an indiscriminate rise in the co-payment rate is an attack against equity, as it reduces the consumption (access) of less affluent population groups to goods of which ultimately they are considered to be tutelaries. This argument is also applicable to the chronically ill, the elderly and in general those population groups that need most medicines. As a result, most countries employ co-payment formulas of some complexity, which require a greater or lesser financial effort depending on income, age or health status. The financing of pharmaceuticals thus becomes an instrument for the redistribution of income.

However, the more complex and intricate the design of the co-payment mode, the greater the management and administrative costs of the system, the greater the incentive for fraud, and the smaller the revenue of the insurer or the national health service. To quote a familiar example, in Spain, where the 'general' co-payment rate for the employed is 40 per cent, public spending on drugs prescribed through the national health service stands at only 8 per cent. Fraud (switching of prescriptions from the employed to pensioners) appears to be widespread. Puig-Junoy[26] quantified it as between 15 per cent and 20 per cent of the total of prescriptions made out in the first half of the 1980s. By comparing aggregate data for pharmaceutical expenditure in the population covered by the general social security system, in which pensioners are excluded from co-payment while the employed contribute 40 per cent, and the population of civil servants belonging to Mutualidad de Funcionarios de la Administración Central del Estado (MUFACE), all of whom pay a flat rate of 30 per cent regardless of whether they are working or in retirement, López et al.[34] provide data on expenditure that would appear to support the hypothesis that this fraud persists today.

Co-payment is an instrument that should not be used on its own. Neither efficiency in drug use nor equity nor the control of pharmaceutical expenditure can rest solely on co-payment. Its effectiveness is reinforced when it is combined with other instruments and incentives. In fact, all European countries combine, in different doses and proportions, multiple instruments that influence the behaviour of the industry, prescribers and patients. It is sufficient to recall that pharmaceutical expenditure is the product of price by quantity, and to consider the enormous international variability of drug prices,[35] in order to understand the limitations of co-payment regulation in comparison with other policies that influence prices. Policies aimed at price control can be as effective as co-payment – or more so – for purposes of cost containment.

For example, the pharmaceutical companies lowered their prices significantly in Germany when this country pioneered reference pricing in 1989.[4]

ACKNOWLEDGEMENTS

I would like to thank Jaime Pinilla Domínguez for his collaboration in the preparation of this chapter.

REFERENCES

1. Zweifel, P. and F. Breyer (1997), *Health Economics*, Oxford: Oxford University Press.
2. Murillo, C. and M. Carles (2000), 'Prospectiva de cambios en el sector asegurador en España y su interrelación con el sistema de salud', study for the Ministerio de Sanidad y Consumo, Madrid.
3. Puig-Junoy, J. (2001), 'Los mecanismos de copago en servicios sanitarios: cuándo, cómo y por qué', *Hacienda Pública Española*, **158** (3), 105–34.
4. Pavnik, N. (2000), 'Do pharmaceutical prices respond to insurance?', NBER working paper no W7865, Washington, DC, August.
5. Feldstein, M. (1973), 'The welfare loss of excess health insurance', *Journal of Political Economy*, 81, 251–80.
6. Feldman, R. and B. Dowd (1991), 'A new estimate of the welfare loss of excess health insurance', *American Economic Review*, 81, 297–301.
7. Nyman, J.A. (1999), 'The economics of moral hazard revisited', *Journal of Health Economics*, 18, 811–24.
8. Pauly, M. (1968), 'The economics of moral hazard: comment', *American Economic Review*, 58, 531–37.
9. Folland, S., A.C. Goodman and M. Stano (1997), *The Economics of Health and Health Care*, Upper Saddle River, NJ: 2nd edn, Prentice Hall.
10. Hillman, A., M. Pauly, J. Escarce, K. Rippley, M. Glaynor, J. Clouse and R. Ross (1999), 'Financial incentives and drug spending in managed care', *Health Affairs*, 18, 189–200.
11. Freemantle, N. and K. Bloor (1996), 'Lessons from international experience in controlling pharmaceutical expenditure: I. Influencing patients', *British Medical Journal*, 312, 1469–71.
12. Soumerai, S.B., D. Ross-Degnan, J. Avorn, T.J. McLaughlin and I. Choodnovskiy (1991), 'Effects of Medicaid drug-payment limits on admissions to hospitals and nursing homes', *New England Journal of Medicine*, 325, 1072–77.
13. Lobato, P., F. Lobo and A. García (2000), *Estrategia, viabilidad e implicaciones económicas de la atención farmacéutica*, Madrid: Colegio Oficial de Farmacéuticos de Madrid.
14. Lyles, A. and F.B. Palumbo (1999), 'The effect of managed care on prescription drug cost and benefits', *PharmacoEconomics*, 15, 129–40.
15. Pauly, M.V. and S.D. Ramsey (1999), 'Would you like suspenders to go with that belt? An analysis of optimal combinations of cost sharing and managed care', *Journal of Health Economics*, 18, 443–58.

16. Mengíbar, F.J. (2000), 'Gasto farmacéutico en atención primaria reformada: implicación de las activadades formativas en el ahorro en farmacia', *Gaceta Sanitaria*, 14, 277–86.
17. Puigventós, L. et al. (1997), 'Cumplimiento terapéutico en el tratamiento de la hipertensión: Diez años de publicaciones en España', *Medicina Clínica*, 109, 702–706.
18. Mossialos, E. and J. Le Grand (1999), 'Cost containment in the EU: an overview', in E. Mossialos and J. Le Grand (eds), *Health Care and Cost Containment in the European Union*, Ashgate: Aldershot.
19. Nonell, R. and J.R. Borrell (1998), 'Mercado de medicamentos en España: Diseño institucional de la regulación y de la provisión pública', *Papeles de Economía Española*, 76, 113–31.
20. Noyce, P.R. et al. (2000), 'The cost of prescription medicines to patients', *Health Policy*, 52, 129–45.
21. Zweifel, P. and W.G. Manning (2000), 'Moral hazard and consumer incentives in health care', in *Handbook of Health Economics*, vol 1A, Amsterdam: North Holland pp. 409–59.
22. Newhouse, J. et al. (1993), *Free for All? Lessons from the Rand Health Insurance Experiment*, Cambridge: Harvard University Press.
23. Manning, W.G. et al. (1987), 'Health insurance and the demand for medical care: evidence from a randomized experiment', *American Economic Review*, 77, 251–77.
24. Hitiris, T. (2000), 'Prescription charges in the United Kingdom: a critical review', University of York, Department of Economics and Related Studies discussion papers in economics No 00/04, York.
25. Lavers, R. (1989), 'Prescription charges, the demand for prescriptions and morbidity', *Applied Economics*, 21, 1043–52.
26. Puig-Junoy, J. (1988), 'Gasto farmacéutico en España: efectos de la participación del usuario en el coste', *Investigaciones Económicas*, 12, 45–68.
27. Lundberg, L. et al. (1998), 'Effects of user charges on the use of prescription medicines in different socio-economic groups', *Health Policy*, 44, 123–34.
28. Fisher, S., I. Cockburn, Z. Griliches and J. Hausman (1997), 'Characteristics of the demand for pharmaceutical products: an examination of four cephalosporins', *Rand Journal of Economics*, **28** (3), 426–46.
29. Stuart, B. et al. (2000), 'Issues in prescription drug coverage, pricing, utilization and spending: what we know and need to know', report prepared for US Department of Health and Human Services, Office of the Assistant Secretary for Policy and Evaluation, Office of Health Policy, Washington, DC, February, accessed at http://www.aspe.hhs.gov/health/reports/drugstudy/appa.htm.
30. Lillars, L.A. et al. (1999), 'Insurance coverage for prescription drugs: effects on use and expenditures in the Medicare population', *Medical Care*, 37, 926–36.
31. Stuart, B. and J. Grana (1998), 'Ability to pay and the decision to medicate', *Medical Care*, 36, 202–11.
32. Rowgowski, J., L.A. Lillard and R. Kington (1997), 'The financial burden of prescription drug use among elderly persons', *Gerontologist*, 37, 475–82.
33. Canton, E. and Y.E. Westerhout (1999), 'A model for the Dutch pharmaceutical market', *Health Economics*, 8, 391–402.
34. López-Casanovas, G., V. Ortún and C. Murillo (1999), *El sistema sanitario español: informe de una década*, Bilbao: Fundación BBV.
35. Danzon, P.M. and L. Chao (2000), 'Cross-national price differences for pharmaceuticals: how large and why?', *Journal of Health Economics*, 19, 159–95.

8. Economic evaluation and pharmaceutical policy

J.L. Pinto Prades and X. Badía Llach

INTRODUCTION

The rapid increase in expenditure on pharmaceuticals has awakened growing interest in the economic evaluation of medicines. New drugs are introduced periodically and the pharmaceutical companies claim price rises to cover their research and development (R&D) expenses. In some cases the health benefits produced by these new drugs is small, but expenditure on health care in general and pharmaceuticals in particular is growing at rates in excess of 10 per cent a year in Spain. All this has led to interest in taking a closer look at the value of the health gains we are buying in exchange for this ever greater expenditure on medicines. In analysing this type of issue, economic evaluation can play an important role, as it comprises a series of techniques that allow the estimation of both costs and benefits.

The main types of economic evaluation (EE) are cost-effectiveness analysis (CEA), cost–benefit analysis (CBA) and cost-utility analysis (CUA). CEA uses 'natural' measures of the outcome, that is, it defines the unit of measurement of the outcome in terms of the most immediate objective of health expenditure. In CUA, health benefit is measured in quality-adjusted life-years (QALYs). The QALY is a measure of health that combines the two basic components that define health, namely the quantity and the quality of life. The figure in QALYs is obtained by multiplying years of life by a weight that reflects the quality of life during those years. The quality of life is measured on a scale that has two invariable points for all individuals: 0 (death) and 1 (perfect health). This scale can include values worse than death, which give negative quality of life values. In turn, CBA measures the value of health gains in monetary units. The monetary value of health is obtained through an individual's willingness to pay to prevent a disease or to improve his or her health if ill.

There is some controversy regarding which method to use in economic evaluation studies to estimate costs and benefits, which has led to attempts at standardization in the field of the economic evaluation of pharmaceuticals.

However, this chapter seeks to ascertain how economic evaluation could be used in pharmaceutical policy. The following deals with those areas in which economic evaluation could potentially be useful.

DECISION-MAKING AREAS IN PHARMACEUTICAL POLICY

Some authors[1] have suggested that EE can be used in many pharmaceutical policy situations as a decision-making tool. These situations would include:

1. *Approval of pharmaceuticals by health authorities*   The decision we are faced with here is whether a particular drug should be on the market or not. Normally governments decide whether to approve or reject the marketing of drugs solely on the basis of effectiveness and safety considerations. Should/can economic evaluation play a part in this?
2. *Drug prices*   In many countries drug prices are regulated by the government. The main reason for this lies in the monopoly that patents provide for new products. Should/can economic evaluation play a part in this?
3. *Financing of products*   Even if the government decides that the medicine can be sold, it is not obliged to finance it. What drugs should be financed and what drugs should not? This issue also affects those private institutions that offer a series of medical services at a fixed price. These institutions have what are called 'formularies', which list the medicines that a patient can consume in exchange for payment of an insurance policy. What drugs should be included in these formularies? Should/can economic evaluation play a part in this?
4. *Medical treatment guidelines*   Here we are faced with the decision as to which medicine to recommend for a particular treatment. These guidelines are usually the result of a consensus between experts and they are intended to influence medical decision-making. Insofar as consensus guidelines can also take into consideration economic matters, again we are led to the question: should/can economic evaluation play a part in this?
5. *Reimbursement*   The decision to finance or not finance a drug is usually accompanied by the decision as to how much to finance; in other words, what part of the price is to be provided by the insurance company or the public sector. Should/can economic evaluation play a part in this?
6. *Patent policy*   One very important aspect of pharmaceutical policy is the protection given by patents to new drugs. Patents can be overprotective, causing detriment to consumers in the form of excessively high prices, or underprotective, destroying the pharmaceutical companies' incentives to develop R&D policies. Should/can economic evaluation play a part in this?

In order to answer the question of whether economic evaluation can or should play a particular part in the decisions mentioned above, carry out a two-step procedure. First, we introduce some theoretical aspects that may help to find the right approach to these issues, and then, having studied the matter from a normative viewpoint, we attempt to show how economic evaluation can contribute towards these putting solutions into practice.

REGULATION AND PHARMACEUTICALS: THEORETICAL ASPECTS

Approving a Pharmaceutical

The first regulatory phase related to pharmaceuticals is their approval, that is, permission to put them on the market. Before a product can be marketed it has be proved to be safe and effective. The main objective of the regulation that affects drugs in the pre-marketing phase is to avoid the approval of medicines that are not effective or that have major side effects. However, a drug is very unlikely to have no risk of causing a side effect. It is almost impossible to find a medicine that guarantees that the probability of it causing some sort of side effect, however small, is zero. Legislation has to accept that the zero-risk drug does not exist, and therefore regulators have to decide what level of risk they are prepared to assume in order to approve a given drug. As in almost everything, legislators are faced with a disjunctive at this point. The more demanding they are about the safety of the drug, the greater the cost. First, more safety means that more tests are necessary to prove it. Second, the time needed to reach approval increases, and therefore there will be patients who cannot receive the drug in time. Finally, the more demanding one is with the safety level of drugs, the fewer effective drugs there will be available to the patient.

Thus, simplifying somewhat, we can say that regulation concerning the approval or rejection of a drug can give rise to four possible situations:[2]

1. The drug is safe and effective but the approval system rejects it, because it demands more proof. We will call this a 'type I error'.
2. The drug is safe and effective and the approval system approves it, because it considers that it has provided sufficient proof. The system works.
3. The drug is not safe and effective and the approval system rejects it, because it detects these characteristics of the drug. The system works.
4. The drug is not safe and effective but the approval system approves it, because it is not sufficiently demanding with the proof it requests. We will call this a 'type II error'.

Type I errors can be either permanent or temporary. An error is said to be permanent when the regulator rejects a drug that is safe and effective and it cannot be marketed. An error is temporary when the regulator rejects a drug provisionally because more proof is needed of its safety, or because proof of effectiveness on a particular group is lacking, and so on. This delays the date of its arrival on the market and is to the detriment of those patients who could have benefited from its being marketed earlier. Type II decisions involve the approval of drugs that are unsafe and/or less effective than those already available. These drugs may cause hitherto undetected side effects.

If a government tightens up its drug approval policy it will have fewer type II errors but more type I errors, and vice versa. Therefore, an ideal drug approval policy should take into account both the costs and the benefits of a stricter or less strict policy when approving a pharmaceutical. Insofar as the costs and benefits stated above are important factors in the decision to approve or reject a drug, the role of economic evaluation is clear.

Pricing

Once a medicine has been approved for use, the next decision to take is what price it will have. The main justification for government regulation of drug prices is the monopoly that patents give to producers. This monopoly is considered to be necessary for the companies to recover the R&D expenses they have had to carry out to develop the product, and at the same time it enables the companies to amass funds for future research. It should also be noted that even in the absence of patents the pharmaceutical industry would tend not to be a perfectly competitive industry, and would display monopolistic, or at least oligopolistic, characteristics. The reason for this is that R&D expenses are fixed costs, in the sense that they do not vary with the scale of production. Because R&D expenses are fixed costs, those industries in which they are high face decreasing average cost curves until relatively high levels of production are reached. Industries with high fixed costs thus tend to have relatively few companies; competition is usually limited. Therefore, if we admit that it makes sense for the price of new drugs to be regulated, the need arises to study the various possible ways of doing so that economic theory can offer.[3,4]

Price Regulation

1. *Marginal cost*   The most obvious candidate for providing an efficient price scheme is the marginal cost. The typical problem for monopolists who set the price according to the marginal cost is that they need a subsidy to cover costs, as the marginal cost for a monopolist is lower than the average cost.

2. *Average cost*   An alternative that avoids the need to subsidize the monopoly is to set the price according to the average price. A proportional amount of the fixed costs are paid at the moment of consumption. The problem with this, from a theoretical point of view, is that it might prevent efficient consumption, that is, it might prevent a consumer with a willingness to pay between the marginal and the average cost from buying the product. Furthermore, for those who wish to consume, it results in a level of consumption that is lower than the efficient one.

3. *Non-linear pricing*   Non-linear prices usually consist of a two-part tariff. One part is fixed and does not depend on the quantity of the product consumed. The simplest way to establish this tariff is to estimate the potential loss (L) at the point where price = CMg and divide it by the number (N) of potential users, that is, the tariff equals L/N. The other part varies with the quantity consumed. In the case in which the variable component is fixed according to the marginal cost, the price structure is efficient and at the same time the company can avoid incurring a deficit.

The advantage of this system over average-cost pricing is that at the moment of consumption it is only the marginal cost that influences the decision to consume. The problem with this tariff structure is that for some consumers the consumer surplus may fall between the total tariff and the variable tariff. The need to pay the fixed part may prevent the consumer from entering the market and consuming, in spite of being willing to pay the marginal cost of production.

4. *Ramsey prices*   The theory on price structures in a monopoly developed by Ramsey affects those monopolies that produce more than one type of product. Ramsey showed that the best way to share fixed costs and cause minimal welfare losses was not the non-linear pricing system described above; instead, the rule he proposed consisted in increasing prices above the marginal cost in an inverse proportion to demand elasticities. Ramsey prices are therefore linear prices that fulfil the condition that total revenue equals total costs, and moreover minimize welfare losses.

5. *Sunk costs*   Often the way prices are determined will influence the volume of these fixed costs for the company. This is particularly true in the case of sunk costs, that is, those costs that once they have been assumed by a company cannot be recovered except through the sale of the products whose production incurred them. In order for a regulated company to make this sort of investment (such as spending on R&D by pharmaceutical companies), it has to have certain guarantees from the regulator that it will be able to recover the sunk costs with the corresponding profitability. Most of the investments that generate sunk costs are made when it is still too early for the company to know what price it will be able to charge for the product. The regulator could opt to assume

some sort of commitment to provide a 'fair' return on the investment once it has been made. However, we would add that it seems logical that this commitment should only be made on condition that the capital is both used and useful. Therefore, in order to ensure suitable regulation of industries with high sunk costs, it is very important for the regulator to have a fairly exact idea of the value of the product that the company is offering.

Pharmaceutical Price Regulation

The above seems to suggest that there are two possible options for regulating drug prices:

1. Pricing based on the average cost, thus enabling pharmaceutical companies to recover their R&D expenses with the corresponding profitability.
2. Two-tariff pricing: the fixed part of the tariff would be related to the company's fixed costs, that is, basically R&D costs. This fixed part would serve to compensate the company for its spending on R&D and encourage it to continue dedicating additional resources to discovering new products. The variable part of the tariff would be established according to the marginal cost. If the government wished to discriminate between users, depending on their characteristics, it could apply a scheme based on Ramsey prices.

In the case of countries with public financing of pharmaceuticals, these two systems can in practice be very similar. This is so because at the moment of consumption users normally only pay a percentage of the price. Therefore, setting prices according to the average cost and subsidizing the consumer heavily may be equivalent to a two-tariff system, with a variable tariff equivalent to the percentage paid by the patient.

Later on we will see how economic evaluation can help to put these types of pricing policies into practice. The following is a brief account of how drug prices are regulated in various countries.

International Experience in Pharmaceutical Price Regulation

Prices are regulated differently in different countries, each country having its own distinguishing peculiarities. Nevertheless, at the risk of oversimplifying, we will follow the classification proposed by some authors,[5] which concentrates on the basic traits of each system. The reason for including this brief overview here is that the role played by economic evaluation has to be different in each of these drug price regulation systems.

1. *Systems with freedom of prices*   These are the countries in which pharmaceutical companies are free to fix the price they see fit for their medicines. This is the case in the USA and the UK. However, freedom of prices does not mean the absence of any type of regulation. Thus, in the UK the Pharmaceutical Price Regulation Scheme[6] establishes limits to the return that can be obtained by the companies. Indirectly, this limits the price of the drugs.

2. *Systems with two administrative stages*   In countries that use this system (for example, France), drugs are first evaluated according to the therapeutic benefit they provide. Once this evaluation is complete, the price of the drug is fixed by means of negotiation between the company and the state regulatory agency. In this negotiation it is common for prices to be fixed by comparing the new product with similar products that are already on the market, or with the price of the same product in other countries. As a method, then, this does not seem to be very sophisticated or based on theoretical principles such as those described above.

3. *Systems based on reference pricing*   These are systems in which drugs are classified according to their chemical, pharmacological or therapeutic equivalence. The regulator commits itself to financing the drug up to a certain price (the reference price). The company is free to fix the price it sees fit, but the patient has to pay the total of the difference between the reference price and the price fixed by the company.

4. *Systems based on economic evaluation*   These systems require the company to present an economic evaluation as part of the documents needed for the granting of the product's marketing authorization. This economic evaluation is used to decide whether or not the drug will receive public financing. To date, the only countries where it is compulsory to present economic evaluations are Australia and Canada, although it is not clear how these evaluations are used in practice. The outcome of the evaluation certainly influences the decision as to the reimbursement or otherwise of the drug, and also the price it will have, but it seems to be used as just another factor in the negotiations. As such, there is no clear relationship between the outcome of the economic evaluation and the price.

Pharmaceutical Financing

Another decision-making area in pharmaceutical policy is that of the financing of drugs. An institution (be it public or private) that finances medical care must decide first whether or not it will reimburse its insurees in the event of their consuming the product, and then what percentage of the price it will reimburse.

Deciding Whether or Not to Finance a Pharmaceutical

Economic evaluation has shown[7] that in order to maximize benefits in a context of budget restraint, it is necessary to calculate the updated costs and benefits of various possible investments. The resulting decision rule will depend on the nature of the decision:

(a) *Problem*   Several independent programmes compete for a limited budget.
   Rule   Arrange the programmes in order of rising cost–benefit ratio and select them in this order until the resources run out.
(b) *Problem*   One programme is to be chosen out of several mutually exclusive programmes.
   Rule 1   Arrange the programmes in order of effectiveness.
   Rule 2   Calculate the incremental cost–benefit ratios.
   Rule 3   Exclude programmes according to the extended dominance rule, that is, if some cost–benefit ratios are lower than the previous ones in the sequence of increasing effectiveness, those with less effectiveness must be excluded.
   Rule 4   Move upwards in the list of incremental ratios and choose the most effective programme, within the existing budget restraint.
(c) *Problem*   The best combination of programmes is to be chosen out of several independent sets of mutually exclusive projects.
   Rule   Apply the same methodology as in the case of several mutually exclusive programmes, but in this case to all the independent sets. In this case, as the aim is not to choose one single programme, we will select programmes following increasing cost–benefit ratios until the budget is exhausted.

As these rules are somewhat difficult to understand in the abstract, we will suggest an example.[8] Let us assume that there are three independent sets of programmes, such as spending on education, health care and roads. Within each of them there are several mutually exclusive options (only one of them will be implemented) with varying costs and benefits. The steps to be taken are as follows:

1.   Arrange the programmes in order of effectiveness and calculate the incremental cost–benefit ratios (Table 8.1).
2.   Eliminate the dominated alternatives (extended dominance). Project C is eliminated from the health care projects, and project L from the roads projects (Table 8.2).
3.   Recalculate the incremental cost–benefit ratios with the remaining alternatives.

Table 8.1 Costs and benefits of social programmes

Health care				Education				Roads			
Project	C	B	$\Delta C/\Delta B$	Project	C	B	$\Delta C/\Delta B$	Project	C	B	$\Delta C/\Delta B$
A	100	10	10	F	200	12	17	K	100	5	20
B	200	14	25	G	400	16	50	L	200	8	33
C	300	16	50	H	550	18	75	M	300	12	25
D	400	19	33								
E	500	20	100								

Table 8.2 Costs and benefits of non-dominated alternatives

Health care				Education				Roads			
Project	C	B	$\Delta C/\Delta B$	Project	C	B	$\Delta C/\Delta B$	Project	C	B	$\Delta C/\Delta B$
A	100	10	10	F	200	12	17	K	100	5	20
B	200	14	25	G	400	16	50	M	300	12	29
D	400	19	40	H	550	18	75				
E	500	20	100								

Table 8.3   Ordering of programmes according to incremental cost–benefit ratios

Project	$\Delta C/\Delta B$	Costs
A	10	100
F	17	200
K	20	100
B	25	200
M	29	300
D	40	400
G	50	400
H	75	550
E	100	500

4.   Select the programmes in rising cost–benefit order until the budget is exhausted. For greater ease of decision-making, all the programmes can be ordered according to incremental cost–benefit ratios (Table 8.3).

Therefore, the projects selected would depend on the budget. For example:

- Budget = 300 → A + F.
- Budget = 500 → F + K + B. This case shows that the rule does not always mean choosing the project with the lowest incremental cost–benefit ratio out of the mutually exclusive projects. If we have a budget of 500 we should in theory choose A + F + K, but then there would be 100 left over. With the extra 100 we can implement B instead of A, since it produces more benefits.
- Budget = 800 → 50 per cent B + 50 per cent D + F + M. This is an interesting case because it shows one of the limitations of this rule, namely that it assumes projects to be divisible. If we have 800 the projects chosen are F + B + M, but this leaves 100, so we look for a project with higher costs and more benefits. The next in the list is D, but B cannot be replaced by D because this would require 900. The option is to do 50 per cent of B (cost = 100) and 50 per cent of D (cost = 200). The rule implies, therefore, that projects are divisible. If they were not, the choice should have been F + B + M, yielding a benefit of 38, although the benefit would have been greater with D + F + L (a total of 39), that is, L should not have been excluded and the extended dominance rule is not legitimate. Moreover, it is assumed that returns are constant to scale, as

otherwise it could not be supposed that 50 per cent of B produces half as much benefit as 100 per cent of B.

Deciding what Percentage to Finance

There are few references in economic theory on how to subsidize the prices paid by the users of products that receive public financing. For reasons of efficiency, the financing of consumption of a certain product can be justified in terms of the positive externalities that this consumption generates. This is the case, first and foremost, with the subsidizing of treatment for most infectious diseases. However, this reasoning does not legitimate the subsidizing of present AIDS treatments, as they do not prevent contagion. Some authors[9] have introduced the term 'caring externalities'. This term is a reference to the fact that individuals are not insensitive to the suffering of others, and derive utility from seeing that no one who suffers a disease is denied necessary medical care. This justifies subsidies according to level of income, as it is the poor who are likely to have most problems in gaining access to necessary medical care when they need it.

One last theoretical reasoning to throw light on the problem of the percentage of price subsidizing has to do with the 'excess consumption' problems raised by the financing of drug prices. It is usually taken as understood that users who do not pay the marginal cost consume too much. Excess consumption is defined in terms of what users would consume if they assumed the entirety of the costs. All those individuals who attach a value to the product that lies between the marginal cost and the price they actually pay should not be consuming the product they are consuming. Only those who obtain a benefit greater than the marginal cost should consume the product. This gives rise to an argument in favour of larger subsidies for those who have more to gain from consuming the product, and vice versa. This could legitimate the Italian system of co-payment, whereby medicines are divided into three groups. Group A contains essential medicines, the price of which is reimbursed 100 per cent; group B comprises medicines that are effective but not essential, or have little cost-effectiveness, and is 50 per cent subsidized; and group C is made up of effective, cheap drugs for short-duration problems and medicines that are shown not to be effective, and receives no subsidy.

Along the same lines, a proposal has been made for the UK that would divide medicines into four groups: 'The A list would contain a selection of effective medicines, no more than 200–300, but sufficiently comprehensive to allow treatment of all major conditions, and free of charge to all. B list medicines are either no more effective than A list medicines, or offer minor benefits at a disproportionate cost. These might require a low co-payment, perhaps related to the cost of the prescription, to a preset maximum. A maximum cumulative annual co-payment per patient should also be set. C list medicines are those for which effective alternatives are already listed, for example, branded preparations where a generic equivalent is available or which are largely directed at patient convenience, such as many modified release preparations. Patients might pay perhaps 50 per cent of the cost of these medicines. D list medicines would not be funded by the NHS at all, as in the current selected list'.[10]

To sum up, the above arguments indicate that it is advisable to establish drug subsidies in such a way that they provide most benefit to:

(a)   Those who have contagious diseases.
(b)   The poor.
(c)   Those who stand to benefit most from using the drugs.

REGULATION AND ECONOMIC EVALUATION

Approving a Pharmaceutical

As explained earlier, the approval of a drug requires a prior evaluation period to test its safety and effectiveness. It has been shown that the more demanding the evaluation period, the more we can guarantee the safety and effectiveness of the pharmaceutical. At the same time, the longer the evaluation period and the larger the sample of patients needed, the higher the cost of obtaining the desired guarantee of safety and effectiveness. Nevertheless, as the Food and Drug Administration (FDA) states, 'Although medical products are required to be safe, safety does not mean zero risk. A safe product is one that has reasonable risks, given the magnitude of the benefits expected and the alternatives available'.[11]

This disjunctive between costs and benefits resulting from the regulation of the pharmaceutical approval process can be dealt with by means of economic evaluation. The various projects can be represented using a decision tree as shown in simplified form in Figure 8.1.

Thus, the decision we are faced with consists of choosing either regulatory process A or B. Once we have chosen one of these two processes, there is a certain probability of the drug being safe and effective and a certain probability of it not being safe. These probabilities are the same in both regulatory processes. The difference between the two regulatory processes emerges in the probabilities of the next event, namely the approval or rejection of the drug. A very strict process generates high probabilities of drugs being rejected owing to a lack of evidence, whether they are safe and effective or not, whereas a laxer process increases the complementary probabilities. Therefore, economic

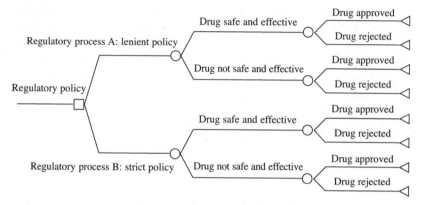

Figure 8.1   Decision tree for regulatory policy

evaluation shows that these probabilities constitute one of the key elements when regulating the approval of a pharmaceutical. The utilities are the second key element associated with the outcomes.

By applying the above decision tree we obtain four outcomes:

1. Safe and effective drug approved (SEA).
2. Safe and effective drug rejected (SER).
3. Non-safe and effective drug approved (NSEA).
4. Non-safe and effective drug rejected (NSER).

In order to associate a number to represent the utility of these four outcomes we have to choose between several types of economic evaluations, basically between cost-effectiveness analysis, cost-utility analysis and cost–benefit analysis. The first of these is ruled out because it measures the health outcome in natural units. Given that the side effects of drugs are of a varied nature, we need to be able to aggregate the different seriousness of these side effects in order to obtain a single utility, at least for the NSEA event. Furthermore, this utility must be comparable with that of, for example, the SER event. This is not possible with cost-effectivity. If we chose cost-utility, the utility associated with each event would be measured in QALYs gained or lost in each option. As QALYs are a universal measure of health benefit, cost-utility analysis could be appropriate for this type of decision. Lastly, cost–benefit analysis would also be appropriate, as it measures the utilities associated with each outcome in monetary terms, which reflect the willingness to pay for one of the outcomes in terms of safety and effectiveness.

The above approach may be excessively academic and simplistic. We do

Table 8.4   Probabilities and utilities of each regulatory policy

	Strict policy	Lenient policy		Utilities (case A)	Utilities (case B)
PSE	0.8	0.8	SEA	20	0.1
PNSE	0.2	0.2	SER	−20	−0.1
PA	0.3	0.9	NSEA	−25	−20
PR	0.7	0.1	NSER	−20	−0.1

Notes: PSE: probability of the drug being safe and effective; PNSE: probability of the drug not being safe and effective; PA: probability of the drug being accepted; PR: probability of the drug being rejected.

not deny this, but it is not the objective of this chapter to attempt an in-depth analysis of the casuistry of individual decision-making. In any event, the approach serves to highlight some important points in the regulatory process of approving a drug. First of all, it shows that the advisability of adopting one regulatory process or the other (A or B) varies from one drug to another. The strictness of the regulatory process serves above all to provide certain probabilities for each event, but the decision to choose one process or the other also depends on the utilities associated with each event. For example, let us assume that we have obtained the data shown in Table 8.4.

Case A is that of a disease, which, if untreated, will cause patients to lose 20, QALYs. If the pharmaceutical is effective and safe patients will gain 20 QALYs. If the pharmaceutical is not safe and effective and it is administered nonetheless, the side effects will entail a loss of 5 QALYs more than would have been the case if they had not been given the medicine. In this case, the more lenient policy has a higher expected value than the stricter one. This is logical, as the consequences for the patients are very serious if they are not provided with the drug and they gain a great deal if they are provided with it. Therefore, this benefit compensates for the potential risks of the side effects. Case B is that of a medicine for a minor ailment. Patients lose 0.1 QALYs if they do not receive the drug and gain 0.1 if they receive it. However, the side effects may be very serious. In this second case the higher expected value is that of the stricter policy.

This example is very simple and restrictive, but it is useful to illustrate the idea that economic evaluation can help to regulate the approval of pharmaceuticals. It also shows that one of the lessons to be learnt from applying the rules of economic evaluation is that the way drug approval is regulated should change from one drug to another, depending on the costs and benefits of each option.

Pricing

The role that economic evaluation can play in pharmaceutical pricing varies with the type of regulation carried out in each country; it cannot play the same role in a country such as the USA, where there is freedom of prices, and in a country where pricing is regulated.

1. *Countries with freedom of prices* In these countries, the role of economic evaluation would in theory appear to be minor, as companies are free to set their own prices. However, clearly the price a company puts on its new product has to follow some logic, as otherwise neither consumers will buy it nor insurance companies will include it in their formularies of reimbursable products. If a company wants to sell its product at a higher price than that of the best alternative product, it needs to justify the higher price with greater benefit, and this is where economic evaluation comes into its own. In these cases, economic evaluation becomes a marketing tool for the company. Is one type of economic evaluation better than the others for this purpose of justifying a higher price? In theory, the most appropriate type of study for a pharmaceutical company wishing to fix a price would be cost–benefit analysis, performed not from the social point of view but from the point of view of the company. In other words, the costs and benefits to be considered in the analysis would be those affecting the pharmaceutical company. In this case, we would be dealing with a typical investment evaluation study rather than a CBA.

2. *Countries with price regulation (two administrative stages)* In this case the price is fixed in two administrative stages: the first serves to calculate the health benefit of the product and the second to fix the price. Clearly, economic evaluation has little to do with the first stage. It is in the second stage, when the price of the drug is fixed, that economic evaluation could be more useful. As explained earlier, a logical scheme would be one in which the patients' co-payment could be designed in such a way that it equals the marginal cost, and public financing, which originates from taxes, could be regarded as the way of financing the R&D expenses (sunk costs) of companies. In this case, the problem lies in how to set up a suitable structure of incentives for spending on R&D. In our opinion, the part that economic evaluation can play in this matter is related to the need to estimate the value of the product in order to be able to estimate the return to which the pharmaceutical company is entitled in exchange for its R&D expenses. In the case of pharmaceuticals, it falls to economic evaluation to say whether the R&D has produced a drug that is useful for society, and hence whether the company should receive reward for the expense it has

incurred on R&D. The type of economic evaluation that can answer this question is primarily cost–benefit analysis. CBA can be used to measure the consumer surplus, and therefore the maximum remuneration the company should receive for its R&D spending. Cost-utility analysis could also be used, as long as the authorities state how much they are willing to pay for each additional QALY the new drug produces.

3. *Systems based on reference pricing* (RP)   Once a product's patent has expired, there do not seem to be many arguments for subsequent regulation of drug prices by the public authorities. Once the company has succeeded in obtaining a satisfactory return on its R&D expenses, it would appear that the price should be based on the marginal cost, and in principle the best guarantee of that happening is competition.

4. *Systems based on economic evaluation*   At present, Canada and Australia[12-15] appear to be the only two countries in which economic evaluation is used to fix drug prices. Although both countries have produced quite extensive guidelines on how economic evaluation studies should be presented, there is no clear evidence of the influence these studies are having on the price of the product. It is true that the economic evaluation studies are presented with the pharmaceutical company assuming a certain price. However, the confidentiality of the negotiations makes it difficult to know how the company has calculated the price in the economic evaluation study it presents, what price is finally reached and what reasoning is used to get to that point.

Perhaps the institutions that most use economic evaluation are the Health Maintenance Organizations (HMOs), Pharmacy Benefit Management firms (PBMs) and hospitals in the 'managed competition' sector[16-18]. However, these studies are not being used to fix prices, but to decide whether a medicine should be included among those financed by the institution. Thus, some HMOs have already developed their own guidelines for the inclusion of medicines in their formulary (the range of drugs available to the user), and these guidelines make it compulsory to conduct a study of the impact, as regards both costs and outcomes, of the inclusion of the drug in the formulary.

Pharmaceutical Financing

Deciding whether or not to finance a pharmaceutical

Once the price has been fixed, the next decision is whether or not the drug should be financed. This decision falls either to the patient, if it is he or she who pays, or a third party, which could mean the government, an insurance company, an institution such as an HMO, or some other. In the first case, the patient does the economic evaluation when he or she decides whether to buy the product. In the second case, our question is: how can economic evaluation help the institution that finances the product to come to a decision?

As explained above, the decision as to whether or not to finance a drug is where economic evaluation comes into its own. In reality, all we have to do is replace the headings 'health care, education, roads' with, for example, 'Alzheimer's, hypertension, chronic obstructive pulmonary disease (COPD) and consider projects A, B, C and so on, as pharmaceuticals, in order to formulate the problem in the framework of drug financing decision-making. The numbers in the examples can be either QALYs or the monetary value of the health benefits. That is, they are quantities estimated by means of either CUA or CBA. CEA is not useful in deciding whether or not to finance a drug. Once we have measured the outcome of the drug in QALYs or monetary units, all we have to do is to use the rules mentioned above to ascertain whether it should be financed.

The answer given by economic evaluation to the question of whether a given product should be financed or not seems to be fairly clear. However, the decision rules mentioned above clash with certain problems, and neither these problems nor some possible solutions should be overlooked.

- *Problem 1*   The decision rules assume that the budget is closed; therefore, if a new drug has a ratio that makes it acceptable, the budget can be obtained by ceasing to finance another one.

  The problem is even more serious, if that is possible, because the new drug might replace not only one which is mutually exclusive but also another that treats a different disease. Let us assume that the current budget finances one pharmaceutical for Alzheimer's, one for hypertension and one for COPD. Let us suppose that a very good but very expensive COPD drug comes out. We might find that the decision rule suggests that, in addition to replacing the other COPD drug, we should also cease to finance the drug for Alzheimer's, thus leaving Alzheimer's sufferers without treatment.

- *Problem 2*   Patients are very heterogeneous and a particular drug may have a favourable ratio for some patients and a poor one for others. Therefore, we will be financing the treatment of some patients and not that of others.

  This generates problems of discrimination between some patients and others, which can on occasions amount to a major political problem. It may be more normal to assume that, once a drug is financed, it will be consumed by a wide variety of patients. Furthermore, it may not be feasible in practice to discriminate between patients for whom the treatment is highly effective and those for whom it is less so.

- *Problem 3*   The decision rules mentioned above assume that projects are perfectly divisible.

This would entail, if necessary, only supplying the medicine to a certain number of patients because there is no budget for the rest. This generates very serious discrimination problems.

There are ways to cope with all these problems, and others not mentioned here. In general, these problems can be solved by designing resource allocation models that incorporate them in the form of new constraints. For example, some authors[19] include the constraint that each group of patients will choose the medicine that provides them with the largest possible number of QALYs. They also include the constraint that there must always be at least one medicine for a particular disease or health problem. Therefore, problems 1 and 2 can be dealt with by introducing these constraints into the model. As for problem 3, the solution is use the constraint that the programmes chosen must be whole numbers.

To sum up, economic evaluation (CUA and CBA) is a suitable decision-making approach to the issue of whether or not to finance a drug. As constraints are imposed to overcome problems, the model used for the economic evaluation becomes increasingly complex.

Deciding what percentage to finance

As mentioned above, there are arguments to support the percentage of pharmaceutical financing being larger for:

(a)   Those with contagious diseases.
(b)   The poor.
(c)   Those who stand to benefit most from using the drugs.

Clearly, economic evaluation has a part to play in two of the above cases. It cannot be used to justify a scheme of subsidies according to income, as this is a problem of equity whereas economic evaluation is more concerned with efficiency motivations. From the viewpoint of efficiency, the benefit of financing one drug or another grows with the QALYs gained by preventing contagious diseases. The more serious the consequences of the disease, the larger the percentage of financing it should receive. Therefore, the decision to finance medicines for this type of health problem admits, without problems of any sort, an approach that employs CUA or CBA.

The decision to relate the percentage to be financed with the therapeutic benefit of each drug is rather more complicated to justify. Briefly, the arguments used to justify a larger percentage of financing for products with greater therapeutic value are based on the assumption that products with greater therapeutic value are more expensive and the marginal utility of income is decreasing. This translates as a decreasing willingness to pay for the same health gains, as the product becomes more expensive (see Table 8.5).

Table 8.5 Example of a utility function

Income (monetary units)	Marginal utility of income	Total utility
1	10	10
2	9	19
3	8	27
4	7	34
5	6	40
6	5	45
7	4	49
8	3	52
9	2	54
10	1	55

Let us suppose that the population attaches a constant value to gains of identical health units, in this case QALYs. This means that the sacrifice, in terms of utility, that they are willing to make to gain a QALY is constant. However, the willingness to pay for each additional QALY is decreasing, as a result of the decreasing marginal utility of income.

Let us suppose that there is one type of patient (A) with a disease that reduces their health status by 2 QALYs, and another type of patient (B) with a disease that reduces theirs by 10 QALYs. They are assumed to have several drugs available to them, and the more expensive the drug, the more effective it is and the more QALYs it enables them to gain. Finally, we assume that the price of a drug is related to its effectiveness, and that the price of a drug rises by 1 monetary unit for each additional QALY it enables us to gain. Therefore, type A patients need a drug that costs 2 monetary units, and type B patients need one that costs 10 monetary units.

To be cured (that is, to gain 2 QALYs), type A patients will have to incur a loss of 2 monetary units, and hence a sacrifice of 3 utils. Type B patients will be cured (that is, will have gained 10 QALYs) when they have made a loss of 10 monetary units, and therefore a sacrifice of 55 utils. The sacrifice per QALY gained is, for type A patients, 1.5 utils/QALY, whereas for type B it is 5.5 utils/QALY. We now suppose that the government proposes to help the patients to finance their expenditure on medicines. The money it has available for this is 10 monetary units. How should it spend this sum in order to raise social welfare to the maximum? It ought to give 9 to type B patients and 1 to type A patients. This suggests that more financing should go to those patients who need pharmaceuticals that are more expensive and produce more QALYs.

Moreover, it is logical to assume that there is a limit to the sacrifice people can make to buy health, as they need the money for other things. Continuing with our example, if we suppose that the maximum sacrifice a person can make is 11 utils, type B patients will only spend 6 monetary units and thus will not be able to fully recover their health. Again, this suggests that the government should provide more complete financing for those patients who need more expensive medicines and produce more QALYs.

The above example is extremely simple and is based on the assumption that the price of a drug is related to its therapeutic value. Nevertheless, it serves to illustrate how the principles of economic evaluation can be applied to the problem of fixing the percentage of drugs that should be covered by public financing.

CONCLUSION

We have reviewed the main decision-making areas in the drug regulation process. In all of them, economic evaluation has some part to play. In the process of approving a pharmaceutical, economic evaluation can help to design optimal policies for regulating the evidence that must be provided for each drug regarding its safety and effectiveness. In the pricing process, the role of economic evaluation varies according to the regulatory system of the country concerned (freedom of prices, two administrative stages, reference pricing (RP), economic evaluation) and how the price structure is fixed (single price, non-linear pricing). In the decision whether or not to finance the drug, economic evaluation suggests decision rules that can maximize the health status of a protected population with a closed budget. In the decision regarding the percentage to finance, economic evaluation suggests that this percentage should be larger for more expensive products and products with greater therapeutic value.

REFERENCES

1. Johannesson, M. (1995), 'Economic evaluation of drugs and its potential uses in policy making', *PharmacoEconomics*, 8, 190–98.
2. Viscusi, W.K., J.M., Vernon and J.E. Harrington (1996), *Economics of Regulation and Antitrust*, 2nd edn, Cambridge: The MIT Press.
3. Laffont, J.J. and J. Tirole (1993), *A Theory of Incentives in Procurement and Regulation*, Cambridge: The MIT Press.
4. Spulber, D.F. (1989), *Regulation and Markets*, Cambridge: The MIT Press.
5. Drummond, M., B. Johnson and F. Rutten, 'The role of economic evaluation in the pricing and reimbursement of medicines', *Health Policy*, 40, 199–215.
6. Department of Health (1999), 'The pharmaceutical price regulation scheme', accessed at: http://www.dh.gov.uk/assetRoot/04/01/99/93/04019993.pdf.

7. Weinstein, M.C. and R. Zeckhauser (1973), 'Critical ratios and efficient allocation', *Journal of Public Economics*, 2, 147–57.
8. Karlsson, G. and M. Johannesson (1996), 'The decision rules of cost-effectiveness analysis', *PharmacoEconomics*, 9, 113–20.
9. Culyer, A. (1998), 'The normative economics of health care finance and provision', *Oxford Review of Economic Policy*, 5, 34–58.
10. Walley, T. (1998), 'Prescription charges: change overdue?', *British Medical Journal*, 317, 487–8.
11. US Department of Health and Human Services – Food and Drug Administration (1999), *Managing the Risks from Medical Product Use*, May.
12. Aristides, M. and A. Mitchell (1994), 'Applying the Australian guidelines for the reimbursement of pharmaceuticals', *PharmacoEconomics*, 6, 196–201.
13. Langley, P. (1996), 'The November 1995 revised Australian guidelines for the economic evaluation of pharmaceuticals', *PharmacoEconomics*, 9, 341–52.
14. Glennie, J., G. Torrance, J. Baladi, C. Berka, E. Hubbard, D. Menon, N. Otten and M. Riviere (1999), 'The revised Canadian guidelines for the economic evaluation of pharmaceuticals', *PharmacoEconomics*, 15, 459–68.
15. Hill, S., A. Mitchell and D. Henry (2000), 'Problems with the interpretation of pharmacoeconomic analyses', *Journal of the American Medical Association*, 283, 2116–21.
16. Lipsy, R. (1992), 'Institutional formularies: the relevance of pharmacoeconomic analysis to formulary decisions', *PharmacoEconomics*, 1, 265–81.
17. Langley, P. (1999), 'Formulary submission guidelines for Blue Cross and Blue Shield of Colorado and Nevada', *PharmacoEconomics*, 16, 211–24.
18. Grabowski, H. (1998), 'The role of cost-effectiveness analysis in managed care decisions', *PharmacoEconomics*, 14, 15–24.
19. Olmstead, T. and R. Zeckhauser (1999), 'The menu-setting problem and subsidized prices: drug formulary illustration', *Journal of Health Economics*, 18, 523–50.

9. Prescriber incentives

L. Cabiedes and V. Ortún

One in eight Japanese hospitals accepted a prospective tariff per type of disease . . . the amount of drugs supplied to inpatients decreased by 83 per cent. Japanese doctors prescribed and dispensed the drugs . . . the Ministry of Health and Welfare wants to put a stop to this practice.

The Economist, 19 October 1996

It's a pity cheaper doesn't always mean better, more appropriate.

Your GP

INTRODUCTION

Ideally, the prescriber (the patient's agent) should indicate the most appropriate medicine for each situation, taking into consideration the variables affecting the patient (diagnosis, prognosis, ease of administration, side effects and others) and the social opportunity cost. The criterion generally adopted in evaluating the prescription is one of social appropriateness or suitability. It is important to bear in mind that there are two alternative viewpoints to that of society to evaluate appropriateness: the clinical perspective and that of the individual patient. Clinical appropriateness is established in terms of expected benefits and costs for the average patient. The viewpoint of the individual patient is incorporated when guidelines for good clinical practice are adapted to the patient's attitude to risk, or the various quality-of-life factors that each person perceives differently. Finally, the social perspective – that which is adopted in this chapter – encompasses the notion of opportunity cost and seeks to maximize the 'welfare function' that each society freely establishes.

Spain stands in an unenviable position of leadership in Europe as regards bacterial resistance, the great and apparently arbitrary variability in prescription rates and the high degree of inadequacy with regard to drug indication, choice and administration, treatment review and communication between the components of the 'chain of medication'.[1] For example, inadequate prescription occurs both when a prescription is given without the pertinent indication (antibiotics in acute viral respiratory infections) and when a prescription is not provided in a situation that requires one (under-treatment of asthmatic patients).

This chapter addresses the issue of how to narrow the gap between the real and the ideal by influencing the prescribers, who are moved by a mixture of motivations that can be either extrinsic (in terms of the consequences they are likely to bring about), intrinsic (the consequences they themselves are likely to undergo) or transcendental (consequences of their actions on another subject or subjects).[2] A whole series of variables (primarily concerning the patient, but also the physician him or herself, the organization, the profession and society at large) account for the prescription: they are the factors that influence it. We will consider that a factor becomes an incentive when it can be channelled by a policy, affecting prescriber behaviour in a way that is advantageous to social welfare.

Prescription is a professional act carried out by doctors, although they do not always carry the initiative for this act: some studies with general practitioners show that they do not feel responsible for all the prescriptions they write and attach particular importance to the inducement of prescriptions by specialists, and to a lesser extent also by patients.[3]

Prescription: a complementary task or a substitutive one? Two tasks are complementary when an effort made towards the first increases the effort required for the second. In contrast, tasks are substitutive when an effort made towards one of them lessens the cost of the effort needed to do the other.

Prescription can be regarded as either an input of the health care process or a product of it. Nevertheless, it usually substitutes other production factors (for example, time) or other products (for example, consultation).

The explanatory factors of prescription that affect the prescriber and have a certain amount of importance and vulnerability (and as such are incentives) can be organized either hierarchically[4] or in parallel.

Hierarchical factors occur under the commonest assumption, namely that of physicians in contracted employment: the insurer sets a series of targets (not all of them explicit) for the health care organization. It should not be taken for granted that these targets pursue efficiency. In turn, the health care organizations – the providers – attempt to transfer the targets (and incentives) received from the insurer or insurers to the clinics, who in the case of prescription allocate the totality of the resources.

Parallel factors take the form of the pressure exerted by colleagues, and can influence both the reputation and the career of the physician.

As a professional act performed by a doctor, prescription occurs in a context. In the first section we analyse the institutional context (state regulation, market rules, clinical standards and population culture); the second section is dedicated to establishing a typology of policies capable of encouraging appropriate prescription, and to valuating the available knowledge on the effectiveness of these policies, with special emphasis on the European Union (EU). The third and final section summarizes what applied economics (and research on health services in general) can tell us about the issue of prescriber incentives.

THE INSTITUTIONAL CONTEXT

All societies have their rules of play: their institutions. These institutions can be defined as the restrictions created by humanity to give structure to political, economic and social interaction. A society's institutions are at the same time its rules of play and its safeguard mechanisms. They can be formal, such as the Constitution, laws, property rights and ethical codes, or informal, such as customs, traditions and expected codes of conduct in a professional group.

The institutions in any society depend on their previous trajectory and show considerable inertia. Institutions are desirable insofar as they reconcile the interest of the individual with that of society.[5]

There are usually three relevant institutions for clinical management: state regulation, market rules and clinical professional standards.[6]

State Regulation

The state regulation of the production, distribution and use of pharmaceuticals has been discussed in depth in other chapters of this book. Here we merely review those regulatory measures that are designed to influence prescription. The measures considered here have been classified as shown in Table 9.1; first, according to whether or not they are directly intended to reduce public pharmaceutical spending; second, according to whether they act on the demand side (that is, the patient/user) or the supply side (basically physicians, pharmacists and the industry itself); and finally according to whether or not they are coercive. Non-coercive measures are generally formulated on the basis of positive and/or negative incentives. Note that the list is open and merely comprises a number of illustrative examples.

The philosophy in which Table 9.1 is inspired requires some elucidation: given the role of doctors as their patients' agents, they could be placed on either the demand side and the supply side. Here we have opted for the latter approach, in view of their function as prescribers, who prefigure the available supply and simultaneously help towards defining the demand. The reference pricing system figures twice, insofar as it seeks to influence both demand and supply at the same time. As far as demand is concerned, it is designed to break the consumer/decision-maker/payer dissociation that characterizes the

Table 9.1 Measures aimed at influencing prescription

1. Measures aimed directly at reducing public pharmaceutical expenditure:		

1.1 On the demand side	Coercive:	Co-payment
	Non-coercive:	Reference pricing
1.2 On the supply side	Coercive:	Positive list
		Negative list
		Price control
		Profit control
		Package size
		Number of items per prescription
		Coercive budgets
	Non-coercive:	Indicative budgets
		Explicit support for generics
		Substitution by pharmacists
		Remuneration system for pharmacies
		Economic evaluation
		Reference pricing

2.   Measures aimed at altering behaviour (in users, the industry itself and health professionals, in order to attain a more rational use of pharmaceuticals and more ethical codes of conduct) from which indirect effects on expenditure may be derived:

2.1 On the demand side	Coercive:	Prescription requirement
	Non-coercive:	Health education
		Involvement in a pharmaceutical care programme
2.2 On the supply side	Coercive:	Limits to spending on advertising
		Penalization of malpractice
	Non-coercive:	Monitoring of prescribing patterns
		Measures encouraging rationalization of prescription
		Pharmaceutical care
		Remuneration system for pharmacies

Notes: The coercive nature of a measure is a question of degree: depending on how they are applied, and in what context, non-coercive measures could ultimately become coercive.

financing of prescription drugs with public funds, thus overcoming user insensitivity to prices. On the supply side, it aims to provide the industry with incentives to fix the prices of drugs included in the scheme close to the reference prices (RPs). For its part, pharmaceutical care (which consists of granting the pharmacist responsibility for the outcome of the pharmacological therapeutics in each patient) is related to both supply and demand, as this new approach to professional practice necessarily hinges on patient/physician/pharmacist collaboration.

The label 'economic evaluation' designates the use of studies of this type as a decision-making aid in the pricing, registration and financing with public funds of the drugs evaluated. Although it is true that studies of this type can be included among the measures taken to encourage rational prescribing patterns, they have been classified as indirect measures, and as such differentiated from the previous ones. They are interpreted more as guidelines that are intended to influence the doctor's prescription process. Finally, budgets involve positive and/or negative economic incentives aimed directly at containing pharmaceutical expenditure. In contrast, measures designed to monitor prescribing patterns and encourage more rational patterns are classified as indirect measures, although in practice it may be questionable whether the former can really be regarded as such, if the monitoring goes no further than a straightforward control (based exclusively on quantitative indicators unlinked to the population profile and other possible explanatory factors) mainly for the purpose of detecting cases of fraud.

Table 9.2 lists some of the measures applied in EU countries in order to influence prescription. As the table shows, the most frequently used measures are co-payment (present in all the countries studied, since its recent introduction in the Netherlands), positive and/or negative lists of medicines, price control and prescription monitoring/control (carried out in all the countries studied). In all cases attempts are made to control expenditure by acting on demand through co-financing by the patient, although the centre of gravity of the policies implemented is located around coercive measures acting directly on the supply side.

Market Rules

The market rules for a service such as the health service are not determining factors in Europe. Nevertheless, if there is one clinical act in which it is particularly important, it is that of prescription.

A large part of the information doctors receive, of the financing of the research they do, of the congresses they attend, of the journals they read and so on, all come from the pharmaceutical industry.

Table 9.2   Measures aimed at influencing prescription as applied in some EU countries

	B	D	DK	E	F	GR	I	IRL	NL	P	S	UK
Co-payment	X	X	X	X	X	X	X	X	X	X	X	X
Reference pricing		X	X	X			X		X		X	
Positive list	X		X		X	X	X		X	X	X	
Negative list		X		X		X	X[a]	X				X
Price control	X			X	X	X	X	X	X	X	X	
Profit control				X[b]								X
Package size		X					X					
No. of items per prescription							X					
Coercive budgets		X			X	X[c]	X[a]					X
Indicative budgets	X					X[c]						X
Support for generics[d]		X	X					X	X			X
Substitution by pharmacists	X		X	X			X	X	X[e]			X
Fixed payment for pharmacy		X							X		X	X
Economic evaluation					X[f]							X[f]
Health education									X			X
Pharmaceutical care	P	P	P	P				P	P	P	P	P
Limits to spending on advertising												X
Penalization of malpractice	X	X			X	X[c]						
Prescription monitoring	X	X	X	X	X	X	X	X	X	X	X	X
Rationalization of prescription	X		X		X			X	X			X

Notes:
a.   Law 537/1993, in force since 1 January 1994. The law set a ceiling of 10 000 billion Italian lira on the total amount the national health service could spend on medicines.
b.   Indirect control since the early 1990s, when cost-dependent pricing was introduced.
c.   Only in the case of IKA (the largest of the sickness funds in the Greek health care system).
d.   We have marked those cases in which an explicit and ongoing policy is applied in favour of generics. However, we could also add other countries in which generics are beginning to be promoted, sometimes indirectly, such as Spain, France and Portugal.
e.   At the patient's request.
f.   Both the UK and France are promoting some form of economic evaluation of pharmaceuticals.
P = pilot projects.

Source: Bibliographical references 7–14.

Pharmaceutical advertising[15]

According to the Spanish regulations, the cost of promoting medicines must not exceed 12 per cent of their price. This percentage [. . .] appears to be far removed from reality [. . .] Some estimates indicate that commercial processes, comprising promotion and marketing, may amount to between 22 and 28 per cent of the volume of sales by laboratories in Spain [. . .] the extent of individual promotion activities directed at doctors is such they have probably succeeded in undermining any attempt at introducing [. . .] economic incentives, amply exceeded by the payments 'in kind' that serve to support these forms of promotion.

Another peculiarity of the Spanish situation as regards advertising is its lack of control. The transcription of a Community directive on this issue gave rise to control over advertising being devolved to the autonomous communities, resulting in the virtual disappearance of control over advertising due to the interterritorial nature of promotion activities.

A recent study[16] on advertisements for antihypertensive and hypolipidaemic drugs published during 1997 in six leading Spanish medical journals attempted to establish the veracity of the statements (which mainly concerned effectiveness and were referenced to previous scientific research) made in the advertisements. Out of the 125 advertising statements studied, the references were located for 102, yet in 43 per cent of these the bibliographical reference did not support the statement made. This situation was found more frequently with the antihypertensive drugs than with the hypolipidaemic drugs. The main manifestation of untruthfulness was that the slogan recommended the drug for a different population from that mentioned in the study, or for a particular population whereas the study did not refer to this population or made no analysis by subgroups that might have justified the recommendation.

Pharmaceutical sales representatives
Each physician in a primary care centre who kept an electronic diary and recorded actual visiting times dedicated 2.6 weeks a year to receiving laboratory sales representatives, which translated into costs totals approximately 475 000 pesetas per doctor per year.[17]

There is ample evidence to suggest that the pharmaceutical industry often has a negative effect on the prescribing behaviour of doctors.[18] Continuing education, research, congresses, even the organization of leisure time, are overwhelmingly dependent on the pharmaceutical industry. It is unacceptable that pharmaceutical sales representatives should be the main source of information on pharmaceuticals, and that compliance with existing regulations on advertising of medicines for human use should be enforced so poorly.

Research is also strongly influenced by the admittedly legitimate interests of the pharmaceutical industry: examples of this include contract clauses reserving copyright, the initial selection of researchers and topics, and the recent consolidation of the position of companies specializing in clinical trials (to the detriment of academic centres). Frequently there is a conflict of interests between social welfare and private welfare that does not necessarily amount to fraud or malpractice, but which should be made public – through explicit references to sources of funding, for example – so that the users of the research can judge for themselves how important it is.

Clinical Professional Standards

In addition to the health care aspect, the act of prescribing involves an economic aspect, doctors in effect making payment orders, although their orders do not require prior auditing or examination, as is the case for most public administration expenses.[19]

It is important to remember the great degree of discretion left to health professionals, and the obvious fact that it is they who actually allocate most health resources. These professionals belong to a group governed by a set of clinical standards. Clinical professional standards comprise both the conduct that the profession considers to be acceptable (and which it upholds through prestige, eponymy, ostracism and so on) and the values and expectations shared by the reference group of professionals.

These clinical standards are influenced not only by the state and the market but also by the population culture: 'We move in a refined culture of the pharmaceutical, which hypertrophies its benefits, even to the point of creating unjustified dependence, and at the same time undervalues more rational forms of treatment and prevention'.[20]

PRESCRIBER INCENTIVE POLICIES

Prescriber incentive policies have been subject to more thorough analysis in the USA than in Europe. However, the potential impact of measures of this sort depends so strongly on the organizational structure and the sociocultural context in which they are applied that it would be very rash to draw general conclusions from the existing reviews on this topic. We can start by using a list of the most representative prescriber incentive policies as a rough guide, and then go on to analyse the situation in a European context (see Table 9.3). Regardless of whether they are applied simultaneously, three types of incentives can be distinguished: financial, non-financial and a combination of both in a single formula.

For the purpose of analysing incentives of a financial nature in a European context, it is advisable to attach more emphasis to the formula of budgets than to the various physician payment mechanisms. From our point of view, these mechanisms are taken into account indirectly as regards the impact that the articulation of budgets might have on prescriber fees (as in the German case). There are two reasons for this approach: first, in most of Europe's public health systems the salary is the predominant form of payment for physicians,

Table 9.3 Prescriber incentive policies

Type of incentives	Aspects considered	Impact
Financial COERCIVE: Physician payment system (even salaries can be translated into incentives if their level is adjusted according to criteria such as induced expenses, patient satisfaction and quality of care) Prescribing budgets (included or not included in comprehensive budgets; England and Germany) NON-COERCIVE: Indicative budgets (Northern Ireland)	Health expenditure (total or almost total) (England) Pharmaceutical expenditure (Germany)	On the budget of the prescribing unit (England) On prescriber fees (Germany)
Non-financial Information Training Formularies and treatment protocols, without economic sanctions or incentives Prescription monitoring (with/without feedback)	Rationalization of prescription, sometimes merely a supervisory approach	

175

Table 9.3   (continued)

Type of incentives	Aspects considered	Impact
Non-financial (continued)		
Cost-effectiveness guidelines		
Hospital pharmacy: therapeutic guidelines and other innovative instruments (creation of pseudo-competition in the hospital pharmaceutical sector in the community of Valencia)		
Interaction with other professionals (pharmacologists and pharmacists). See 'hospital pharmacy' above, other innovative instruments		
Pressure from patients		
Combination of incentives	Pattern in accordance with prescription guidelines or profiles (clinical criteria) (France, Ireland)	On prescriber fees (France) On the budget of the prescribing unit (Ireland)
COERCIVE:		
Treatment guidelines, when failure to comply can entail positive and negative economic incentives (France: *Références Médicales Opposables*)		
NON-COERCIVE:		
Indicative prescription targets, linked to the possibility of reinvesting the savings obtained (Ireland: indicative drugs targets)		

occasionally with minor variable complements depending on the number of patients on the doctor's list; and second, although the coexistence of sharply contrasting payment schemes in the USA has led to the stressing of their impact on the use of services and (to a lesser extent) expenditure on pharmaceuticals, methodological problems make it impossible to reach totally validated conclusions, even in this context.

Budgets

Medical budgets in the strict sense have only been employed in the UK, in the wake of the reform initiated at the beginning of the 1990s, which grants GPs purchasing power and budget responsibility for the acquisition of successively extended hospital services and pharmaceuticals. The incentive for pharmaceutical saving hinged on the possibility of reinvesting part of the savings obtained in pharmacy – by physicians now transformed into GP fundholders – in other items.[21] GPs who did not adopt this scheme were governed by indicative budgets, but in this case there were neither negative nor positive incentives. This system has subsequently been changed: each GP practice in a given geographical area of the National Health Service (NHS) will mandatorily belong to the recently created primary care groups (PCGs). These PCGs will cover a population of around 100 000 inhabitants. The health authority will allocate them an annual budget, and they will be responsible for practically all the health needs of the population. Each GP practice belonging to a PCG will be controlled by means of an indicative budget.

The formula for calculating the budget of a GP practice must offer an unbiased estimator of the expected level of expenditure if each GP practice had a standard response to the needs of its population. Even if the considerable technical difficulties of establishing this formula could be overcome, the actual expenditure of a GP practice would differ from the budgeted amount due to characteristics of the patients not taken into account in the formula (socioeconomic characteristics, chronic diseases, private coverage and so on), variations in clinical practice between GP practices, random variations in the level of disease and price variations. For a population of 10 000 inhabitants (a reasonable mode for a GP practice) there is a one-third probability that the actual expenditure will deviate more than 10 per cent from a well-designed budget.[22]

This limited reliability of the budgets may induce a wide range of responses from the GP practices, from spending the 'leftovers' so that none of the budget remains unimplemented to selecting patients or providing below-average health care in order to stay within the budget. There are a number of ways of mitigating these negative consequences: the larger population size resulting from the voluntary grouping of GP practices and their budgets allows better compensation for risks and less probability of deviations. A similar effect can be produced by grouping together several years for a single GP practice, so that its deviations can be compensated over time. The exclusion of cata-strophic diseases or the delimitation of a portfolio of services, thus excluding high-cost treatments, help to devise more reasonable budgets. Finally, GP practices can reinsure each other by constituting a fund that at the end of each year enables those who have generated a surplus to compensate those who have incurred a justifiable deficit.

More specifically, pharmaceutical budgets were introduced in England in 1991 as part of the reformed GP fundholder scheme. It represented an attempt to overcome the historical budget system both to control growth in spending and to reduce the great variation in pharmaceutical spending between GP prac-tices. As of 1993–1994 a capitation was applied that was adjusted for age, sex and temporary residence: the ASTRO-PU (age, sex and temporary resident originated prescribing unit).[23] A more refined formula was introduced as of 2000–2001 that also allows for four needs-based variables and attempts to ignore the effect of supply on use.[24] Needs-based and supply-independent prescribing budgets will constitute targets towards which PCGs and GP prac-tices will gradually move. Insofar as prescribing budgets are integrated into the general budget of the PCG and the GP practice, there will be the possi-bility of substitution between, for example, expenditure on pharmacy and programmable specialized care. The maximum amount that GP practices can retain from their possible savings on the budget for all items is £45 000.[25]

In Germany in 1993, a system began to be introduced whereby each area covered by a regional association of physicians was allocated a budget for pharmaceutical expenditure, such that any excess over the established limit would be paid out of their own fees. In this context, the medical associations were responsible for notifying those doctors who exceeded the average for their region by 15 per cent and requiring rectification of their prescribing pattern from those who exceeded the average by 25 per cent.[26] Although they do not have medical budgets as such, a certain amount of control is practised in Belgium, France, Ireland and Italy,[27] and orientative budgets are used in most of Spain's autonomous communities in order to enable the monitoring of expenditure.

When the budget scheme was introduced in the UK and the Irish Republic, with the possibility of reinvestment of the savings obtained, the main concern that was voiced was that savings might be achieved at the cost of prescribing less than would be desirable for patients' health. There does not appear to be any evidence for this, whereas there does seem to have been an impoverish-ment of the stimulus implicit in the incentives, as the budget can be seen to fit more tightly as each year passes, incentives thus disappearing together with the margin for manoeuvre.[28,29]

According to the report prepared by the Audit Commission in the UK and published in May 1996, doctors assigned to fundholdings contained pharmaceutical spending better than those assigned to indicative budgets, following prescribing patterns characterized by a better cost-effectiveness ratio, basically by means of more extensive use of generic products and a more cautious attitude to innovations. However, some studies conclude that there are few consistent differences in prescription costs between the two cases that cannot be explained by underlying sociodemographic variables.[30]

In contrast to the British system, in the pharmaceutical budget applied in Germany since 1993 to each area covered by a regional medical association, part of the financial risk is transferred to the GPs; that is, the fact of exceeding the target fixed for expenditure may entail economic penalties (shared by the physicians and the pharmaceutical industry). In this framework, the positive results in terms of pharmaceutical cost containment were accompanied by an increase in referrals to specialists and hospitals. Indeed, an important difference between the German and the British system is that in the latter the doctors assume the risk associated with a complete package of services and not only pharmaceutical services, and this risk is not transferred to their salaries. The immediate impact in Germany was a drop in the number of prescriptions, and substitutions with generic and less innovative drugs. This formula has led to a reduction in spending on drugs with no or questionable value, and also on useful drugs, although to a lesser extent[3]. In just one year, savings were made to the value of over DM 2000 million, with fewer problems than were initially envisaged. In a word, rationality was increased, at least in the area of pharmacy, given that this saving is a good indicator of the degree of overprescription that held sway prior to the measure being applied. Nevertheless, it would appear to be crucial to address the rationality of the process of replacing drugs with medical consultations.

Non-financial Incentives

First of all, in general terms it is fair to say that not only are financial and non-financial incentives usually applied in parallel but moreover in some contexts measures that at first sight would appear to be of a non-financial nature (for example, continuing education) may in the long run have a impact on doctors' fees.[31] It is also important to note that measures that in principle appear to be the most logical for the purposes of improving physicians' prescription practices can come up against practical obstacles that impair their potential. This can be the case with formularies or lists of restricted or essential drugs, an intervention that is logical – insofar as a selection that is reached in consensus with health professionals and regularly reviewed is clinically rational and at the same time may be cost-effective – but may clash with the perspective of industrial policy.

At present there is a fairly widespread tendency to use formularies and protocols. Thus, by way of example, Italy legislated to this effect in 1997 (seeking to generate incentives for responsible behaviour, mainly through guidelines dealing with the treatment of particular diseases). The success of this step depends on the involvement of health professionals, consensus, peer reviews and continual updating.

The effectiveness of interventions of an educational nature, with requisites such as group discussion and ongoing feedback has been demonstrated in such a wide range of countries as Australia, Germany, Iceland, Ireland, Netherlands, Norway, South Africa, the UK and the USA.

In turn, 'reminders' at the moment of prescribing may be more administrative than educational in nature, their impact disappearing when the intervention ceases, although their reference to previously agreed prescription standards is of especial relevance. Little is known about whether mechanisms of this type might help to relieve pharmaceutical-related problems derived from pressure exerted either by colleagues or by patients.

It should be stressed that the methodological problems present in the design of some studies on the impact of this type of measure impose the need for a great deal of caution in interpreting the results; when analysing the observed effects one should take into account the influence of a whole series of factors that in principle are alien to the study. This would account for the fact that positive changes are sometimes detected in the prescribing behaviour of doctors belonging to the control group. However, Soumerai et al.[32] carried out a review of 44 studies (1970–1988) on a number of non-financial incentives featuring certain conditions for inclusion, such as the evaluation of their impact. This survey provides evidence of the importance of the organizational structure as a starting point and also of the method applied, showing that when information is personalized for each patient and the influence and authority of colleagues is legitimated, 'administrative reminders' and feedback systems appear to fit into group practices, and that in less consolidated structures, individual face-to-face educational sessions (following the format of pharmaceutical sales representatives) are more effective, amply complemented with printed material.

The dissemination of well-designed educational material constitutes a complement to other strategies, especially as a basis for training measures (face-to-face interviews or feedback systems), its relatively low added cost being a factor to take into consideration. However, disseminating this type of material alone hardly has any effect on prescriber behaviour.

All the countries studied carry out prescription monitoring processes of one sort or another, following the lead of the UK, although not always systematically. Moreover, most countries do not reach the extreme of penalizing malpractice. In Spain, personalized information is gathered, more with the aim of cost containment and fraud detection than in order to rationalize prescription; an approach that is also prevalent in other countries. Most Danish counties constitute an exception to this, sending statistics to each physician on his or her prescribing pattern and the average for the area. It has been shown that in order to achieve changes in conduct it is more effective for the counties to monitor conduct and convene those doctors whose practices differ significantly from the average. Nevertheless, experience has also shown that doctors quickly revert to their old habits when the county authority concludes the monitoring initiative.[33] In the review by Soumerai et al.[32] four studies confirm these results: without ongoing monitoring and suggestions for changes in prescribing patterns, physicians' prescription behaviour is very unlikely to be altered.

Thus, in terms of achieving changes in conduct, the impact of these initiatives on prescription does not seem to be either very effective or long-lasting, unless they form part of a package of measures aimed at rationalizing prescription, the effectiveness of which on prescription behaviour can vary considerably depending on the method used. In contrast to a predominantly supervisory approach (which moreover rarely leads to the imposition of penalties), the UK stands out as one of the countries where monitoring has been conducted most systematically and with the clearest will to rationalize prescription. The measures introduced to support the optimization of prescription range from information and education campaigns to the use of cost-effectiveness guidelines, formularies and treatment protocols.

In the area of hospital pharmacy, therapeutic guidelines have long been used that, despite their voluntary nature, in practice seem to be followed by clinics. In this context, we would draw special attention to the innovative move concerning centralized drug purchasing in the public hospital network of the Ministry of Health of the Community of Valencia in Spain: after a careful process leading to the design of the mechanisms necessary to adopt the measure, including the involvement of health professionals in the project through the creation of a pharmaceutical advisory committee and the preselection of the active ingredients with most economic importance, a 'pseudo-market' was set up. The competition for centralized purchasing was designed to enable suppliers to be selected individually for each pharmaceutical product, taking two aspects into account simultaneously: quality valuation (among others, packaging requirements for unit doses, bioavailability studies if appropriate, and bidding for all presentations) and monetary valuation. The results obtained through this measure (for the centralized purchase of five active ingredients in 1998) showed a major monetary saving, together with a guarantee that the products acquired met a series of quality requirements.[34] This is an example of how public network hospitals can take advantage of their market power to generate competition among bidders and hence greater efficiency, at the same time offsetting the pressure exerted by laboratories on prescribers.

Formulas Combining Financial and Non-financial Incentives

The introduction of *Références Médicales Opposables* in France constitutes a example of combined financial and non-financial incentives: consensus of treatment guidelines (in fact, a package of agreed recommendations on what not to prescribe – in the way of treatments and complementary examinations – owing to either their lack of utility or their hazardous nature) together with positive and negative economic incentives (a 5 per cent increase in the fees of doctors who follow the recommendations and the possibility of economic penalties for those who ignore them in their practice).[35] These types of incentives form part of what the French call *maîtrise médicalisée*, which incorporates compulsory continuing education for all practising physicians. Although exceeding the set spending target can entail economic penalties shared by doctors and the pharmaceutical industry, it remains to be seen how this type of overall objective will ultimately be allocated to each individual doctor.

In Ireland, economic and non-economic incentives have gradually been combined since the early 1990s by means of a formula that, unlike the French system, lacks a coercive character. The system, which employs 'indicative drugs targets' for GPs, was implemented as a result of an agreement reached between representatives of GPs and the Ministry of Health in 1991 that sought to rationalize prescription. In this context, whereas doctors retain the right not to follow the targets, they are encouraged to do so and reinvest the savings thus obtained.[36]

To summarize, it should be highlighted that in general terms the issue of prescribing incentives is approached with a marked lack of consideration of such fundamental concerns as their impact on health, although this aspect is indirectly addressed by non-financial incentives and mixed formulas such as those discussed above. Financial incentives alone appear to lack effectiveness as instruments of pharmaceutical policy. Incentives aimed at prescribers should under no circumstances create a clash of interests between their fees and the quality of the care they provide for their patients, and therefore adjustment must be made in these terms. In turn, we cannot ignore that the effect of this type of mechanism on physicians' behaviour will depend on, among other factors, the quality of available information on the aspects taken into consideration in their application.

Finally, we would stress that although it is not straightforward to achieve changes in prescribing patterns, there is a minimum of evidence to support the effectiveness of a coherent and systematic strategy that combines several formulas simultaneously, involves health professionals, and ultimately leads to the rationalization of prescription in the full sense. As these are early days to judge the effectiveness of the recently implemented French formula, it would seem to be recommendable to apply a combination of non-financial incentives following the method described above, regardless of their complementary nature with other formulas.

CONCLUSIONS

This chapter on prescriber incentives brings together various midpoints, all of them difficult to find. One of these midpoints concerns incentives (if there is one distinguishing feature of health care organizations; it is the advisability of moderating the power of incentives in order to stop financial considerations from short-circuiting clinical considerations); another concerns the balance between health policy issues and industrial policy ones; and a third concerns the influences exerted on prescription by the market, the state and clinical standards (the combination of financial and non-financial incentives).

As regards the last of these, from the points raised in the first section above the wisdom of the following measures is clear:

1. To promote a code of good practice for the promotion of pharmaceuticals in order to clarify the relationship between the industry and doctors and thus improve the quality of prescription, especially now that evidence is beginning to accumulate to the effect that action taken on the basis of scientific evidence can have a favourable impact on the appropriateness of prescription.[37]
2. To declare conflicting interests. It is not unusual to find oneself amid a conflict of interests between individual welfare and social welfare, which do not necessarily amount to fraud or malpractice, but which it is desirable to make public – for example by making explicit reference to sources of funding – thus enabling the users of research to judge for themselves how important it is.
3. To be watchful of the degree of dependence of medicine on the pharmaceutical industry, combining the best of public intervention and the best of market mechanisms.

In prescription, as in the other areas of clinical management, doctors – key decision-makers in the health system – are to be provided with the necessary incentives, information and infrastructure to take clinical decisions in a cost-effective way. When possible, appropriate personnel selection, valuing not only skills but also attitudes, can compensate for the characteristic weakness of incentives in the health sector. This focus on selection as an organizational alternative to incentives is particularly relevant in a public sector with an urgent need for a professional and public-service ethic.

It would appear to be advisable to combine financial and non-financial incentives. Among non-financial incentives, we would stress: support for training and research, improvements in the workplace and working conditions, promotion and career development, job security, a feeling of belonging and voluntary geographical mobility, among others. The involvement of workers in issues that affect the company and self-organization have a high motivation rating, helping to produce a feeling of fulfilment and achievement. In primary care, greater autonomy of management, which can be brought about by decentralization, has proved to be a highly motivating element.[38]

Several factors endorse the need for individual incentives[39] in prescription (professional independence, variability in styles of practice, internalization of the opportunity cost and so on), but given that health care involves technical conditions that require teamwork, and moreover that prescription as an input is fairly substitutable with other inputs in the health care process, prescribing budgets have to be included in comprehensive budgets. And on top of all this, it is important to act with the good judgement urged by the aspects discussed in the second section of this chapter as regards needs-based budgets (independent of supply), the limitations that make it advisable initially to work with indicative budgets, and the need to regulate budget surpluses as far as their limits and destinations are concerned.

REFERENCES

1. Meneu, R. (2000), 'Los costes de las actuaciones sanitarias inadecuadas', *Formación Médica Continuada*, 7, 378–85.
2. Martín, J. and M.P. López (1994), 'Incentivos e instituciones sanitarias públicas', Escuela Andaluza de Salud Pública *Documentos Técnicos EASP no 5*. Granada.
3. Gervás, J. and M. Pérez (1995), 'Farmacoeconomía y medicina general', in J. Sacristán, X. Badía and J. Rovira (eds), *Farmacoeconomía: Evaluación Económica de Medicamentos*, Madrid: Editores Médicos, pp. 185–202.
4. Macho, I. (1999), 'Incentivos en los servicios sanitarios', in P. Ibern (ed.), *Incentivos y contratos en los servicios de salud*, Barcelona: Springer-Verlag, pp. 19–47.
5. North, D. (1990), *Institutions, Institutional Change and Economic Performance*, Cambridge University Press.
6. Ortún, V. and J. Del Llano (1998), 'Estado y mercado en sanidad', in J. Del Llano, V. Ortún, J.M. Martín Moreno, J. Millán and J. Gené (eds.), *Gestión sanitaria: innovaciones y desafíos*, Barcelona: Masson, pp. 3–16.
7. Abel-Smith, B. and E. Mossialos (1994), 'Cost containment and health care reform: a study of the European Union', *Health Policy*, 28, 89–132.

8. Cabiedes, L. (1995), 'La regulación de la industria farmacéutica', in J. Velarde, J.L. García-Delgado and A. Pedreño (eds), *Regulación y competencia en la economía española*, Madrid: Civitas, pp. 213–29.

9. Cabiedes, L. (1998), 'Información sobre pacientes derivada de la atención farmacéutica', in S. Peiró and L. Domingo (eds) (1998), *Información sanitaria y nuevas tecnologías*, Vitoria: Asociación de Economía de la Salud, pp. 169–82.

10. Gómez, M.E., J.A. Ruiz and J. Martínez (1999), 'Políticas de uso racional de medicamentos en Europa', *Administración Sanitaria*, 3, 93–107.

11. Jacobzone, S. (2000), 'Pharmaceutical policies in OECD countries: reconciling social and industrial goals', OECD, labour market and social policy occasional papers no. 40, Paris.

12. López, Bastida J. and E. Mossialos (1996), 'Políticas de contención del gasto farmacéutico en los Estados miembros de la Unión Europea', in R. Meneu and V. Ortún (eds.), *Política y gestión sanitaria: la agenda explícita*, Barcelona: SA editores and Asociación de Economía de la Salud, pp. 321–46.

13. Mossialos, E., P. Kanavos and B. Abel-Smith (1994), 'The impact of the single European Market on the pharmaceutical sector', in E. Mossialos (ed.), *Cost Containment, Pricing and Financing of Pharmaceuticals in the European Community: the Policy-makers' View*, London: London School of Economics and Pharmetrica SA, pp. 17–87.

14. Zara, C., L. Segú, M. Font and J. Rovira (1998), 'La regulación de los medicamentos: teoría y práctica', *Gaceta Sanitaria*, 12, 39–49.

15. Rey, J. (ed.) (2000), *El futuro de la sanidad española: un proyecto de reforma*, Madrid: Fundación Alternativas, 107–108.

16. Villanueva, P., S. Peiró and I. Pereiro (2003), 'Accuracy of pharmaceutical advertisements in medical journals', *Lancet*, **361** (9351), 27–32.

17. Ausió, J. (1998), 'Prescripción farmacéutica y médicos de familia', *Atención Primaria*, 22, 545–6.

18. Wazana, A. (2000), 'Physicians and the pharmaceutical industry: is a gift ever just a gift?', *Journal of the American Medical Association*, 283, 373–80.

19. Antúnez, F. (1999), 'Análisis del gasto farmacéutico en la provincia de Granada', *Hacienda Pública Española* **149** (2), 3–20.

20. Castellón, E. (1998), 'Sobre listas negativas', *El País*, 23 February, p. 28.

21. Glennerster, H. and M. Matsaganis (1994), 'The English and Swedish health care reforms', *International Journal of Health Services*, 24, 231–51.

22. Smith, P.C. (1999), 'Setting budgets for general practice in the new NHS', *British Medical Journal*, 318, 776–9.

23. Roberts, S.J. and C.M. Harris (1993), 'Age, sex, and temporary resident originated prescribing units: new weightings for analysing prescribing of general practices in England', *British Medical Journal*, 307, 485–8.

24. Rice, N., P. Dixon, D. Lloyd and D. Roberts (2000), 'Derivation of a needs based capitation formula for allocating prescribing budgets to health authorities and primary care groups in England: regression analysis', *British Medical Journal*, 320, 284–8.

25. Majeed, A. (2000), 'New formula for GP prescribing budgets', *British Medical Journal*, 320, 266.

26. Schmeinck, W. (1994), 'Overview of the German health insurance system', in E. Mossialos (ed.), *Cost Containment, Pricing and Financing of Pharmaceuticals in the European Community: the Policy-makers' View*, London: London School of Economics and Pharmetrica, pp. 161–6.

27. Gómez, M.E., J.A. Ruiz and J. Martínez (1999), 'Políticas de uso racional del medicamento en Europa', *Revista de Administración Sanitaria*, 3, 93–107.
28. McGavock, H. (1997), 'Strategies to improve the cost effectiveness of general practitioner prescribing. An international perspective', *Pharmacoeconomics*, 12, 307–11.
29. Rafferty, T., K. Wilson-Davis and H. McGavock (1997), 'How has fundholding in Northern Ireland affected prescribing patterns?', *British Medical Journal*, 315, 166–70.
30. Majeed, A. and S. Head (1998), 'Setting prescribing budgets in general practice', *British Medical Journal*, 316, 748–53.
31. Chaix-Couturier, C., I. Durand-Zaleski, D. Jolly and P. Durieux (2000), 'Effects of financial incentives on medical practice: results from a systematic review of the literature and methodological issues', *International Journal for Quality in Health Care*, 12, 133–42.
32. Soumerai, S., T. McLaughlin and J. Avorn (1989), 'Improving drug prescribing in primary care: a critical analysis of the experimental literature', *The Milbank Quarterly*, 67, 268–317.
33. Bartels-Petersen, J. (1994), 'Pharmaceutical consumption in a low consuming country: the case of Denmark', in E. Mossialos (ed.), *Cost Containment, Pricing and Financing of Pharmaceuticals in the European Community: the Policy-makers' View*, London: London School of Economics and Pharmetrica, pp. 173–81.
34. Trillo, J.L., J.L. García and D. Pablo (1999), 'Creación de pseudocompetencia en el sector farmacéutico hospitalario: aplicación de un procedimiento de adquisición centralizada de medicamentos en el ámbito de la Comunidad Valenciana', in G. López, J. Callau (eds), *Necesidad sanitaria, demanda y utilización: XIX Jornadas de Economía de la Salud*, Barcelona: Asociación de Economia de la Salud, pp. 411–26.
35. Segouin, C., M. Doussaud and D. Bertrand (1998), 'La réforme du système francais de soins et de son financement', *Epístula Alass*, 26, 14–17.
36. O'Donoghue, N. (1994), 'Pricing and reimbursement of medicines: the Irish experience', in E. Mossialos (ed.) (1994), *Cost Containment, Pricing and Financing of Pharmaceuticals in the European Community: the Policy-makers' View*, London: London School of Economics and Pharmetrica, pp. 281–301.
37. Bernal-Delgado, E., M. Galeote-Mayor, F. Pradas-Arnal and A. Ceresuela-López, (2000), 'Atención sanitaria basada en la evidencia: primeros argumentos empíricos en nuestro entorno', mimeo.
38. Tamborero, G., J.M. Pomar, A. Pareja and J. Fuster (1996), 'Descentralización de la gestión y motivación profesional', *Cuadernos de Gestión*, 2, 177.
39. Cunillera, R. (1998), 'La incentivación económica de los profesionales en atención primaria', *Cuadernos de Gestión*, 4, 157–65.

PART III

10. Economic considerations regarding pharmaceutical expenditure in Spain and its financing

G. López-Casasnovas

INTRODUCTION

This chapter seeks to provide some reflections on the behaviour of health expenditure and the evolution of public health financing, with particular attention to spending on pharmaceuticals. The first part attempts to lay the foundations for a series of considerations on the effects of policies aimed at restraining public health expenditure, in particular drug expenditure. In the second part we offer the reader some reflections on what could constitute an alternative framework which would help to rationalize decision-making processes on pharmaceutical financing and spending.

THE PROBLEMS INVOLVED IN FINANCING HEALTH CARE

For some years now, the sustainability of the social protection systems that have shaped what we call the welfare state has been a recurring theme in the European political and economic debate. In this debate, the future of the financing of public health care has been one of the most controversial issues, for at least two reasons: because health spending is one of the items that receives most attention from citizens, and because this spending has risen significantly (the proportion of Spain's income spent on public health care has risen nearly 25 per cent in the last decade). Furthermore, the factors that contribute to this growth do not appear to be abating, thus raising doubts as to the financial sustainability of the system.

Spain undoubtedly constitutes an atypical case in the context of the European Union (EU) as regards the growth of public health expenditure within health expenditure as a whole. A cursory look at the figures reveals that the percentage of public spending within overall health expenditure remains very stable (if anything, showing an upward trend) throughout the period considered. This means that the pressure of increases in health spending, in a period of relative growth in income (between 1980 and 2000 the income gap between the Spanish figure and the average for the EU shrank by 15 points, up to the present 85 per cent level), was directed just as much at public as at private financing, if not more. Income elasticity (the extent to which a good is considered a 'luxury') has proved no different for public and private provision. This observation is contrary to what we would expect (beyond a certain threshold, 'normal' social development substitutes public spending with private spending), although perfectly explicable from the perspective of politics and social choice (in the disjunctive between funding at the expense of the taxpayer and at the expense of the user, ultimately the former weighs more heavily!).

Neither does cross-national comparison of Spanish health spending yield straightforward conclusions. Although it is true that aggregate data on Spanish public health expenditure show a major difference (some 25 per cent) from the average for many advanced countries, it is important to understand that the comparison is misleading, as it fails to take into account either the different development levels of different countries or the inordinate weight of countries with a tradition of insurance (whether social as in Germany, the Netherlands and France or private, as in the USA) in the Organisation for Economic Co-operation and Development (OECD) sample. Thus, using this benchmark is tantamount to accepting that Spain should increase its expenditure to match that of these countries (a move that we doubt is shared by some of those who propose changes to the system), and that we do not consider the concept of income elasticity in the growth of this social expenditure (which contradicts their own arguments). Both extremes strike us as erroneous.

Therefore, if we take into account the income gap and/or limit the comparison to European countries with public health systems similar to those established by the Spanish General Law on Health, or alternatively, if we look into how much these countries spent – in the past, because they have a lead over Spain – when they had the same level of income as Spain has now, we find that Spain's expenditure is as it should be for its level of development and not less. The overall valuation is, therefore: (a) if Spain has the right level of health expenditure, why are mistaken arguments for increases in public health spending wielded for the (indiscriminate?) satisfaction of various pressure groups or lobbies (trade unions, the industry) without any point of reference as regards coordinated actions for health improvement? (b) as the relative income of the Spanish population increases, it seems likely that the growth in health expenditure will likewise do so, the evolution of its distribution (between public and private health spending, that is, at the expense of either the user or the taxpayer) being at any rate a crucial endogenous decision for health policy.

In effect, there is an additional error in the conventional argument in favour of new (and indiscriminate) increases in spending: not only is the destination not selected, but there is not even any self-interrogation as to how it would be financed. In practice this means ignoring the need to balance the budget (nothing is free in this world: so what taxes are to be increased? Indirect regressive taxes?), or even opting to return to public deficit (as if debt did not have perverse intergenerational redistribution effects: how can we be concerned about the environmental legacy we leave to our children but not the financial burden of debt?).

Common sense thus requires us to shun fundamentalist approaches and pay more attention to the details of public spending policies, that is, what Atkinson calls the 'subtle' structure of welfare programmes (type of spending, aims, institutional aspects, profit regulation, conditions of access, selection of beneficiaries, method of financing and so on). In short, it is not true that 'all's fair'.

To sum up, the question that should concern decision-makers now is not so much whether Spain's current level of expenditure can be put on a par with that attained by its neighbouring countries, but rather to what extent current growth rates of public health spending are compatible with the income scenarios fixed by the Spanish public sector in the process of European convergence and its frameworks of stability.

Prognosis

However, in order to voice an opinion on this issue, it is first necessary to gain an understanding of the behaviour of expenditure and the factors that do most to stimulate its growth.

As we have stated elsewhere (López-Casasnovas[1]), there is ample reason to believe that the rise in health spending in Spain can be traced to the diagnostic and therapeutic content of average health provision, for which the forecasts to date predict an increase in use as a consequence of the ageing of the population.

Although it is true to say that health care prices are to a large extent endogenous in the public sector (doctor's salaries, at least in the short term) and demographic change is predictable, the evolution of average real provision depends to a lesser degree on governmental decisions.

In fact, the evolution of the factor utilization depends on a series of variables (the system's ability to solve problems using lower-cost alternative treatment, frequency of service use and the evolution of the intensity of care and/or the degree of 'intensity' of technology per care episode), the control of which by the authorities is complicated at best. The technological frontier is being pushed back rapidly in the health sector (combinations of drugs in the treatment of AIDS as the main challenge), new drugs such as statins, antiasthmatics, antipsychotics and antidepressants are appearing (adding to rather than substituting existing ones), the population is ageing, life expectancy is increasing (although some unknown quantities remain in the association between ageing, average functional disability and morbidity) and we aspire to improvements in the quality of life (thus blurring the dividing line between health expenditure and social expenditure). Indeed everything is pointing in the direction of new rises in spending due to the diagnostic and therapeutic content of average real health provision.

If this is the case, the relevant question is not whether health expenditure will increase or not (in our opinion it will undoubtedly increase) but rather how its financing will evolve: will both curing and caring be provided through public funds? Note that this question is easier to answer if the variation in average real health provision occurs mainly in terms of effectiveness, in which case it is possible to discuss its cost-effectiveness ratio as regards public financing. It is much less so, however, when the evolution of the provision incorporates elements of utility or welfare. Although the line between 'curing' and 'caring' is not always easy to draw, it would seem logical for 'exchange value' components (for example, utility derived from freedom of choice) to have a financial treatment that is closer to the individual user than to the joint or collective user, considering the greater importance of subjective (and as such less definable) judgements in the former than in the latter.

Thus, in the absence of a general process of rationalization of decision-making in the health sector, social pressure on public health expenditure can put its financing in a very complex situation. The influence of an increasingly 'medicalized' society that expects the health care system to be able to solve practically all its health problems on the rise of new technologies (personalized treatments) and in the face of new diseases, forces authorities to practise a very cruel prioritization: the possibilities that health science opens up are global, but the resources available for applying it are local. Hence, any rationing is seen largely as a frustration of collective welfare, and political confrontation can yield major electoral rewards.

A minimum of realism in the definition of health policies would thus advise governments to start drawing up alternative scenarios in order to direct all the foreseeable pressure that will be generated by the growth in health expenditure along channels other than those that at present affect the public financing of this expenditure. In the coming context, perhaps the optimal approach would be to concentrate this financing selectively, on provision that passes cost-effectiveness criteria, thus 'decompressing' the general tax burden. This is the case not so much because of the level this burden has reached again in Spain (the ratio between compulsory government receipts and gross domestic product (GDP) lies in the low bracket in cross-national comparisons) as because of the difficulty of introducing new tax increases when rates are strait-jacketed by the fierce competition in international trade.

PHARMACEUTICAL EXPENDITURE WITHIN HEALTH EXPENDITURE AS A WHOLE

Let us now take a look at some aspects of the role played by medicines within average real health provision (that is, the growth of pharmaceutical spending within health spending). This implies a return to the view that drugs constitute an element of the overall combination of functional expenditure for health production and not an isolated input. Under this approach, and as mentioned above, the expectations of a medicalized society regarding the ability of modern medicine to cure and care, together with the appearance of new lifestyle drugs (drugs against depression or obesity, Viagra®, and so on), all contribute to raising the pharmaceutical bill (see Table 10.1).

The realities concealed by the figures are, however, far more complex than a straightforward reading would imply. Although it is true from a temporal perspective that Spain went from spending 14.9 per cent of its overall public health expenditure on pharmaceuticals in 1987 to figures in the region of 23 per cent – not including hospital pharmacy – in 2003 (as opposed to the European average of around 13 per cent), the figures for spending in terms of population are far less anomalous. Pharmaceutical expenditure per capita paints a very different picture, actually showing lower levels for Spain than for the average of Western countries. For the purpose of these comparisons, the inferences vary according to whether the yardstick is captitative (populational) or based on the GDP (income), and whether we consider pharmaceutical spending as a proportion of overall or public health expenditure. Therefore, simply contemplating the multifaceted nature of the problem enables us to

Table 10.1   Distribution by categories of the 50 top-selling drugs in the world, years: 1988–2002 (estimate) (number of products)

Category	1988	1993	1998	2002
Elderly	27	28	22	25
All ages	21	15	18	15
Lifestyle[a]	2	7	10	10

Note: a.   Defined as drugs that make one feel better rather than just well, for example, drugs for treating impotence, high lipids or menopause symptoms, and contraceptives.

Source: *The Economist*, Special Supplement on Drugs (2000).

reach diagnoses that come closer to reality, as we explain in the sections below.

Some More Facts and Figures

In Spain, pharmaceutical expenditure has recently been subject to all possible cost containment measures (negative lists, reference pricing (BP), price control, generic introduction, transfer of return above an agreed threshold, and price reduction by decree). Nevertheless, it should be stressed that drug prices in Spain appear to be below the EU average (see Table 10.2), in view of which the problem with pharmaceutical expenditure is above all a problem of overconsumption and dispensing costs. Given the existence of an active parallel trade, control over expenditure entails more factors than one-to-one negotiation with the laboratories directly involved: pharmacies, users and especially prescribers are key, despite which many of the measures used in pharmaceutical cost containment often do not seem to be fully directed at these protagonists.

We would draw attention to some additional information shown in the tables below. Spending on drugs shows for Spain: (a) a public pharmaceutical expenditure/GDP ratio 50 per cent higher than the average, (b) a per capita PPP expenditure much closer to (but still below) the average, and (c) the highest

Table 10.2   Weighted average price of pharmaceuticals in the main EU countries in 2001 (Spain 100)[a]

Country	Retail price + VAT %
Germany	203
Netherlands	176
UK	186
Belgium	169
Italy	116
Spain	100
France	93

Note: a.   A valuation that is properly adjusted to reality ought to consider the weightings of these prices in greater detail (given the diversity in amounts of consumption affected) and their different composition between prices of old and new products (given the effect this can have on their dynamics). Other studies provide a variety of data, quantifying with various weightings and at PPP values, but to date we have not encountered any statistic that offers a synthetic price index that is higher than the EU average. Obviously, if this were not the case, the well-known problem of parallel trade would not exist.

Source: *La industria farmacéutica en cifras*, Farmaindustria (2001).

Table 10.3   Spanish Social Security drug consumption through pharmacies (retail price plus VAT) (1988–2001)

Year	Consumption (current million pesetas)	Annual increase (rate)
1988	310 845	16.2
1989	360 363	15.9
1990	413 208	14.7
1991	481 189	16.5
1992	558 534	16.1
1993	600 027	7.4
1994	635 007	5.8
1995	720 949	13.5
1996	800 853	11.1
1997	842 264	5.2
1998	926 262	10.0
1999	1 016 003	9.7
2000	1 097 472	8.0
2001	1 211 582	11.1

Source: *La industria farmacéutica en cifras*, Farmaindustria (2001).

public drug expenditure expressed as a percentage of the total out of all the countries considered (Table 10.3). A good analysis of this can be found in Puig-Junoy.[2]

In this context, Table 10.4 shows a certain amount of convergence in the relative weight of public pharmaceutical expenditure within the GDP. Over the last two decades those countries that started at lower levels have come to have higher rates than those that started at higher levels (Germany, Belgium, France), with the result that the 2000 percentages are closer than those for 1980. Finland and Denmark are extreme cases, considering the constancy of their low ratios in time.

Table 10.5 shows the evolution of public pharmaceutical expenditure as a percentage of total public health spending. Note at this point that the very high Spanish figure rises over time, whereas Germany and Italy seem to stand still. Although they have managed to 'anchor' their total spending on drugs at a low percentage of their GDP, the Nordic countries unmistakably also register significant rises in the public pharmaceutical component within public health spending: Sweden doubled its proportion, and Denmark and Finland's rose by 50 per cent or more. Table 10.6 shows some indicators which might help to understand these facts.

Table 10.4 Public pharmaceutical expenditure as a percentage of GDP

Country	1980	1985	1990	1995	2000
Austria	0.5	0.5	0.5	0.6	0.8
Belgium	0.7	0.6	0.5	0.6	0.9
Denmark	0.3	0.3	0.2	0.4	0.4
Finland	0.3	0.3	0.4	0.5	0.5
France	0.8	0.9	0.9	1.0	1.2
Germany	0.9	0.9	0.9	0.9	1.1
Ireland	0.5	0.5	0.5	0.6	0.7
Italy	0.7	0.9	1.0	0.5	0.7
Netherlands	0.4	0.4	0.5	0.9	0.9
Portugal	0.8	1.0	1.0	1.3	1.3
Spain	0.8	0.7	0.9	1.1	1.3
Sweden	0.4	0.4	0.5	0.8	0.9
UK	0.5	0.5	0.6	0.7	0.7

Source: OECD health data (2002).

Table 10.5 Public pharmaceutical expenditure as a percentage of total public health expenditure

	1980	1985	1990	1995	2000
Austria	10.3	10.0	10.3	11.1	14.4
Belgium	11.9	9.8	8.2	8.9	14.9
Denmark	3.7	3.7	3.1	5.5	5.6
Finland	6.3	5.5	5.5	8.6	10.4
France	13.0	13.9	13.6	12.5	17.4
Germany	12.5	12.8	13.6	11.4	11.6
Ireland	7.1	7.9	10.4	10.8	13.0
Italy	12.1	15.7	15.6	10.2	12.2
Netherlands	7.0	7.5	8.8	12.7	17.2
Portugal	21.2	30.1	23.7	26.3	22.8
Spain	16.8	15.7	16.2	18.7	23.7
Sweden	5.0	5.4	6.4	10.6	11.7
UK	9.3	10.5	10.9	12.0	14.3

Source: OECD health data (2002).

Table 10.6   Some other (financing) pharmaceutical indicators, 2000

	Public/total pharmac. costs	Public pharmac. exp./public pharmac. costs	Patient co-pay/ public pharmac. costs
Austria	90.3	85.9	14.1
Belgium	69.8	82.9	17.1
Denmark	79.7	54.2	45.8
Finland	66.6	61.7	38.3
France	83.0	76.4	23.6
Germany	79.0	92.6	7.4
Greece	53.9	82.0	18.0
Ireland	78.1	91.3	8.7
Italy	50.3	90.7	9.3
Netherlands	100.0	93.9	6.1
Portugal	69.4	76.0	24.0
Spain	78.0	93.3	6.7
Sweden	92.6	63.6	22.4
UK	83.4	95.1	4.9

Source: OECD health data (2002).

An initial reading of the evolution of pharmaceutical consumption within the Spanish Social Security system enables us to conclude, albeit in isolation and tentatively, that in per capita terms drug consumption has grown more than the nominal GDP, but that it has maintained its position within public health expenditure as a whole. Therefore, in terms of evolution, rising consumption does not represent a differential feature within the general growth in health spending.

Finally, Tables 10.7–10.10 provide various additional data.

As Figueras and Saltman note in their report for the WHO,[3] however, cross-national comparisons prove to be extraordinarily misleading: (a) depending on our choice of benchmarks, and on whether we consider public or overall health spending, or per capita pharmaceutical expenditure, (b) in view of the fact that final pharmaceutical expenditure includes taxes and intermediaries' markups, when both of these factors vary greatly from country to country, and (c) given the variety of combinations of functional expenditure, type of care and regulation of access to health services. Figueras and Saltman show that if we calculate spending using ex-factory prices and applying the same markups to both prescription and non-prescription drugs, the UK (which according to the conventional indicators of the first group is always in the low spending

Table 10.7   Total drug consumption in the EU in euros per person per year, 2000

Country	€
Austria	234
Belgium	388
Denmark	287
Finland	318
France	470
Germany	373
Greece	245
Ireland	253
Italy	283
Netherlands	254
Portugal	290
Spain	265
Sweden	334
UK	238
EU total	325

Source: *La industria farmacéutica en cifras*, Farmaindustria (2002).

Table 10.8   Pharmaceutical consumption and expenditure in Spanish Social Security prescriptions per insured person per year (1995–2001) in pesetas/year

Pharmaceutical consumption	1995	1997	1999	2001
Pharmaceutical consumption[a]	21 552	25 036	30 035	33 724
Consumption of products	19 406	22 588	27 156	30 647
Pharmaceutical expenditure by the Social Security[a]	19 645	22 978	27 825	31 379
Beneficiary's contribution[a]	1 908	2 059	2 210	2 358
Number of prescriptions[a]	14.1	15.1	15.2	15.7

Note: a. Includes consumption of products, formulas, effects and accessories, through prescriptions dispensed through pharmacies.

Source: *La industria farmacéutica en cifras*, Farmaindustria (2002).

Table 10.9   *Average sum per prescription of pharmaceutical products in the Spanish Social Security market (retail price plus VAT) 1992–2001*

Year	Current pesetas	Variation (%)
1992	1133	14.7
1993	1227	10.2
1994	1330	8.4
1995	1419	6.7
1996	1500	5.7
1997	1547	3.1
1998	1703	10.1
1999	1837	7.9
2000	1901	3.0
2001	2014	6.0

Source: *La industria farmacéutica en cifras*, Farmaindustria (2002).

Table 10.10   *Pharmaceutical expenditure in Europe by categories in 1999 (in million US$)*

	France	Germany	Italy	Spain	UK
Cardiovascular	3706	3802	2140	1219	1740
Alimentary/metabolism	2144	2558	1363	843	1501
CNS	2009	1920	1054	862	1463
Anti-infective	1584	1381	1207	538	455
Respiratory	1327	1481	775	577	1230
Urinogenital	878	956	504	223	477
Musculoskeletal	688	697	506	252	448
Skin care	528	656	310	202	388
Cytostatic	233	712	495	245	234
Blood agents	307	361	343	142	72
Sensory organs	265	235	185	100	143
Mixture	90	218	33	8	37
Hormones	240	339	179	155	96
Diagnostic agents	179	315	99	3	95
Hospital solutions	14	45	29	3	10
Parapsychology	32	24	7	3	37
Total	14 224	15 700	9229	5375	8426

Source: IMS Health (2000).

bracket) appears to have the largest percentage of pharmaceutical expenditure as a fraction of overall spending. It even surpasses Germany, which as a gross percentage without accounting for margins had a figure no less than 25 per cent higher, and more than doubled the British one in terms of per capita in US dollars.

Having said this, we nevertheless have no answers to many other questions relating to the behaviour of pharmaceutical expenditure. What is the degree of efficiency of Spain's pharmaceutical consumption? Is it high or low? Will a solution be forthcoming with the introduction of a generic market (considering the poor prospects for introducing one), or the liberalization of markups, or the opening of pharmacies, or the vertical integration of the wholesalers? In short, is pharmaceutical spending excessive in Spain?

PUBLIC FINANCING AND PHARMACEUTICAL POLICY

Quite apart from the above reflections, it should be stressed that no single approach to the problem can provide an ultimate justification for a general policy of decreasing or increasing this item of expenditure. Pharmaceutical expenditure is really just another input in health production policies, and complementariness or substitutability with other inputs, and cross-effects in general make it necessary to take an overall approach to any rationalization process.

Seen from this angle, measures like the '*medicamentazo*' (the popular name given to Spain's first major negative list, passed by governmental decree in 1993), despite their immediate aim of cutting expenditure by discouraging the unnecessary use of medicines, often have a rebound effect on other items of expenditure. Thus, 'all's fair' is an unacceptable approach for a health care rationalization policy. The design and structure of co-payment offers a descriptor of the extent to which the objectives of more funding (without reducing consumption, higher unit prices) and less spending (cost containment by reducing consumption in the face of higher prices) are affected by health care regulation. As a result, only when the measure has a strong effect on the reduction of 'unnecessary' drug consumption are we dealing with a case of effective health care prioritization.

Specifically, Spain's experiences in the selective financing of pharmaceuticals up to 1997 (Order of 6 April 1993, developing Royal Decree 98/93 of 22 January 1993, which regulates the selection of medicines for purposes of financing by the National Health System, BOE No. 88, 13 April 1993, Madrid, *Boletín Oficial del Estado*) lead us to conclude that the effectiveness of these measures has been small as regards their cost containment objectives. The decrees on the selective financing of pharmaceuticals of 1993 and

1997 were aimed at the exclusion of drugs judged to have a low therapeutic value; although empirical studies value this aspect positively, the results in terms of reduction in spending are less conclusive. Indeed, the recent increase in the market for the prescription of drugs amounts to 9 per cent (2000), 11.3 per cent (2001), 9.9 per cent (2002), up to the 11.7 per cent increase for 2003.

From an overall perspective, everything seems to indicate that on the whole there has been no downward trend to date in pharmaceutical expenditure in Spain, but quite the opposite.

In general, the results confirm the short-term nature of the pharmaceutical cost containment strategy. The trend followed by spending in the long term effectively shows a return to the initial levels prior to the measures.

This has led some observers to support the introduction of direct measures aimed at containing consumption, such as raising the co-payment rate or the imposition of a general *ticket modérateur* on consumption.[4] In effect, Spain has one of the lowest beneficiary contributions to public pharmaceutical consumption in Europe: 6.7 per cent in 2001 (a third and a sixth of those for Sweden and Denmark, approximately). Intrinsic to this are the growing ranks of pensioners, whose numbers increased by 21.8 per cent over the period 1985–2002, the number of prescriptions per person per year rising steadily (15.7 in 2002). All this leads us to similar conclusions to those seen when analysing the previous issue. These are utilization factors for which the ceiling is an unknown quantity, with very difficult management measures (as they affect society's expectations of the system), the de-marketing of which is highly problematic. In addition to the liberalization measures already undertaken and efforts to restrict the profits of the pharmaceutical industry, there seem to be clear indications that it is also advisable to attempt to moderate users' consumption and achieve a better integration for pharmaceutical provision within professional practice. The dissociation between pensioners and the poor should perhaps accompany any new policies undertaken in the future.

Having stated the above, it is absolutely essential to make some comments on the current package of measures regulating the Spanish pharmaceutical market. As we mentioned earlier, the expected effectiveness of tackling the problem of pharmaceutical consumption in a single sphere of intervention (supply, demand or wholesalers) is small. Equally, the study of the impact of any measure of this sort must therefore incorporate an integral approach to the problem (see Table 10.11).

In addition to the economic objective of savings for public health care funds, the regulation of the Spanish pharmaceutical sector pursues other goals, both economic and social. Thus, from a social welfare viewpoint, it is important to bear in mind the repercussions of regulation on the health status of the

Table 10.11   Some cost-containment measures in the pharmaceutical sector

Devolution of the implementation of pharmaceutical legislation to several autonomous communities (Catalonia, Navarre, Canaries, Galicia, and Castile and León)

Relative deregulation of pharmacies (marginal extension of the number of authorized establishments and opening hours) and continual adjustments to markups (decrees of 1997 and 1999)

Promotion of generic policy and setting up of the Spanish Pharmaceutical Agency in June 1999, in an attempt to achieve more rational pharmaceutical policies

The potential effects of the decree passed on 19 June 1999, regulating the RP system, on the financing of pharmaceuticals by Social Security funds. Similarly for 2003 (implemented January 2004)

- The move towards selection in the latest decree on public financing of pharmaceuticals (1998) and as a result from a new RP system due to start in 2004
- Agreements with Farmaindustria for health care cost sharing in 1998, continuing those of 1995 and 1997 and raising them with annual contributions of 39 000 and 26 000 million pesetas for 1998 and 1999, 2001

population, the equity of the health system either generally or from a more sectoral perspective, and innovation and localization processes in the pharmaceutical industry as a whole.

We can divide the package of measures regulating the Spanish pharmaceutical market up to 1997 into those that directly affect the supply side and those (such as the *medicamentazo*) that fall on the demand for drug consumption.

Measures Affecting the Supply Side

One of the most important factors on the supply side has been the agreements between the Department of Health (DH) and the pharmaceutical industry (Farmaindustria), first for the period 1995–1997, which imposed a ceiling on the pharmaceutical industry rate of return, at 7 per cent in 1996 and 4 per cent in 1997. These agreements established the refunding of the gross margins corresponding to increases in expenditure above the fixed percentage, together with a series of recommendations for pharmacies to offer discounts (up to 2 per cent of the retail price) to the users of the drugs. The contributions of the pharmaceutical industry to the Spanish Social Security as a result of this agreement amounted to ptas 14 173 million, 17 909 million and 18 043 million (Ministry of Health and Consumer Affairs estimate) for 1995, 1996 and 1997 respectively. This sort of agreement was extended until 2003, when the new reference pricing system was approved with the opposition of Farmaindustria.

On a different front, a debate has been initiated on the suitability of single linear markups, alternative proposals being made for differentiated markups according to the services offered, by likewise differentiated sectors or groups.

Indeed, the recent history of the financial regulation of pharmacies provides us with practically the whole range of possibilities: a fixed 25 per cent markup in 1945, subsequently increased to 30 per cent (but with a 6.6 per cent reduction for 'Compulsory Insurance' drugs), then progressive markups inversely proportional to the retail price, which were introduced in 1963 and 1964 for those that exceeded a certain amount and then modified in 1977, then the single markup again in 1981, although with modifications to the rate for various reasons in 1985, 1988, 1993 and 1997, and finally a return to special markups (Royal Decree Law 5/2000 on the rationalization of drug use). This established a maximum markup of 27.9 per cent for drugs with a retail price of up to ptas 20 000, a fixed sum of ptas 5580 for drugs costing more than this amount, and a markup of 33 per cent for generics. It also authorizes a discount on over-the-counter drugs of up to 10 per cent. On a different note, the decree also regulates the deductions (refunds to the public health system) to be applied as a function of the monthly turnover of drugs dispensed in pharmacies.

The alternatives to this system of remuneration are well known, although their effects on the present status quo appear to be an obstacle to their being applied. For example, one possibility would be to determine a fixed component (for active service or stand-by) or a semi-fixed one (according to the number of pharmacists in service), and a variable component per prescription/package dispensed, a percentage of the price and a fee for special services. There is no need here to enter into the details of the incentive compatibility problems raised by one type of contractual rule or another, whether it is viewed in the context of the agency relationship between health authorities and pharmacist or the more liberal or private one between user and pharmacist (see Cabiedes and Ortún[5]). The actual effects of the markups resulting from the various combinations can be calibrated in relation to their present values, depending on: (a) the size of the municipality, (b) sales (and how they are distributed between prescription and over-the-counter drugs), (c) the evolution predetermined by the fixed component of the formulations (nominal GDP or consumer price index (CPI) basically), and of course (d) the weight of the amount per prescription versus the markup on the retail price. Simulations and subsequent calibrations have been carried out in Catalonia with real data for the provinces of Girona and Tarragona. An excellent analysis of these changes can be found in Andreu.[6]

Some of the above changes have been proposed as a reaction to the incipient introduction of a generic market in Spain.[7] However, taking into consideration that this market barely accounts for 3 per cent of total prescription costs, together with the scant development of European regulation as regards patents in the pharmaceutical sector (and the little impact of the progress made in this direction in Spain) we can forecast that the effect on pharmaceutical expenditure will be small. This may take the form of a mere 'exchange of copies', which represent 30 per cent of the country's prescriptions. The OECD recommendations for the future that are being introduced into several works hinge on the need to carry out a thorough evaluation of variations in prescription patterns within and between countries, and to advance towards selective deregulation of the retail market.

Measures Affecting the Demand Side

As regards distribution, there is a clear need for a broader structural reform than the political situation sometimes allows, although the law passed by the autonomous community of Navarre (Statutory Law 12/2000 on Pharmaceutical Care) seems to have opened up something of a breach in this respect. In our opinion the necessary reform, which affects both organizational and financial aspects, requires a coherent strategy centred on a new regulatory arrangement for pharmacies.

This could be based around the following points:

1. A minimum coverage health plan could be established that would guarantee one pharmacy for a certain number of inhabitants and/or a certain distance to travel to one. For example, one pharmacy for a town with 800 inhabitants and/or at a distance of no more than 250 metres (the Statutory Law in Navarre mentioned above attaches each pharmacy to a Basic Health Zone, moreover adding that unless this coverage is guaranteed no new pharmacies will be authorized to open anywhere in Navarre, as in this respect the public interest predominates over business initiative). If to this end it is necessary to invite inverse tenders (public non-private financial compensation for sharing capital gains derived from the barriers to competition thus generated) the previous thresholds should be guaranteed.

2. Once this minimum pharmaceutical care is covered, pharmacists would be free to set up any other initiative. The erosion of earning power that this might spell for existing pharmacies could be offset by means of minimum market protection periods and by prohibiting chains of pharmacies without a single owner per pharmacy.

3. Initially the system of public grants for pharmacists would only affect pharmacies that correspond to planned authorization. The initial realistic approach would require the maintenance of the grants with existing pharmacies, although the system of allocating the best clause tendered (possibly guaranteeing the established minimums) could be imposed. This would be particularly plausible after an initial period (for example, three years) before the pharmacies broaden their range of pharmaceutical care services to raise the initial requirements of the health authorities for public pharmaceutical care. In this way, the awards could be made by invitation to tender (even with different levels: basic, and complementary with pilot programmes) to a given number of pharmacies, at least equivalent to the number planned according to population size and not necessarily coinciding with the number that had previously enjoyed public grants.

It would be desirable for the above process to result in the future pharmaceutical grants taking in the entirety of pharmaceutical services. Possible lines of implementation would be: (a) the definition of the range of services offered by each pharmacy, (b) the purchase of these services from each pharmacy by the corresponding health services, (c) selective grants depending on the services offered, and (d) changes in the dispenser's remuneration system to bring it more in line with priority pharmaceutical care activities.

This strategy might help to generate a level of professional competition between pharmacies that would encourage them to perform pharmaceutical care activities with the ultimate goal of improving the quality of the care received by citizens. This would include aspects such as the management of the product (as regards guaranteeing the accessibility of the drug: availability, product quality and dispensing), clinical management (appropriate use of the drug by the patient, including evaluation of the outcome of pharmaceutical intervention, treatment monitoring, observance, information, detection of therapeutic problems and so on) and a series of preventive activities (for example, health promotion in primary pharmacy, and screening in specialized pharmacy).

Summary

To sum up, the diagnosis derived from the foregoing aggregate analysis shows that:

1.　The problem of Spain's pharmaceutical expenditure appears to lie in its growth rate over the last two decades. But this cannot be judged without considering the point of departure: its share in terms of GDP was already high in 1980 and has remained high to the present. International price convergence is behind its dynamics but this does not fully explain the values. In most countries the diagnosis is the opposite: it is primarily a problem of growth rate from an already high spending level.

2.　The problem of Spain's pharmaceutical expenditure does not lie in its absolute level but in the large proportion financed publicly (74.4 per cent of the total, whereas the European average is 58.3 per cent). The absence of significant co-payments for the population as a whole and little screening in the type of drugs financed may explain this.

3.　In spending per capita, Spain also stands above average, although less strikingly so. But contrary to what we find in many neighbouring countries, in Spain the problem has more to do with excess consumption than with relative prices. Thus, for example, more than half the growth in spending between 1995 and 2002 can be explained by the number of prescriptions per capita. The effect of prices is especially strong on the component (which stands at around 15 per cent of the total) of consumption of new products (those that have been on the market for less than five years), as they more than double the prices of old products (those marketed for 10 to 15 years). Indeed, over the period 1980–1996 the price of new products had an average impact on the upward trend in health expenditure of 442 per cent.[8]

CONCLUSIONS

It is extremely difficult to forecast what the Spanish health system of even the near future will be like, particularly if it continues to be 'anchored' in the dynamics offered today by national health services: 'services' as if they were just another administrative service, 'national' implying a strong tendency towards uniformity and 'health' denoting an intention that is not always translated into the best integration (for instance, between ultimate objectives and the provision of services, or between health sector policies and all the other economic and social sector policies).

It seems likely that in the future we will need to tackle health problems from an angle that has more in common with the idea of a social insurance system. 'System' for a better interlocking of ultimate objectives and health care services between public and private actors, and between different public actors, all politically legitimated throughout the territory, and for their better coordination, crucial for the success of any health policy. 'Insurance' because of the inescapable nature of the idea of specifying levels of health care coverage and selective limitation of provision. 'Social' because of the foreseeable continuity of the implicit objective of solidarity in its system of financing, protection through the coverage of all or part of the population, and a closer integration of the social health needs of the population.

As we mentioned above, the health sector may easily remain stuck in the present status quo, and as such incapable of responding to the new needs of society. This can be attributed, among other reasons, to the very roots of universalism (benefits that tend to be presented as 'necessary' for all), the short-term approach of health policies (which works against major changes), the customary corporatism of today's prevalent interests and the frequent use of health care as a political weapon in elections.

Thus, reorientation towards a new social insurance system may take a very long time to impregnate the health care of the future. This would come to replace the British model of the NHS (imported for the Spanish General Law on Health, more than 50 years too late), a service that was, after all, created under very different circumstances from the present (in a postwar period of extreme poverty with 'compassionate' Conservative governments and a strong predominance of social over individual responsibility). It is difficult to see this instrument, which was so successful in the past in improving the welfare of the population, as being extrapolable today in the face of a future marked by hitherto barely imaginable possibilities such as the appearance of genetic testing and personalized treatments, the irruption of new and costly 'lifestyle' drugs, technological capabilities in which 'caring' is of greater value than 'curing', and strong expectations to introduce elements of individual welfare – not only clinical effectiveness – into health care provision. And of course, in consonance with all this, greater acceptance within society of shifts of responsibility from collective state action to the individual sphere.

Between the 'old' that puts off its death and the 'new' that puts off its birth, doubts are rife, but discussion on the subject is invaluable.

In this context, and in the specific case of pharmaceutical provision, the prognosis provided by the series of considerations raised in this chapter leads us to emphasize the following points.

First, if, as we have seen, the problem is one of overconsumption first and cost level (including dispensing costs) second. Therefore, it should be the former and not the latter that dominates policy agendas.

Despite this fact, beyond the pressure exerted on the laboratories, almost none of the measures that have been implemented in Spain (negative lists, RP, control of authorized prices, generic introduction, transfer of return above an agreed threshold and price or markup reduction by decree) have any direct influence on the day-to-day development of expenditure and its key protagonists: users, pharmacies and above all prescribers.

As we understand it, only combined action involving the participation of decisive parties, and a return to the view that drugs constitute an element of the overall combination of functional expenditure for health production (and not an isolated input), can lead to the creation of a stable framework for the sector, thus pointing it in the right direction to face the future challenges of the Spanish health system.

Second, there is every reason to believe that the externalities that pharmaceutical development has in technological innovation, the industrial policy of a country and patients' welfare require a more stable framework than is the case at present. In this regard, we would stress that general public regulation should be sufficiently broad and long term to be able to guide the sector through short-term upheaval in the financing of expenditure. Most of the utilities in any country (electricity, gas, telecommunications) enjoy a stable 'legal' framework that enables the parties to know where they stand, according to a semicontractual arrangement with obligations and duties for both parties. The constraint of discretionality is particularly necessary for those economic sectors that require long-term investments entailing major fixed costs (research and development (R&D) that are often irrecoverable. Although this demands a more thorough public regulation study than is possible here, it strikes us that pre-fixing a particular line to follow according to variables such as the evolution of the GDP, plus an additional index for diagnostic and therapeutic value (similar to that developed by Berndt et al.[9]) provides a better formula than sporadic adjustments made to variables that fail to discriminate sufficiently between either industries or products or turnover (volumes versus margins).

This may encompass the substitution of drugs with greater therapeutic value (economy clause), levels of advancement in selective financing (favourable evolution of private financing in the joint financing of the expenditure), positive adjustment for convergence of prices in the single world market (against parallel trade) and other factors concerning industrial economic policy (weight of R&D spending over the total for the sector in relation to volume of business).

We consider that working towards a stable framework for the sector in Spain is one of the main challenges for the evolution of public financing of health expenditure. The necessary consensus to achieve this could be built on the discussion already formalized in parliament around a broad agreement for the pharmaceutical sector, although we are very much afraid that in the end electoral issues will outweigh what is advisable and rational.

ACKNOWLEDGEMENTS

The author would like to acknowledge the financial support for this research line provided by the Spanish Ministry of Science and Technology (SEC2004).

REFERENCES

1. López-Casasnovas, G. (1999), 'Health care and cost containment in Spain', in E. Mossialos, J. Le Grand (eds), *Health Care and Cost Containment in the European Union*, London: Ashgate, pp. 401–42.
2. Puig-Junoy, J. (1999), 'Reptes en la gestió de la prestació farmacèutica', *Fulls Econòmics del Sistema Sanitari*, **33**.
3. World Health Organization (1997), *Las reformas sanitarias en Europa: análisis de las estrategias actuales*, R.B. Saltman and J. Figueras (eds), Madrid: Ministerio de Sanidad y Consumo.
4. Ibern, P. (1996), 'Gasto farmacéutico, responsabilidad individual y social', *Cinco Días*, 2 December.
5. Cabiedes Miragaya, L. and V. Ortún Rubio, 'Prescriber incentives', (Chapter 9 of this volume.
6. Andreu, J. (2001), *'Revisió i anàlisi de sistemes alternatius de retribució de l'oficina de farmacia'*, mimeo, dissertation for master's degree in health economics, IDEC, Barcelona..
7. Lobo, F. (1997), 'La creación de un mercado de medicamentos genéricos en España', in G. López and D. Rodríguez (eds), *La regulación de los servicios sanitarios en España*, Madrid: Civitas.
8. Mossialos, E. and J. López (1997), 'Spanish drug policy at the crossroads', *The Lancet*, 350, 679–80.
9. Berndt, E.R. et al. (1998), 'Price indexes for medical care goods and services: an overview of measurement issues', *National Bureau of Economic Research working paper no 6817*, Cambridge, MA.

11. Review of economic studies of the pharmaceutical industry published over the last 20 years by Spanish economists

F. Lobo, M. Cabañas Sáenz and R. González Pérez

SCOPE AND WORK PLAN[*]

This review encompasses works published between 1 January 1980 and 31 December 1999. To avoid it extending interminably, we give priority to economic studies by economists, although we apply this restriction flexibly, especially in the bibliographical appendix.[**]

In principle, the works we deal with must have been published in a scientific journal of some sort. This condition is treated fairly broadly. We include Spanish journals that did not use (and in some cases still do not use) anonymous referees, as long as their level of quality is admitted in the profession. Naturally, we also consider articles published in foreign scientific journals with anonymous referees. We also mention books and book chapters in this field.

We pay close attention to doctoral theses, owing to their importance for

---

[*] The Health Economics Association (AES) asked F. Lobo to prepare this review, one of several that marked the occasion of its 20th annual conference, held in Palma de Mallorca. With help from Laura Pellisé, he presented a preliminary version of this review at the conference. The chairman of the Scientific Committee gave him six criteria: identification of the works, accessibility, theoretical development, statistical data and techniques, recommendations for measures and action, valuation of the importance of the study and repercussion on health policy. These reviews were published in F. Antoñanzas, J. Fuster and E. Castaño (eds) (2000), *Libro de ponencias de las XX Jornadas de Economía de la Salud. Avances en la gestión sanitaria: implicaciones para la política, las organizaciones sanitarias y la práctica clínica*, May 3–5; Palma de Mallorca, España. Barcelona: Asociación de Economía de la Salud, p. 197–205.

[**] After much thought on the matter, the authors have decided to transfer the comments on Leopoldo Arranz's great work to a separate study. However, there can be no doubt as to the value of its contributions for economics.

research. Researchers, especially young researchers, spend a large amount of time, effort and motivation on their theses, and go to great lengths to ensure that the data, analyses and models they use are very rich, as it constitutes a fundamental stage in their academic career. The result is also a reflection of the contribution of the thesis supervisor, other researchers and the members of the panel. Given the recognized importance of doctoral theses, generally they are all willing to lend support and critical opinion. The intrinsic interest of the economics of pharmaceuticals and the pharmaceutical industry has attracted the attention of a considerable number of doctoral theses in Spain in recent years.

This review does not cover pharmaceutical economic evaluation studies, as the *Associación de Economía de la Salud* (AES) commissioned a separate review on this subject.

Although we cannot make extensive reference to all the works published, in the Appendix we offer a bibliographical list that we would hope is exhaustive.

The review is organized as follows. In the section below we set out the main conclusions we have reached on the evolution of economic research in this area. We then go on to single out some pending issues, and finally we survey those works that fulfil the criteria set, divided into subject areas.

MAIN CONCLUSIONS ON THE EVOLUTION OF ECONOMIC RESEARCH IN SPAIN IN THIS FIELD

Having read and reflected on the works cited, we reached the following conclusions:

- The number of works published per period is tending to rise, although for a total span of 20 years the overall number of works is not very large.
- In recent years the rate of publication has accelerated.
- The quality of the works is on the rise, in consonance with economic research in Spain generally. There is an increasing proportion of works published in journals with anonymous referees and of a high category, especially international ones.
- We could say that in Spain today there is an 'invisible college' uniting Spanish researchers interested in the economics of pharmaceuticals and the pharmaceutical industry. This can be seen by analysing the cross-references. It is also symptomatic that practically every year a special session dedicated to this topic is held at the Conference on Health Economics.

- This fact is compatible with plurality of methodological and disciplinary perspectives. As is to be expected, there is a particularly strong interrelationship between industrial economics and health economics.
- Whereas at the beginning of the period, in common with economic research as a whole, 'sectoral' studies often originated in the sphere of the government and were published in their official organs. In the present day the mainstream is formed by research done and journals published by Spanish universities.
- In this area as in others, the doctoral theses presented are, for their quantity and quality alike, the main vector for the creation and transmission of knowledge.
- There have been recognized specialists in the subject for some years now. Recently we have witnessed the rise of organized specialist research units linked to universities. Examples are the Research Centre for Economics and Health (CRES) at Pompeu Fabra University and the Health and Pharmaceuticals Social Studies Seminar at Carlos III University in Madrid.
- As in other areas of economic research, the flow of knowledge is becoming internationalized. Contacts, meetings and seminars attended by Spanish economists together with foreign (especially British and American) economists are innumerable, and held both in Spain and abroad. The Health Economics Association, European Union (EU) projects and doctoral degrees taken by Spanish researchers in foreign universities have all played an important part in these exchanges. This trend can be seen in the publication of a growing number of studies carried out by Spanish researchers in international scientific journals.

PENDING TASKS

This is not the place to propose topics for future research. The richness of economic reality and its extremely strong dynamics of change in this area, together with the progress made in economic research, provide an almost infinite field of possibilities. Therefore, in this section we merely make a few proposals in an attempt to ensure that these research opportunities are not wasted.

First, a solution should be found to the problem of the accessibility of data on the consumption and sale of medicines at the various levels of aggregation; both the public data published by the Ministry of Health and Consumer Affairs and the private data by Intercontinental Medical Systems (IMS). We think it would be possible to reach an agreement that would safeguard the privacy of the individual, statistical secrecy and the commercial interests of the drug companies, and at the same time enable interested researchers to gain access to these data. An agreement could be promoted involving the Health Economics Association, interested universities, Farmaindustria, the Ministry of Health and Consumer Affairs and also the firm IMS. It could include a stable set of rules of conduct that make researchers' efforts to find data less of an adventure with an uncertain ending.

Second, it would be desirable to make improvements to the Ministry of Health and Consumer Affairs gazette *Indicadores de la Prestación Farmacéutica* and give it a less restricted distribution. It would also be advisable to improve the questionnaires in health surveys (national, regional and so on) to include the right questions for research in our field. Very positive results will be forthcoming if the relationship between industrial economics and health economics in this subject area is maintained and stepped up. It is important to ward off the danger of economic research on pharmaceuticals becoming isolated. Note what Lobato says on the demand for pharmaceuticals later on in this chapter. As far as 'neglected' subject areas are concerned, we would mention the new regulation introduced to account for product patents.

Finally, we believe that the application of advanced techniques, particularly statistical and microeconometric techniques should become more widespread.

TWENTY YEARS OF CONTRIBUTIONS BY SUBJECT AREAS

Most of the works we mention below share a common interest in the economic causes and effects of the regulation of the pharmaceutical industry and drugs. That is, they are concerned about analysing the role of the state when it intervenes in the market.

Overviews

A brief synthesis of the characteristics of the pharmaceutical industry both worldwide and in Spain in particular was published by Cruz-Roche and Durán[1] in 1987 on the occasion of a meeting held in Madrid by the United Nations Industrial Development Organization. Benefit is still to be derived from reading it today, and moreover it stands as evidence of the development of thought on industrial policy.

Lobo's book[2] is the result of both academic studies and research and also experience in public bodies entrusted with the regulation of the pharmaceutical sector. It includes texts that had already appeared in various publications, some of them updated. After an interesting introduction by Velarde, the book is divided into three parts. The first consists of Chapters 1 and 2 and is dedicated to pharmaceutical policy, both internationally and in Spain. The second part consists of Chapter 3 and deals with public spending on pharmaceutical care in Spain. The book concludes with an extensive chapter dedicated to analysing the pharmaceutical sector from the viewpoint of industrial economics.

The first part deals with topics such as the evolution of the pharmaceutical industry and drug policy, the concept of the National Drug Policy as created by the World Health Organization (WHO), the drug policy of the European Communities, relations between the pharmaceutical industry and the public sector in Spain, the Spanish Law on Pharmaceuticals, an analysis of the number of drugs available in Spain, and a study on pharmacological education and information for health care services. The chapter on public spending in Spain includes a study of data on consumption, an analysis of the policy of public expenditure on pharmaceutical care between the General Law on Social Security of 1967 and the General Law on Health of 1986, and some reflections on the perspectives opened up by the latter. In the chapter on the industrial economics of the pharmaceutical industry the author analyses the growth of the sector in the 1960s and 1970s, the market structure, transfer prices and price intervention, and also includes a study on drug patents in developed countries.

Lobato, Lobo and Rovira[3] is an extensive work published in five volumes with the support of a grant from Farmaindustria. The authors start by studying the basic conditions of the market and its evolution (technology, population, morbidity, health care system, prescribers as demanders). The second part is devoted to the dynamics of the market structure (the new product patent, European regulation of the evaluation, authorization and registration of medicines, restructuring as a result of the single market, parallel trade, and generics). Family firms, an economico-financial analysis of the sector and research and development (R&D) strategies are the object of the third part. This is followed by an account of industrial policy and public drug expenditure regulation policy, changes in the nature of competition and distribution problems. Finally, the work closes with two lengthy chapters on future scenarios and recommendations.

The book by Lobo and Velásquez[4] contains the articles presented at sessions of the Health and Pharmaceuticals Social Studies Seminar of the Flores de Lemus Institute at Carlos III University in Madrid and the World Health Organization Action Programme on Essential Drugs in March 1995. Lobato and Rovira made an interesting summary of the articles and provided the conclusions of the meeting ('Medicines in the face of new economic realities: synthesis and forecasts'). Although they do not deal with pharmaceuticals, Segura's article ('The welfare state, economic policy and health services') is of interest, and although it is not strictly an economic text, the article by Alberto Infante ('Health care reform in Latin America: the role of the state and essential medicines') is worthy of note. From the viewpoint of pharmaceutical economics the rest of the articles are of great interest: Scherer ('The new structure of the pharmaceutical industry'), Le Pen ('Innovation and regulation of the pharmaceutical market'), Correa ('The Uruguay Round agreements and medicines'), O'Brien ('The standardization of the international drug market: its future impact on emerging countries') Dukes ('Growth and change in generic drug markets'), Ignacio Arango ('Regulation, policies and essential medicines', on developing countries) and Elias Mossialos ('The impact of cost containment and health care reforms on medicines', on developed countries).

Rovira's article[5] is a summary of public action affecting the Spanish drug market (patents, registration, public financing, price intervention), with emphasis on the more recent measures adopted (product patenting, selective financing, the 1990 price regulation), together with the possible conflicts arising from these policies and the consequences of the unification of the European market (for example, parallel imports). When analysing these consequences, the author clarifies which national policies are affected and which are not.

The article by Nonell and Borrell[6] contains considerations on regulation theory, 'social' regulation and the public financing of pharmaceuticals in Spain, the bodies in charge of regulation and relations between the government and Farmaindustria, price intervention and the new legislation responsible for introducing product patenting. We mention more contributions of theirs below.

López Bastida's contribution[7] also offers a panorama of the Spanish pharmaceutical market, with special emphasis on the more recent measures within economic policy on pharmaceuticals.

Regulation Theory as a Framework for Analysis

The doctoral thesis of Natalia Martín Cruz[8] is directly influenced by Williamson, and is based on an advanced interpretation of regulation theory. It contains an empirical application to the US and Spanish markets, and gives economic policy recommendations. One of its initial hypotheses is that companies do not take the milieu and regulatory constraints as data or as given elements, but that rather the regulation itself is the object of their business strategies. After an extensive survey of the literature, the author adopts the view of regulation as an incomplete contract that evolves according to the needs of social groups. By calculating the transaction costs associated with exchange, it is possible to compare alternative forms of government and regulation. The unit of analysis is the transaction (each purchase of a medicine) and not the company. Relevant factors here are the uncertainty that affects transactions, their specificity and their frequency.

The form and the process of regulation offer a whole range of possibilities, from hierarchy to the market, via various hybrid situations. The efficient regulator will be that which succeeds in developing an intervention that provides a better response to the characteristics of the transaction. For their part, lobbies are characterized by their nationality, size, reputation and experience. The empirical application considers a sample of active ingredients in three therapeutic groups for which the author identifies the regulatory forms adopted in each of the two countries.

The doctoral thesis of Chaqués Bonafont[9] belongs more to political science than to economics. It is based on a large number of interviews with experts in the sector, and on an exhaustive bibliography. According to the proposed network analysis model, regulation is not merely a reflection of the public interest, pressure from lobbies or the autonomy of the state. It also reflects complex interactions between public and private actors in particular areas, acting by means of decentralized and informal procedures (and not only through institutions such as parliament, government or the government), and is influenced by the structure of the state, the number of actors, the volume and distribution of resources and the nature of the relationship between the actors. One of the conclusions of the work is that neither the industry nor the state are either monolithic or homogeneous.

Evolution of the Pharmaceutical Industry in Spain

Still on the subject of Chaqués's thesis,[9] we could add that it tells the history of the pharmaceutical industry in Spain over the last 40 years. It features chapters on pharmaceutical policy during the Franco regime, the transition to democracy, the Socialist reform of the 1980s and the Popular Party governments. It also considers the effects of globalization and the decentralization process in Spain.

The EU: the Pharmaceutical Industry and Pharmaceuticals

The article by Rovira[10] stands out for the clarity of its ideas. It sets out an up-to-date description of the pharmaceutical industry and the Spanish market before and after the single market, and its chief merit is its suggestions for a common strategy for the EU. The diagnosis focuses on three points: the need for different policies for innovative and non-innovative products, the importance of expected benefits as an incentive for innovation and the existence of conflicts of objectives at national level and between national and EU interests, the solution of which requires compromises of different sorts.

First, the author recommends opting for innovation, which may entail strong patents, high prices and public financing, but with social intervention in the form of fixed research priorities. Second, he proposes expenditure control policies that do not erode the incentive to innovate, encourage competition in the non-innovative sector and provide information transparency and demand-side incentives in both markets. Third, he recommends a single Euro-price, but observes that it cannot be fixed on the basis of economic evaluation studies that merely provide an upper limit, which is not necessarily efficient. Finally, the author suggests that the different purchasing power in different Member States should be reflected through discounts whereby each country's contribution to the central expenditure on R&D would be adjusted accordingly.

The doctoral thesis by Darbà[11] is a complex work dealing with the problems of parallel trade and dynamic pricing. The legal complexity of parallel trade is such that we economists are forced to seek the help of legal experts when analysing the problems it raises. One early and very interesting reference is the article by Bercovitz.[12] After surveying the literature and analysing the market structure, prescription, price intervention, public financing and the EU evaluation, authorization and registration procedures, the author constructs a model of the optimal strategies for a pharmaceutical company to follow when faced with parallel imports in various situations, and of the price differential above which parallel trade is triggered. He also studies price intervention in the UK and a theoretical and econometric model of dynamic pricing with data for 148 new chemical entities marketed there between 1987 and 1998.

The article by Darbà and Rovira[13] is an overview of the problem of parallel trade in the EU, extracted from the former's doctoral thesis, and with an additional section on possible future scenarios.

The journal *PharmacoEconomics* published an interesting controversy between Rovira[14] on the one hand and Danzon and Towse[15] on the other. Rovira defends a system of prices and discounts that takes into account the differences in income to be found between European countries and a European-scale negotiation delimited by (at the bottom) production costs and (at the top) the price determined by economic evaluation. Danzon and Towse, given the difficulty of establishing costs when the production of innovations is joint, defend a country-by-country negotiation that takes into account willingness to pay. They also differ in their methods: Rovira prefers transparent negotiation with public results, whereas Danzon and Towse defend confidentiality.

Market Structure

One of the authors of this chapter dedicated an article to the function of advertising as an instrument of, among other aspects, product differentiation (Lobo[16]).

In his thesis,[17] Borrell makes a cross-country comparison between Spain and the UK, and succeeds in constructing and using comparable databases for

Spanish and British drug consumption. It also includes a number of recommendations for public action. Primarily it warns of the complexity of decision-making in issues such as selective financing and price-cap regulation. One of its contributions is the analysis of dominant positions (concentration of sales by products according the Herfindhal–Hirschman index). It confirms the idea that positions of dominance exist in segmented submarkets. These positions are stronger in the UK, probably owing to the absence of fully operative product patents in Spain when the data were acquired.

The basic aim of the thesis is to estimate the break-even prices in Spain and the UK for the purpose of calculating the margins. To this end, the author devises a model of supply and demand in a market of differentiated products. Consumer behaviour is characterized in the framework of Berry's discrete choice model. Equations are estimated for demand and price and the margins obtained by each company from each product are calculated. The author concludes that in Spain competition is broader (that is, affects more drugs); the margins are larger in the UK and the price elasticities of demand are higher than is usually assumed, and higher in the UK than in Spain. Price regulation causes margins to drop, but more so in Spain than in the UK; old drugs have lower margins than new ones; the characteristics of margins and competition differ according to the therapeutic group and the break-even margins are higher for generics than for brand-name drugs.

Among other considerations on the structure of the pharmaceutical sector in Spain, Cabiedes[18] studies the degree of business concentration in the sector, along with the recent mergers and takeovers.

Demand

Lobato's work[19] makes at least four contributions. First, it seeks to quantify the demand for pharmaceuticals and argues that those variables that are employed in an attempt to approximate physical consumption, such as the number of prescriptions or packages, are not useful because they sum heterogeneous units. Monetary valuation presents the problem (considered below) of what price indexes are to be applied as deflators when studying the evolution of demand and expenditure over time.

Another important contribution of this work is that it reminds us that medicines are means of production that are combined with others in a production function, and that therefore the demand for them is derived from the demand for health care, which is determined by the increase in income. Thus, it is not the demand for pharmaceuticals that should be regulated but the demand for health services as a whole. Moreover, the derived demand for pharmaceuticals depends not only on the demand for health care services but also 'on the production functions of these services and the decisions made by doctors regarding how they should be rendered, depending on the available pharmacological technology, their objectives, and also the availability of other factors or means' (p. 94). Lobato provides two interesting examples of decisions that do not involve the minimum cost (for the cases of fixed remuneration and fee-for-service).

Co-payment

One of the classical topics of pharmaceutical economics, the price elasticity of demand when there is co-payment or shared financing between the insurer and the user, is addressed by Cruz-Roche[20] with some calculations on this elasticity. The same topic is developed by Puig-Junoy,[21] applied to the Spanish case. This study includes a review of the international literature with empirical content, a detailed description of co-payment in Spain, its regulation since 1978, the main data and estimates of the effect of the switching of prescriptions from the employed to pensioners, and the price elasticity of demand (which is found to be small).

The empirical results provided by Borrell[17] indicate that the price elasticity of aggregate demand for each therapeutic chapter appears to be much higher than time-series and cross-national studies have shown. Thus, price restriction may be a powerful explanatory factor for the large amount of pharmaceuticals consumed per person in Spain.

Nonell and Borrell[6] consider co-payment to be 'a useful instrument for containing the real public expenditure on medicines per insured person' (p. 125), as the demand for pharmaceuticals would be slightly sensitive to the price paid by the patient (they obtain an elasticity of 0.08). We do not share the opinion that the reduction in aggregate terms of the participation of the co-payment in the expenditure promotes the growth of pharmaceutical provision. Co-payment continues to influence those who are forced to make it. The fact that those who are not forced to make a co-payment (pensioners and others) account for an increasingly large proportion of the expenditure is entirely another matter.

Price Indexes

Rovira's proposals[22] regarding drug price indexes are still relevant today. Lobato[19] considers that the consumer price index (CPI) is not a suitable deflator for series of pharmaceutical expenditure (it leads to absurd conclusions: real consumption would not have risen between 1969 and 1989). A deflator built on authorized price reviews leads to the opposite result, likewise illogical (the Social Security demand cannot have risen 12.5 times between 1969 and 1989). Consequently, the author constructs an ad hoc deflator which combines both the above and deflates the values for each year by generations of registration and marketing

> The consumption of drugs registered in or before the base year would be deflated with the authorised price index; the consumption of drugs registered in the last year in the series, with the CPI; and that of the intermediate generations, with indexes obtained by combining the evolution of the CPI and the authorised prices. It is assumed that the registration price reflects all the changes in the CPI up to that time, and that as of registration, prices evolve according to the authorised price index for pharmaceuticals (p. 93).

This method yields a cumulative annual increase in real expenditure on pharmaceuticals of 4.7 per cent.

Research and Technological Development

On the subject of patents, see Lobo,[23] which with hindsight the author considers as lacking balance, Lobo[2] and Lobo,[24] which deals with the new international regulations. The article by Carballeira and Velasco[25] analyses the behaviour of companies that did research during 1992 and proposes some technological priorities to take into account in promoting the innovation process.

Burguete and García[26] in their article confirm the self-evident truth that the pharmaceutical sector allocates major budgets to the R&D of products, occupying one of the leading positions in this respect among Spain's industries. In this study they use data provided by the National Institute of Statistics and the Central Balance Sheet Data Office of the Bank of Spain.

Fernández Cano and García Alonso[27] perform, in their chapter dedicated to the promotion of technology, a general analysis of the current state of affairs of the R&D process in the pharmaceutical industry, especially the advances taking place in the field of biotechnology. The same work includes an extensive chapter, with a large contribution by Colom, which deals with R&D activities and strategy. Among other topics, it studies research results in terms of patents granted and products discovered, and the first research promotion plan in the pharmaceutical industry in Spain.

Esteve[28] analyses the correspondence between biomedical research and the pharmaceutical industry, contextual changes that affect this relationship, the present situation of pharmaceutical research in Spain, and measures that the government could take to promote it.

M. Santoro's doctoral thesis[29] compares Argentina's pharmaceutical industry with Spain's, primarily to gain insight into the technological direction followed by companies and their production of innovations, and also the effect of the public R&D promotion plans that have been applied in Spain, particularly the Farma II Plan. The author presents an evaluation of this plan and proposes that it should serve as a point of departure for devising local plans in Argentina.

'Social' Regulation, Technical Barriers, Trade and Diffusion of Innovation

The thesis by Cabiedes[30] is built on a solid theoretical foundation. It examines the relationship between international trade and industrial economics, neoprotectionism and technical barriers, and theories on state regulation.

This thesis has made several contributions. First, it provides an interpretation of the registration and marketing authorization of drugs (a form of social regulation whose declared objective is to guarantee their safety, effectiveness and quality in response to a characteristic market failure caused by doctors' and patients' imperfect information), in terms of the modern theories on international trade, technical barriers to commercial exchange and state regulation. However, registration also functions as an instrument of commercial protection and restriction with effects on the diffusion of technological progress – an objective that is not made explicit. In order to carry out her empirical analysis, the author uses a logit logistic regression model and a highly complex database of drug marketing authorizations and registrations in five European countries.

The main conclusions reached in the thesis are:

- The national drug register functions as a technical barrier to trade. This conclusion is partly related to the fact that after eight years of efforts the pharmaceutical industry was considered to be the single European market's greatest failure.
- Genetic engineering products enjoy rapid and ample diffusion thanks to their specific legal framework.
- The speed at which other products are diffused is related to price control and how registration works in each country.
- The product cycle theory is not applicable to therapeutic innovations.
- The probability of expansion of a therapeutic innovation shows a positive relationship with the degree of innovation it incorporates, the age of the molecule, the size of the laboratory, the economic results obtained from the product and its previous authorization in the UK.
- The diffusion of therapeutic innovations in the five markets studied depends more on the nationality of the inventor and the type of product than on therapeutic traditions. Each country tends to market its own innovations sooner and more extensively than those from abroad.

Public Expenditure on Pharmaceuticals in Spain: Description, Data

Nonell and Borrell[6] also study the evolution of public drug expenditure between 1986 and 1997 and break down its growth into five factors: demography, coverage, index of prices actually paid for the products financed, number of prescriptions per insured person, and the real cost per prescription calculated as a remainder. They conclude that 'the dynamics of the average cost per prescription is the main driving force behind expenditure' (p. 123).

Public Spending Containment Policies

The report by the Abril Committee[31] published in July 1991 marks a milestone not only in health policy but also in Spanish politics in the broadest sense. This work merited discussion and analysis by the social forces and experts convened, as it contained generally very reasonable recommendations. However, it was almost completely neutralized by the political ineptitude with which it was presented and the absurd sabotage of irresponsible media that chose to launch an attack on a limited proposal for the extension of co-payments. The chapter on pharmacy deserves a less favourable opinion. Out of five recommendations, three referred to the extension of co-payment, taking up the idea, put forward earlier by the health minister, Mr Lluch, of raising pensions in compensation by the same amount, in order to emphasize that the measure was not intended for tax-raising purposes. The other two recommendations were to improve doctors' information and training, and to separate the marketing authorization of drugs and their financing. The latter of these was already established by the 1990 Law on Pharmaceuticals, which introduced selective financing.

Precisely the greatest weakness of the proposed extension of co-payment (which falls on the patients), in the Abril Report and on other occasions, is that all attention is focused on this measure, other possible measures affecting the pharmaceutical industry or its distributors being neglected. By 1991, seven years had passed since the Hatch–Waxman Act on generics in the USA, and two since the establishment of the reference pricing (RP) system in Germany. Fortunately, later governments have not continued along this path, instead taking important and committed decisions on selective financing, reductions in prices and margins, generics and RP.

Curiously, there is no correspondence between the report by the Subcommittee on Pharmaceutical Care (which addresses issues such as generics and reference pricing) and the final report by the Committee. The Subcommittee disagreed on fundamental points and its report includes opposing positions, which deprives it of clarity and convincingness.

A brief summary of this issue can be found in English in the article by

López Bastida and Mossialos[32], published in nothing less than *The Lancet*, with some debatable statements on prices.

Nonell and Borrell[6] summarize Spain's pharmaceutical expenditure containment policy, co-payment, negative lists and price caps for new drugs. The containment of the prices actually paid by the government (taking into account discounts, price reductions and refunds by the industry and pharmacists) have not resulted in any growth in spending per insured person, since the price elasticity of demand for pharmaceuticals with respect to these prices would be nil.

They attribute the variation in the number of prescriptions per person in 1993 and 1994 to the exclusion of products from public financing, although other factors could have influenced it. The growth of this indicator in subsequent years could be due to a substitution effect, which would have cancelled out the effectiveness of the negative lists. Prices of new drugs can only be followed in terms of real cost per prescription, which explains 10.2 of the 13.2 percentage points of the growth in spending. There would be two new effective instruments to contain it: the 1990 price intervention method and the threat of exclusion from public financing.

López-Casasnovas[33] has published a book chapter in English summarizing Spain's cost containment policies in the health sector. Within this general context, he introduces some specific considerations on certain measures adopted in Spain concerning medicines. His observations on co-payment, in which he compares the general system with MUFACE, and on negative lists, are interesting. With regard to the latter, it is important to bear in mind the long-term effect caused by an increase in the bargaining power of the government.

The journal *Fulls Econòmics del Sistema Sanitari*[34] published a monograph on pharmaceutical provision in its issue number 33 (November 1999), in which the most notable contribution is the article by Puig.[35] It features comparative data for pharmaceutical expenditure in Europe and an analysis of measures taken recently in Spain to contain this expenditure, on both the demand side and the supply side.

See also Hernández's controversial article,[36] with its strong criticism of the pharmaceutical cost containment policy adopted in Spain.

Public Expenditure on Pharmaceuticals in Spain: Regulation Design

Callejón and Ortún[37] discuss the social utility of pharmaceuticals, an allocation criterion introduced by the Law on Pharmaceuticals for public financing or insurance. They defend an extended concept of welfare whereby the variable to be maximized is health, which depends on health services and other factors. The benefits of the pharmaceutical alternative are not only therapeutic but also include technological external effects and improvements in employment and the balance of payments. They also draw attention to a series of obstacles to the determination of social utility. Previous to this, they examine the market structure and health and industrial policy in this area in Spain, and the effects of the single market.

In chapter 4 of his thesis, Borrell[17] studies selective financing and price-cap regulation. The model he applies, Dixit and Stiglitz's monopolistic competition model, poses certain problems. The preference for variety and the fact that utility depends on the number of units consumed are not so clear as in other markets. The model does not take into account the complex relationship between doctor and patient. The fact that innovation only represents a fixed cost also raises doubts.

In order to analyse the balance in view of the threat of exclusion from public financing, the author devises a demand equation with a two-stage budget allocation. The first step is to choose a therapeutic group, and the second is to choose the differentiated products. The co-payment acts as the price. The main conclusion is that when the product is included in public financing the health service can receive a discount if the political decisions are price-sensitive and the fixed cost of market entry in the event of inclusion is lower than the fixed cost of exclusion. In his study of price-cap regulation, the author insists that the mechanism should be continued in the long term, and that therefore it is necessary to account for the entire lifetime of the product and consider a discount factor. All this takes as its point of departure Abbott's 1995 model.

Price Intervention

A book published by the Directorate-General of Pharmacy and Health Products of the Spanish Ministry of Health and Consumer Affairs and the Subdirectorate-General of the Pharmaceutical Industry of the Ministry of Industry and Energy[38] in 1986 contains an analysis of price intervention in several European countries, data on drug prices in Spain, a cross-national comparison between Spain and other European countries and two chapters evaluating price policy in Spain. Soon after the appearance of this book, Lobato[39] offered an interesting criticism of it. Also around this time (1985), Arnés,[40] Cainzos[41] and Rovira[22] made contributions to the debate that are still of interest today. The last of the three mentioned a package of measures designed to influence demand as a counterpart to price intervention.

Lobato[19] studies the direct control of drug prices in Spain based on the difficulty of inspecting costs; it is complicated to allocate fixed costs and estimate the size of the market for each product. Revisions of authorized prices to make up for inflation would have been insufficient. The main conclusion is the need for a formal agreement between the government and the sector guaranteeing cost containment but also the role of the market.

The document by Revilla[42] (Director-General of Pharmacy and Health Products at the time of its publication) is of great interest. It sets out the system of price intervention and the design of the public financing of pharmaceuticals in Spain. Notably, it presents the aggregate cost structure of the pharmaceutical industry in Spain in 1990, using data provided by the companies themselves to the price regulation authority. It also contains valuable discussion on the treatment of transfer prices.

The article by Puig-Junoy[21] informs about price regulation in the EU and discusses the rate of return method and the price-cap method. He includes cost control in the former. In our opinion, it would have been preferable to distinguish it clearly, as it involves a complex product-by-product intervention, whereas rate of return regulation is concerned with the company as a whole, and uses the rate of return in different industries as a criterion. The author also reflects on the use of the results of economic evaluation in relation to the 1990 price decree. The article's most interesting contribution is its findings on one specific system, price-cap regulation.

Borrell's study[43] attempts to measure the effect of price control in the UK, which is based on limiting the rate of return on capital. Using cointegration techniques, the author concludes that the system has had little effect in terms of price containment.

Generics and Reference Pricing

The primary aim of the book chapter by Lobo[44] is to describe the economics of generic drugs (that is, their relationship with brands, quality, patents and competition). Its secondary aim is to examine the conditions that must be fulfilled to create a generic market in Spain. To this end, the author considers problems of information, regulation and incentives; among the latter the allocation of public financing only to the cheapest drugs by means of RP or substitution by the pharmacist.

Puig-Junoy[21] studies generic policies and RP. He discusses the reasons why in 1998 the generic market could still be described as inexistent in Spain, and the necessary conditions for it to grow. He is not very enthusiastic about the market's response to the increase in competition heralded by generics and the behaviour of prices. He notes that the prices of generics are generally lower, but that those of brand products do not fall and may even rise. This is a case of what Scherer calls the generic competition paradox. The author also mentions the explanation given by Frank and Salkever (1992)[45], who distinguish between more and less price-sensitive consumers, whereby the demand for the brand product falls but at the same time become more inelastic.

Companies would thus be practising cross-subsidies between products under patent and products whose patent has expired, in order to maintain their overall income. Other strategic responses are: patent extension, the creation of second brands and subsidiaries of generics and the differentiation of the brand product through marginal innovations and promotion campaigns.

The author predicts that RP in Spain will provide incentives for the consumption of generic drugs and other relatively low-price drugs, assuming that certain institutional conditions are fulfilled. In other countries public spending has not improved spectacularly because measures taken in this direction have been offset by price rises in new products and rising consumption. In Spain, it should be borne in mind that recently introduced products with high prices fetch the largest market shares in the EU. RP may exacerbate this behaviour even further. It might be wise to draw a sharper line between the mechanism of co-payment and the very different mechanism of RP. In the latter, the patient's share of the burden of the cost is avoidable if the patient or the doctor select a product with a price lower than the RP.

In later works, Puig-Junoy and López-Casanovas[46,47] again examine Spanish RP policy. Perhaps they should have placed more emphasis on the fact that RP is a policy aimed at encouraging competition, in which the RP is in principle intended as a competitive market price, and examined the Spanish version of it in this light. They also discuss the knotty problem of the substitute drugs to be considered when fixing a RP, the basic arithmetic of the system, the relationship with patients' welfare and the negative consequences of applying the system to patented products. On the subject of the Spanish regulations, the authors are fairly pessimistic about their effects on prices and public spending, and draw attention to the relatively low price levels in Spain, the importance of the factor utilization or quantities, and the weight of recently introduced patented products with high prices.

Mestre's study[48] earned him an International Health Economics Association award for young researchers. After analysing the significance of generics for market structure and competition, taking into account Scherer's paradox and the thesis of the competitive advantage of the pioneering company, the author wonders whether a company with a brand product that loses its patent should be interested in producing the generic. Using the segmented market model, he reaches the conclusion that there is indeed an incentive to do so, as the generic is used strategically to raise the profile of the brand product and thus exploit its loyal consumers.

A simple but interesting simulation of the potential saving in public expenditure due to generics, a summary of recent regulatory measures and some data on concentration, prices and expenditure are the main contributions of the text by Segura.[49]

Selective Financing in Spain (Negative Lists)

The concept of selective financing or preferential public financing of pharmaceuticals, in relation to their rational use, was expounded as early as 1986 in a booklet published by the Directorate-General of Pharmacy and Health Products of the Spanish Ministry of Health and Consumer Affairs.[38] This work includes an overview of the public financing of drugs in several European countries and an interesting text by Ignacio Cruz-Roche, presented at a meeting of the WHO in 1984, which analyses pharmaceutical cost containment policies on both the demand side and the supply side, and co-payment or *ticket modérateur* in Spain.

The article by Marino, Marqués and Velasco[50] is a multidisciplinary collaboration between an Insalud official and two lecturers at the Technical University and the Faculty of Medicine of the University of Valladolid, which handles original primary data of great reliability (seldom achieved in applied economics studies) and time-series analysis to evaluate the first (1993) decree on selective financing (negative lists). The authors' theory is simple: if the other circumstances remain constant, the difference between real pharmaceutical expenditure and the expenditure calculated according to forecasting techniques under the assumption of the non-implementation of selective financing will give us a measure of its effectiveness. They make this comparison using the weight of the brand-name drugs that are excluded as a proportion of the total. The variables used are the number of prescriptions per thousand inhabitants and expenditure per thousand inhabitants. For these two variables the authors construct two time series from January 1986 to May/June 1993 with the monthly data corresponding to the province of Valladolid.

The authors note that the brand-name drugs that were excluded had a downward sales trend. Only 13 pharmaceuticals showed consumption of over 10 000 units and expenditure of over five million (concurrently). These 13 drugs are taken as representative of the entirety of the drugs excluded from public financing. The main results are as follows:

- With or without the measure, consumption continues to rise as in previous years.
- Both short-term and mid-term forecasts show a drop in the relative weight of the excluded products that would have occurred even if selective financing had not been introduced.
- The repercussion of selective financing (the difference between forecasted values and real values for 1994) is an 8.2 per cent decrease in the number of prescriptions and a 4.7 per cent decrease in cost.

The main problem here is the uncertainty of the *ceteris paribus* condition. The authors painstakingly attempt to make the adjustments required by other concurrent variations (for example, discounts offered by the laboratories, changes in the billing system and so on) but they acknowledge that the introduction of a programme for rational drug use, the prescription of therapeutic substitutes that are not excluded from financing, and the reformulation of drugs by pharmaceutical companies to convert them into monodrugs with a higher price but the same brand, could all affect the results obtained. The authors' overall conclusion is that the measure has failed. In our opinion, the results do not warrant such a pessimistic impression. Furthermore, the balance should include the increase in the bargaining power of the government against the pharmaceutical companies as a result of the suppression of the previously indiscriminate financing for all the products on the market.

Juez and Tamayo[51] also apply time-series analysis to the evaluation of the consequences of introducing selective financing in 1993. Using the aggregate monthly data on pharmaceutical expenditure of the National Health System between 1991 and 1995, in constant deseasonalized pesetas, the authors compare the observed evolution with the theoretical evolution according to a linear fit. They conclude that the measure had a notable effect in the short term, but was absorbed in the long term.

Studies on Pharmacies

Although only the third came to be formally published, it is worth while mentioning the studies by Cruz-Roche and Alonso[52] and Cruz-Roche[53,54] analysing the cost structure and profit and loss accounts of Spanish pharmacies, their remuneration systems, their monopoly on dispensing, employment and the professional situation of pharmacists.

At this point we should mention, although they are not economic texts, two books with the same title: *La profesión farmacéutica* (*The Pharmaceutical Profession*). One is by the sociologists de Miguel and Salcedo,[55] and contains abundant data and interesting interpretations. The other, by the lecturer in Law at the University of Granada Francisca Villalba Pérez,[56] and is noteworthy for its thoroughness and the fine legal interpretations it contains.

García-Fontes and Motta[57] study the regulation of freedom of establishment or entry and the prices of these distribution services. They use a variant of Hotelling's model (horizontal differentiation by location throughout a 'linear city'). The originality here lies in the fact that the consumers have a high but finite reserve price. This condition means that the market may not be covered, and hence the positive effects of perfect competition may not occur.

The authors develop their model on the basis of these assumptions, inferring the demand and profit functions and the condition that the market is covered. Then they find the collective welfare. Under the conditions they set, a drop in the intervened price would bring about an increase in welfare, which is the policy that Spanish governments have pursued on several occasions. The first variant the authors introduce is to allow price competition (through discounts), which always leads to an improvement in welfare. The second is to admit freedom of entry or establishment, maintaining price-cap regulation, and the result is greater social welfare. This result does not change (although there is a redistribution among pharmacists) if tenders are invited for the licensing rights for setting up pharmacies, which enables the government to absorb part or all of the monopoly benefits of the restriction of free establishment. The authors then go on to admit price competition and free entry simultaneously. They formulate a constrained optimization problem solvable with Kuhn–Tucker conditions, the solution of which is also an improvement in social welfare.

In the last part of their work, the authors design an optimal regulation: freedom of entry, payment of a licence for new pharmacies by means of either a tendering system or a mixed system that takes academic and professional merit into account, and alternative remuneration systems with a fixed component and a variable component or a decreasing margin. They also mention the zero generation problem (that of pharmacists who have paid a transfer fee for their pharmacy but have yet to redeem it), although they do not suggest any solution to it here. The authors insist that they do not defend total deregulation of the sector because medicines are by their very nature merit goods and free competition would generate the risk of the disappearance of pharmacies in areas with little demand, or would cause the quality of service to diminish.

Gisbert, Rovira and Illa[58] highlight the permanence of a very simple regulation in Spain (a fixed markup on sales) whereas other countries, such as the Netherlands, the USA and Canada, have undergone experiences of all sorts. The authors consider that giving a higher profile to the health care facet of the pharmacist and a lower one to the commercial facet would help towards changing the regulation. In contrast to such a trend, laws passed recently in Catalonia and the Basque Country 'perpetuate a nineteenth-century model of pharmacy . . .'. They also study the models of pharmacy to be found in various countries and develop retrospective simulations of the effects that the different remuneration systems would have. As their sample, they use the pharmacies in Catalonia in 1991. These exercises reveal that it is possible to reduce expenditure and maintain the average margin per pharmacy, obviously with the resulting redistribution. The last section includes a calculation of profitability and the break-even point in three scenarios. The authors show that many pharmacies in towns with fewer than 1000 inhabitants and in the city of Barcelona would fall below the break-even point.

Jansson's paper[59] also studies the regulation of freedom of establishment and opening of pharmacies and price regulation. In the first part the author describes a model of competition with horizontal spatial differentiation. In the second part she carries out an empirical study of the Spanish case that includes a comparison with other EU countries, an econometric contrast with the model proposed for the Spanish data and the calibration of the model for data from Spain's autonomous communities. The model is a simplification of that developed by Waterson (1993)[60]. On this basis, the author discusses the possible cases: regulated prices and free entry, regulated entry and free prices, and finally free entry and free prices. She also studies the socially optimal number of pharmacies.

Jansson applies the model to the current Spanish regulation and analyses the effect of the different liberalization measures. In the first case, new pharmacies would open and consumers would benefit, but we can say nothing from a social point of view. In the second case, the evolution of the liberalized prices would depend on the regulation regarding the number of pharmacies. Finally, she studies the effects of total deregulation. She defines the optimal regulation as one whereby a price is fixed and entry is liberalized for that price.

According to the empirical study and using the pattern provided by the model, Spain would appear to have a larger number of pharmacies than it should, taking the EU as a yardstick. The margin is also higher in coherence with this. The econometric contrast reveals that the estimated number of pharmacies would be significantly lower than the number actually observed, although the inaccuracy of the forecasts provided by the model prevents us from reaching firm conclusions. The model is also calibrated using data from Spain's autonomous communities. The conclusion is that according to the forecasts provided by the model, it is only possible to reach the social optimum through regulation.

The work by Cabiedes, Arcos and Álvarez de Toledo[61] makes a novel contribution, evaluating the incremental cost of a broader pharmaceutical care service than the mere distribution of drugs in pharmacies. The authors define this broader service as 'pharmaceutical intervention', understanding this as the activity that is oriented towards preventing, detecting and if necessary solving problems related to pharmaceuticals.

ACKNOWLEDGEMENTS

This work was supported by an unrestricted educational grant from the Merck Company Foundation, the philanthropic arm of Merck & Co. Inc., Whitehouse Station, New Jersey, USA.

REFERENCES

1. Cruz-Roche, I. and J.J. Durán (1987), *Estrategias de desarrollo de la industria farmacéutica: la industria española en el contexto internacional*, Madrid: Ministerio de Industria y Energía.
2. Lobo, F. (1992), *Medicamentos: política y economía*, Barcelona: Masson-SG.
3. Lobato, P., F. Lobo and J. Rovira (1997), *La industria farmacéutica en España tras la unificación del mercado Europeo*, Madrid: Farmaindustria.
4. Lobo, F. and G. Velásquez (eds) (1997), *Los medicamentos ante las nuevas realidades económicas*, Madrid: Civitas.
5. Rovira, J. (1996), 'Are national drug expenditure control policies compatible with a single European market?', *PharmacoEconomics*, 10 (supplement 2), 4–13.
6. Nonell, R. and J.R. Borrell (1998), 'Mercado de medicamentos en España: diseño institucional de la regulación y de la provisión pública', *Papeles de Economía Española* (76), 113–31.
7. López Bastida, J. (1998), 'El mercado farmacéutico español: una panorámica', in J. Del Llano, V. Ortún, J.M. Martin, J. Millán and J. Gene (eds), *Gestión sanitaria: innovaciones y desafíos*, Barcelona: Masson, pp. 105–24.
8. Martín Cruz, N. (2000), 'Una aproximación a la política de los costes de transacción a través del análisis institucional comparado. La regulación de los medicamentos en dos ámbitos institucionales. La industria farmacéutica en España y en Estados Unios', doctoral thesis, Unversidad de Valladolid, Valladolid.
9. Chaqués, Bonafont L. (1999), 'Políticas públicas y democracia en España: la política farmacéutica del franquismo a la democracia', doctoral thesis, Universidad de Barcelona, Barcelona.
10. Rovira, J. (1998), 'Impacto del Mercado Único sobre el sector farmacéutico en España', *Papeles de Economía Española*, 76, 132–40.
11. Darbà, J. (1999), 'The impact of the single European market on the structure, conduct and dynamics of the pharmaceutical sector, doctoral thesis. Universidad de Barcelona: Barcelona.
12. Bercovitz, A. (1986), 'Las importaciones paralelas de productos farmacéuticos en la CEE', *Revista de Derecho Privado*, (December), 995–1019.
13. Darbà, J. and J. Rovira i Coll (1998), 'Parallel imports of pharmaceuticals in the European Union', *PharmacoEconomics*, 14 (supplement 1), 129–36.
14. Rovira, J. (1998), 'The pros and cons of a single euro-price for drugs and the economics of parallel trade', *PharmacoEconomics*, 14, 135–36.
15. Danzon, P. and A. Towse (1998), 'The pros and cons of a single euro-price for drugs and the economics of parallel trade [authors' reply]', *PharmacoEconomics*, 14, 136–37.
16. Lobo, F. (1980), 'La publicidad farmacéutica en España', *Papers: Revista de Sociología*, (14), 99–132.
17. Borrell, J.R. (1999), 'Los precios de los medicamentos en Inglaterra y en España: competencia, regulación y financiación pública', doctoral thesis, Universidad de Barcelona, Barcelona.
18. Cabiedes, L. (1996), 'Estructura del sector farmacéutico en España', in Meneu R. and V. Ortún (eds), *Política y gestión sanitaria: la agenda explícita*, Barcelona: SG Editores, pp. 255–76.
19. Lobato, P. (1990), 'El mercado de medicamentos en España: demanda, gasto farmacéutico e intervención de precios', *Información Comercial Española*, 89–103, 681–2.

20. Cruz-Roche, I. (1986), 'Financiación y control del gasto farmacéutio', in *Dirección General de Farmacia y Productos Sanitarios: Uso racional y financiación pública de los medicamentos en Europa*, Madrid: Ministerio de Sanidad y Consumo, pp. 151–73.

21. Puig-Juroy, J. (1998), 'Regulación y competencia de precios en el mercado farmacéutico', *Papeles de Economía Española*, 76, 96–112.

22. Rovira, J. (1988), 'Política de precios: interdependencia del área sanitaria con el área económica', in F. Lobo (ed.), *Encuentro sobre la ley del medicamento*, Madrid: Ministerio de Sanidad y Consumo, pp. 343–54.

23. Lobo, F. (1983), *La investigación industrial farmacéutica: la política de patentes*, Madrid: Ministerio de Industria y Energía.

24. Lobo, F. (1991), 'Un mercado internacional nuevo para las invenciones y creaciones intelectuales', in J. Velarde, J.L. García and A. Pedreño (eds), *Apertura e internacionalización de la economía España en una Europa sin fronteras*, Madrid: Colegio de Economistas, pp. 307–28.

25. Carballeira, R. and J.L. Velasco (1994), 'La investigación farmacéutica y su entorno', *Economía Industrial*, 296, 105–14.

26. Vázquez, J.L. and M.P. García (1995), 'La I+D de productos farmacéuticos: motor de un servicio asentado en una industria', in *Libro de Ponencias del V Congreso Nacional de Economía, Economía de la salud*, 5–7 December, Las Palmas de Gran Canaria, España. Madrid: Consejo General de Colegios de Economistas de España, 143–52.

27. Fernández Cano, P. and F. García (1997), 'El impulso de la tecnología', in P. Lobato, F. Lobo and J. Rovira (eds), *La industria farmacéutica en España tras la unificación del mercado Europeo*, Madrid: Farmaindustria, pp. 3–38.

28. Esteve, J. (1998), 'La industria farmacéutica como impulsora de la I+D en el sector sanitario', *Revista de Administración Sanitaria*, 11, 1–9.

29. Santoro, F.M. (1997), *Innovación y sendero evolutivo en la industria farmacéutica: los casos de Argentina y España*, doctoral thesis, Universidad de Buenos Aires, Buenos Aires.

30. Cabiedes, L. (1992), *Estructura industrial, intervención estatal y barreras técnicas a las transacciones commerciales: una aplicación a la industria farmacéutica*, doctoral thesis, Universidad de Oviedo, Oviedo.

31. Comisión de Análisis y Evaluación del Sistema Nacional de Salud (1991), *Informe y Recomendaciones, Informes de las Subcomisiones: Subcomisión de Atención Farmacéutica*. Madrid: Comisión de Análisis y Evaluación del Sistema Nacional de Salud.

32. López, J. and E. Mossialos (1997), 'Spanish drug policy at the crossroads', *The Lancet*, 350, 679–80.

33. López-Casasnovas, G. (1999), 'Health care and cost containment in Spain', in E. Mossialos and J. Le Grand (eds), *Health Care and Cost Containment in the European Union*, Aldershot: Ashgate, pp. 401–41.

34. Various authors (1999), 'La prestacó farmacèutica', *Fulls Econòmics del Sistema Sanitari*, 33.

35. Puig-Junoy, J. (1999), 'Reptes en la gestió de la prestació farmacèutica', *Fulls Econòmics del Sistema Sanitari*, 33, 6–13.

36. Hernández, J.M. (1998), 'El gasto farmacéutico en el contexto de la sanidad pública', *Boletín del Círculo de Empresarios*, 63, 179–97.

37. Callejón, M. and V. Ortún (1990), 'Los medicamentos en España: Mercado Único y utilidad social', *Economía Industrial*, 274, 191–206.

38. Dirección General de Farmacia y Productos Sanitarios (1986), *Los precios de las medicinas en España y en Europa*, Madrid: Ministerio de Sanidad y Consumo.

39. Lobato, P. (1988), *La industria farmacéutica ante el Mercado Único Europeo*, Madrid: Farmaindustria.

40. Arnés, H. (1988), 'Desarrollo industrial y política de precios en el área de los medicamentos', in F. Lobo (ed.), *Encuentro sobre la ley del medicamento*, Madrid: Ministerio de Sanidad y Consumo, pp. 299–306.

41. Cainzos, J.M. (1988), 'Factores que condicionan la política de precios de los medicamentos', in F. Lobo (ed.), *Encuentro sobre la ley del medicamento*, Madrid: Ministerio de Sanidad y Consumo, pp. 315–26.

42. Revilla, R. (1994), 'Pricing and financing of pharmaceuticals in Spain', in E. Mossialos, C. Ranos and B. Abel-Smith (eds), *Cost Containment, Pricing and Financing of Pharmaceuticals in the European Community: the Policy-makers' View*, London: LSE Health, pp. 191–205.

43. Borrell, J.R. (1999), 'Pharmaceutical price regulation: a study on the impact of the rate-of-return regulation in the UK', *PharmacoEconomics*, 15, 291–303.

44. Lobo, F. (1997), 'La creación de un mercado de medicamentos genéricos en España', in G. López-Casasnovas and D. Rodríguez (eds), *La regulación de los servicios sanitarios en España*, Madrid: Civitas, pp. 393–436.

45. Frank, R.G. and D.S. Salkever (1992), 'Pricing, patent loss and the market for pharmaceuticals', *Southern Economic Journal*, 59, 165–79.

46. Puig-Junoy, J. and G. López-Casasnovas (1999), 'La aplicación de precios de referencia a los medicamentos', *Cuadernos de Información Económica*, 143, 77–84.

47. Puig-Junoy, J. and G. López-Casasnovas (1999), 'Análisis económico de la aplicación de precios de referencia en la financiación pública de medicamentos: Ventajas, limitaciones e impacto esperado en España. Informe Técnico No 1', *Economía y Salud*, 31.

48. Mestre, J. (1999), 'The impact of generic goods in the pharmaceutical industry', *Health Economics*, 8, 599–612.

49. Segura, M. (1999), 'Consideraciones económicas de las especialidades farmacéuticas genéricas', in M. Dal Val (ed.), *Genéricos: Claves para su conocimiento y comprensión*, Madrid: Editores Médicos, pp. 271–98.

50. Marino, M.A., J.M. Marqués and A. Velasco (1996), 'Impact of selective financing of drugs on pharmaceutical expenditure in the province of Valladolid, Spain', *PharmacoEconomics*, 10, 269–80.

51. Juez, P. and P.A. Tamayo (1997), 'Efectividad de las medidas de contención del gasto público farmacéutico contenidas en el Real Decreto 83/1993 de 22 de enero (de selección de medicamentos a efectos de su financiación por el Sistema Nacional de Salud)', *Estudios Sobre Consumo*, 42, 63–72.

52. Cruz-Roche, I. and J. Alonso (1986), *La profesión farmacéutica del año 2000: parte III, situación económica*, Madrid: Universidad Autónoma.

53. Cruz-Roche, I. (1987), *La distribución de productos farmacéuticos en España: un análisis económico de la oficina de farmacia y de las políticas de racionalización del sector*, Madrid: Ministerio de Sanidad y Consumo.

54. Cruz-Roche, I. (1988), 'Estructura económica de la distribución de los precios farmacéuticos', in F. Lobo (ed.), *Encuentro sobre la ley del medicamento*, Madrid: Ministerio de Sanidad y Consumo, pp. 327–42.

55. de Miguel, J.M. and J. Salcedo (1987), *La profesión farmacéutica*, Madrid: Centro de Investigaciones Sociológicas.

56. Villalba, F. (1996), *La profesión farmacéutica*, Madrid: Marcial Pons.
57. García-Fontes, W. and M. Motta (1997), 'Regulación de las oficinas de farmacia: precios y libertad de entrada', in G. López-Casasnovas and D. Rodríguez (eds), *La regulación de los servicios sanitarios en España*, Madrid: Civitas, pp. 325–47.
58. Gisbert, R., J. Rovira and R. Illa (1997), 'Análisis de modelos alternativos de retribución da las oficinas de farmacia', in G. López-Casasnovas and D. Rodríguez (eds), *La regulación de los servicios sanitarios en España*, Madrid: Civitas, pp. 349–92.
59. Jansson, E. (1999), 'Libre competencia frente a regulación en la distribucion minorista de medicamentos', *Revista de Economía Aplicada*, 7, 85–112.
60. Waterson, M. (1993), 'Vertical integration and vertical restraints', *Oxford Review of Economic Policy*, **9** (2), 41–57.
61. Cabiedes, L., P. Arcos and F. Álvarez de Toledo (1995), 'Evaluación del coste incremental del servicio farmacéutio respecto a la distribución de medicamentos en oficinas de farmacia', in *Libro de Ponencias del V Congreso Nacional de Economía, Economía de la salud*, 5–7 December, Las Palmas de Gran Canaria, España, Madrid: Consejo General de Colegios de Economistas de España, pp. 163–70.

Appendix List of economic studies of the pharmaceutical industry and pharmaceuticals published over the last 20 years by Spanish economists*

BOOKS AND BOOK CHAPTERS 1980–1999

Arnés, H. (1988), 'Desarrollo industrial y política de precios en el área de los medicamentos', in F. Lobo (ed.), *Encuentro sobre la Ley del Medicamento*, Madrid: Ministerio de Sanidad y Consumo, pp. 299–306.

Cabiedes, L. (1995), 'La regulación de la industria farmacéutica', in J. Velarde, J.L. García and A. Pedreño (eds), *Regulación y competencia en la economía española*, Madrid: Civitas, pp. 213–29.

Cabiedes, L. (1996), 'Estructura del sector farmacéutico en España', in R. Meneu and V. Ortún (eds), *Política y gestiòn sanitaria: la agenda explícita*, Barcelona: SG Editores, pp. 255–76.

Cabiedes, L., P. Arcos and F. Álvarez (1995), 'Evaluación del coste incremental del servicio farmacéutico respecto a la distribución de medicamentos en oficinas de farmacia', in *Libro de Ponencias del V Congreso Nacional de Economía. Economía de la salud, 5–7 December,* Las Palmas de Gran Canaria, España, Madrid: Consejo General de Colegios de Economistas de España, pp. 163–70.

Cainzos, J.M. (1988), 'Factores que condicionan la política de precios de los medicamentos', in F. Lobo (ed.), *Encuentro sobre la Ley del Medicamento*, Madrid: Ministerio de Sanidad y Consumo, pp. 315–26.

Comisión de Análisis y Evaluación del Sistema Nacional de Salud (1991), *Informes de las Subcomisiones: Subcomisión de Atención Farmacéutica*, Madrid: Comisión de Análisis y Evaluación del Sistema Nacional de Salud.

Cruz-Roche, I. (1986), 'Financiación y control del gasto farmacéutico', in *Dirección General de Farmacia y Productos Sanitarios: uso racional y financiación pública de los medicamentos en Europa*, Madrid: Ministerio de Sanidad y Consumo, pp. 151–73. (An English version is available entitled Cruz-Roche, I. (1984), 'Financing and control of pharmaceutical

---

* Excluding economic evaluation studies of pharmaceuticals.

spending: meeting on drug policies and management: procurement and financing of essential drugs', October 22–26, Madrid, pp. 48–59.

Cruz-Roche, I. (1987), 'La distribución de productos farmacéuticos en España: un análisis económico de la oficina de farmacia y de las políticas de racionalización del sector', unpublished monograph, Ministerio de Sanidad y Consum, Madrid.

Cruz-Roche, I. (1988), 'Estructura económica de la distribución de los precios farmacéuticos', in F. Lobo (ed.), *Encuentro sobre la Ley del Medicamento*, Madrid: Ministerio de Sanidad y Consumo, pp. 327–42.

Cruz-Roche, I. and J. Alonso (1986), *La profesión farmacéutica del año 2000: parte III, situación económica*, unpublished monograph, Universidad Autónoma, Madrid.

Cruz-Roche, I. and J.J. Durán (1987), *Estrategias de desarrollo de la industria farmacéutica: la industria española en el contexto internacional*, Madrid: Ministerio de Industria y Energía.

Dirección General de Famacia y Productos Sanitarios (1986), *Los precios de las medicinas en España y en Europa*, Madrid: Ministerio de Sanidad y Consumo.

Dirección General de Farmacia y Productos Sanitarios (1986), *Uso racional y financiación pública de los medicamentos en Europa*, Madrid: Ministerio de Sanidad y Consumo.

Fernández, P. and F. García (1997), 'El impulso de la tecnología', in P. Lobato, F. Lobo and J. Rovira (eds), *La industria farmacéutica en España tras la unificación del Mercado Europeo*, Madrid: Farmaindustria, pp. 3–38.

Freire, J.M. (1999), 'Política basada en la evidencia y copago', in A. Berra, J. Artells and J. Ruiz (eds), *Control del gasto sanitario: participación de usuarios y profesionales. Actas del simposio celebrado en Madrid, el 15 de octubre de 1998, bajo el patrocinio de Fundación SB y Fundación Sanitas*. Madrid: Fundación SB, pp. 113–21.

García, M. (1995), 'Un modelo de análisis competitivo del sector farmacéutico', in *Libro de Ponencias del V Congreso Nacional de Economía. Economía de la salud, 5–7 December*, Las Palmas de Gran Canaria, España. Madrid: Consejo General de Colegios de Economistas de España, pp. 153–62.

García-Fontes, W. and M. Motta (1997), 'Regulación de las oficinas de farmacia: precios y libertad de entrada', in G. López-Casasnovas and D. Rodríguez (eds), *La regulación de los servicios sanitarios en España*, Madrid: Civitas, pp. 325–47.

Gisbert, R., J. Rovira and R. Illa (1997), 'Análisis de modelos alternativos de retribución de las oficinas de farmacia', in G. López-Casasnovas and D. Rodríguez (eds), *La regulación de los servicios sanitarios en España*, Madrid: Civitas, pp. 349–92.

Lobato, P. (1988), *La industria farmacéutica ante el Mercado Único Europeo*, Madrid: Farmaindustria.

Lobato, P., F. Lobo and J. Rovira (1997), *La industria farmacéutica en España tras la unificación del mercado europeo*, Madrid: Farmaindustria.

Lobo, F. (1983), *La investigación industrial farmacéutica: la política de patentes*, Madrid: Ministerio de Industria y Energía.

Lobo, F. (ed.) (1985), *Encuentro sobre la Ley del Medicamento, Universidad Internacional Menéndez Pelayo, 11–13 Septiembre*, Madrid: Ministerio de Sanidad y Consumo.

Lobo, F. (1991), 'Un mercado internacional nuevo para las invenciones y creaciones intelectuales', in J. Velarde, J.L. García and A. Pedreño (eds), *Apertura e internacionalización de la economía española: España en una Europa sin fronteras*, Madrid: Colegio de Economistas, pp. 307–28.

Lobo, F. (1991), 'Política económica del medicamento: competencia e intervención', in *Sociedad Española de Salud Pública y Administración Sanitaria: de política sanitaria a políticas de salud*, Valencia: Gráficas Ronda, pp. 32–42.

Lobo, F. (1992), *Medicamentos: Política y Economía*, Barcelona: Masson-SG.

Lobo, F. (1992), 'La evaluación económica, el registro y la intervención de precios de los medicamentos', in J.L. García and J.M. Serrano (eds), *Economía española, cultura y sociedad. Homenaje a Juan Velarde Fuertes*, Madrid: Eudema, pp. 149–76.

Lobo, F. (1992), 'Intervención y mercado: reforma sanitaria y medicamentos', in J. Martínez, D. Figuera and P. Sánchez-García, *Debate sanitario: medicina, sociedad y tecnología*, Bilbao: Fundación BBV.

Lobo, F. (1992), 'El control del gasto farmacéutico', in F. Antoñanzas and J. Pérez-Campanero (eds), *La reforma del sistema sanitario*, Madrid: Fedea, Mundi Prensa, pp. 95–9.

Lobo, F. (1997), 'La creación de un mercado de medicamentos genéricos en España', in G. López-Casasnovas and D. Rodríguez (eds), *La regulación de los servicios sanitarios en España*, Madrid: Civitas, pp. 393–436.

Lobo, F, and G. Velásquez (eds) (1997), *Los medicamentos ante las nuevas realidades económicas*, Madrid: Civitas (an English language version is available entitled Lobo, F. and G. Velásquez (eds), *Medicines and the New Economic Environment*, Madrid: Civitas.)

López, J. (1998), 'El mercado farmacéutico español: una panorámica', in J. Del Llano, V. Ortún, J.M. Martin, J. Millán and J. Gené (eds), *Gestión sanitaria: innovaciones y desafíos*, Barcelona: Masson, pp. 105–24.

López, J. and E. Mossialos (1996), 'Políticas de contención del gasto farmacéutico en los Estados Miembros de la Unión Europea', in R. Meneu and V. Ortún (eds), *Política y gestión sanitaria: la agenda explícita*, Barcelona: SG Editores, pp. 321–46.

238   *The public financing of pharmaceuticals*

López-Casasnovas, G. (1999), 'Health care and cost containment in Spain', in E. Mossialos and J. Le Grand (eds), *Health Care and Cost Containment in the European Union*, Aldershot, Ashgate, pp. 401–41.
López-Casasnovas, G. and D. Rodríguez (eds) (1997), *Le regulación de los servicios sanitarios en España*, Madrid: Fedea.
Miguel, J.M. and J. Salcedo (1987), *La profesión farmacéutica*, Madrid: Centro de Investigaciones Sociológicas.
Revilla, R. (1994), 'Pricing and financing of pharmaceuticals in Spain', in E. Mossialos, C. Ranos and B. Abel-Smith (eds), *Cost Containment, Pricing and Financing of Pharmaceuticals in the European Community: the Policy-makers' View*, London: LSE Health, pp. 191–205.
Rovira, J. (1988), 'Política de precios: interdependencia del área sanitaria con el área económica', in F. Lobo (ed.), *Encuentro sobre la Ley del Medicamento*, Madrid: Ministerio de Sanidad y Consumo, pp. 343–54.
Segura, M. (1999), 'Consideraciones económicas de las especialidades farmacéuticas genéricas', in M. Del Val (ed.), *Genéricos: Claves para su conocimiento y compresión*, Madrid: Editores Médicos, pp. 271–98.
Vázquez, J.L. and M.P, García (1995), 'La I+D de productos farmacéuticos: motor de un servicio asentado en una industria', in *Libro de Ponencias del V Congreso Nacional de Economía. Economía de la salud, 5–7 December*, Las Palmas de Gran Canaria, España, Madrid: Consejo General de Colegios de Economistas de España, pp. 143–52.
Villalba, F. (1996), *La profesión farmacéutica*, Madrid: Marcial Pons.

Doctoral Theses 1980–1999

Borrell, J.R. (1999), 'Los precios de los medicamentos en Inglaterra y en España competencia, regulación y financiación pública', doctoral thesis, Universidad de Barcelona, Barcelona, supervised by Dr. Antón Costas.
Cabiedes L. (1992), 'Estructura industrial, intervención estatal y barreras técnicas a las transacciones comerciales: una aplicación a la industria farmacéutica, doctoral thesis, Universidad de Oviedo, Oviedo, supervised by Dr. Félix Lobo and Dr. Rigoberto Pérez.
Chaqués, L. (1999), 'Políticas públicas y democracia en España: la política farmacéutica del franquismo a la democracia, doctoral thesis, Universidad de Barcelona, Barcelona, supervised by Dr. Pere Vilanova.
Darbà, J. (1999), 'The impact of the single European market on the structure, conduct and dynamics of the pharmaceutical sector, doctoral thesis, Universidad de Barcelona, Barcelona, supervised by Dr. Joan Rovira.
Martín, N. (2000), 'Una aproximación a la política de los costes de transacción a través del análisis institucional comparado. La regulación de los medicamentos en dos ámbitos institucionales. La industria farmacéutica en España

y en Estados Unidos', doctoral thesis, Universidad de Valladolid, Valladolid, supervised by Dr. Juan Manuel de la Fuente Sabaté and Dr. Juan Hernangómez Barahona.

Santoro, FM. (1997), 'Innovación y sendero evolutivo en la industria farmacéutica: los casos de Argentina y España', doctoral thesis, Universidad de Buenos Aires, Buenos Aires.

Papers Published in Foreign Scientific Journals 1980–1999

Borrell, J.R. (1999), 'Pharmaceutical price regulation: a study on the impact of the rate-of-return regulation in the UK', *PharmacoEconomics*, 15, 291–303.

Darbà, J. and J. Rovira (1998), 'Parallel imports of pharmaceuticals in the European Union', *PharmacoEconomics*, 14 (supplement 1), 129–36.

López, J. and E. Mossialos (1997), 'Spanish drug policy at the crossroads', *The Lancet*, 350, 679–80.

Marino, M.A., J.M. Marqués and A. Velasco (1996), 'Impact of selective financing of drugs on pharmaceutical expenditure in the province of Valladolid, Spain', *PharmacoEconomics,* 10, 269–80.

Mestre, J. (1999), 'The impact of generic goods in the pharmaceutical industry', *Health Economics*, 8, 599–612.

Rovira, J. (1996), 'Are national drug expenditure control policies compatible with a single European market?', *PharmacoEconomics*, 10 (supplement 2), 4–13.

Rovira, J. (1998), 'The pros and cons of a single Euro-price for drugs and the economics of parallel trade', *PharmacoEconomics*, 14, 135–6.

Papers Published in Spanish Scientific Journals 1980–1999

Arnés, H. (1983), 'El sector farmacéutico en la CEE', *Economía Industrial*, 233: 95–106.

Arnés, H. (1983), 'Análisis global de la industria farmacéutica', *Economía Industrial*, 233, 39–48.

Arnés, H. and J.A. Zamora (1984), 'Libre circulación de medicamentos en la CEE: importaciones paralelas y patentes', *Economía Industrial*, 239, 73–9.

Ausió, J. (1999), 'Els professionals en les polítiques de gestió de la prestació farmacèutica', *Fulls Econòmics del Sistema Sanitari*, 33, 26–7.

Bercovitz, A. (1986), 'Las importaciones paralelas de productos farmacéuticos en la CEE', *Revista de Derecho Privado*, (December), 995–1019.

Cabiedes, L. (1994), 'Barreras técnicas a la difusión de innovaciones farmacéuticas', *Revista de Economía Aplicada*, 2, 151–62.

Callejón, M. and V. Ortún (1990), 'Los medicamentos en España: mercado único y utilidad social', *Economía Industrial*, 274, 191–206.

Carballeira, R. and J.L. Velasco (1994), 'La investigación farmacéutica y su entorno', *Economía Industrial*, 296, 105–14.

Casado, A. (1987), 'La ley de patentes de 1986 y los sectores químico y farmacéutico', *Economía Industrial*, 256, 151–62.

Conejos, J. and J.M. Hernández (1990), 'La industria farmacéutica en Cataluña', *Economía Industrial*, 276, 91–9.

Costas, E. (1998), 'El gasto farmacéutico público y el acuerdo de la Subcomisión: una nota', *Papeles de Economía Española*, 76, 141–5.

Esteve, J. (1998), 'La industria farmacéutica como impulsora de la I+D en el sector sanitario', *Revista de Administración Sanitaria*, **11** (7), 1–9.

Fernández, M.D. and J.L. Velasco (1983), 'La penetración extranjera en la industria farmacéutica española', *Economía Industrial*, 233, 83–93.

Ferrandiz, F. (1983), 'Estrategias de la industria farmacéutica hacia el futuro', *Economía Industrial*, 233, 135–50.

Foguet, R. (1999), 'L'impacte de la indústria farmacèutica catalana en l'economia productiva del nostre país', *Fulls Econòmics del Sistema Sanitari*, 33, 15–16.

Granda, E. and A. Arias (1983), 'El mercado farmacéutico en el ámbito de la Seguridad Social', *Economía Industrial*, 233, 67–81.

Hernández, J.M. (1998), 'El gasto farmacéutico en el contexto de la sanidad pública', *Boletín del Círculo de Empresarios*, 63, 179–97.

Hernández, J.M. (1999), 'Farmaindustria en l'actual context de la gestió de la prestació farmacèutica', *Fulls Econòmics del Sistema Sanitari*, 33, 14–15.

Ibern, P. (1997), 'Las importaciones paralelas de medicamentos: una controversia sobre la libre competencia en el mercado', *Boletín ICE Económico*, 2537, 43–9.

Jansson, E. (1999), 'Libre competencia frente a regulación en la distribución minorista de medicamentos', *Revista de Economía Aplicada*, 7, 85–112.

Juez, P. and P.A. Tamayo (1997), 'Efectividad de las medidas de contención del gasto público farmacéutico contenidas en el Real Decreto 83/1993 de 22 de enero (de selección de medicamentos a efectos de su financiación por el Sistema Nacional de Salud)', *Estudios Sobre Consumo*, 42, 63–72.

Llor, C. (1999), 'Posició dels professionals de la salut en les polítiques de gestió de la prestació farmacèutica', *Fulls Econòmics del Sistema Sanitari*, 33, 24–5.

Lobato, P. (1990), 'El mercado de medicamentos en España: demanda, gasto farmacéutico e intervenión de precios', *Información Comercial Española*, 89–103, 681–2.

Lobo, F. (1980), 'La publicidad farmacéutica en *España Papers: Revista de Sociología*, 14, 99–132.

Lobo, F. (1998), 'Medicamentos y Sistema Nacional de Salud: mejoras recientes en la financiación pública', *Boletín del Círculo de Empresarios*, 63, 199–212.

Lobo, F. (1999), 'Genéricos y precios de referencia', *Cartas CEDEF*, 4, 1–3.

López, J.P. (1985), 'La organización de los intereses empresariales en la industria farmacéutica española', *Papeles de Economía Española*, 22, 144–60.

Mestre, J. (1999), 'Relación entre un sistema de precios de referencia y medicamentos genéricos', *Hacienda Pública Española*, 150, 173–9.

Nonell, R. and J.R. Borrell (1998), 'Mercado de medicamentos en España: diseño institucional de la regulación y de la provisión pública', *Papeles de Economía Española*, 76, 113–31.

Pla, F. (1999), 'Els serveis farmacèutics en la gestió integral dels serveis sanitaris', *Fulls Econòmics del Sistema Sanitari*, 33, 16–18.

Puig, J. (1988), 'Gasto farmacéutico en España: efectos de la participación del usuario en el coste', *Investigaciones Económicas*, 12 (1), 45–68.

Puig, J. (1998), 'Regulación y competencia de precios en el mercado farmacéutico', *Papeles de Economía Española*, 76, 96–112.

Puig, J. (1999), 'Reptes en la gestió de la prestació farmacèutica', *Fulls Econòmics del Sistema Sanitari*, 33, 6–13.

Puig, J. and G. López-Casasnovas (1999), 'Análisis económico de la aplicación de precios de referencia en la financiación pública de medicamentos: Ventajas, limitaciones e impacto esperado en España. Informe Técnico No 1', *Economía y Salud,* 31.

Puig, J. and G. López-Casasnovas (1999), 'La aplicación de precios de referencia a los medicamentos', *Cuadernos de Información Económica*, 143, 77–84.

Reol, J.M. (1983), 'La asistencia farmacéutica y el medicamento: libertad y responsabilidad', *Economía Industrial*, 233, 151–5.

Rincón, A. (1983), 'La industria farmacéutica española', *Economía Industrial*, 233, 51–65.

Rodríguez, A. (1981), 'La patente de invención y la industria farmacéutica', *Información Comercial Española*, 569, 67–73.

Rovira, J. (198), 'Impacto del mercado único sobre el sector farmacéutico en España', *Papeles de Economía Española*, 76, 132–40.

Sáenz, M.T. (1990), 'El futuro de la industria farmacéutica en España', *Boletín ICE Económico*, 2246, 3191–3.

Santaló, M. (1999), 'El posicionament de l'Institut Català de la Salut sobre les noves polítiques de gestió de la prescripció farmacèutica', *Fulls Econòmics del Sistema Sanitari*, 33, 23–4.

Segú, L., P. Solans, P. Gavilan, I. Vargas, B. Ruiz and C. Manté (1999), 'La utilització de medicaments: la perspectiva dels proveïdors', *Fulls Econòmics del Sistema Sanitari*, 33, 18–23.

Urbanos, R.M. (1995), 'El consumo de medicamentos en España y su impacto social: una aproximación a partir de la Encuesta de Salud (1995)', *Cuadernos de Información Económica*, 131, 148–52.

Various authors (1999), 'La prestació farmacèutica', *Fulls Econòmics del Sistema Sanitari*, 33.

Papers Presented at the Conference on Health Economics 1980–1999

Anitua, C. and B. Fernandino (1998), 'Evolución del gasto sanitario directo en medicamentos', paper presented at the 18th Conference on Health Economics, 27–29 May, Vitoria-Gasteiz, Spain.

Antoñanzas, F., J. Rovira and C. Juárez (1999), 'La demanda de medicamentos: un método para calcular las repercusiones presupuestarias', in G. López-Casasnovas and J. Callau (eds), *Libro de Ponencias de las XIX Jornadas de Economía de la Salud, June 2–4* [abstract only], Zaragoza, Huesca: Asociación de Economía de la Salud, pp. 407–408.

Badía, X., M. Brosa, A. Casado, L. Segú and A. Álvarez (1999), 'Análisis coste efectividad de estrategias de diagnóstico-tratamiento del Ulcus Péptico asociados a *Helicobacter Pylori*', in G. López-Casasnovas and J. Callau (eds), *Libro de Ponencias de las XIX Jornadas de Economía de la Salud, June 2–4*, Zaragoza. Huesca: Asociación de Economía de la Salud, pp. 279–90.

Badía, X., J. Rovira, L. Segú and M. Porta (1993), 'La evaluación económica de medicamentos en España (1982–1992) y su repercusión en la toma de decisiones', paper presented at the 13th Conference on Health Economics, 2–4 June, Granada, Spain.

Cots, F., J. Monterde, X. Castells and S. Grau (1993), 'Cálculo y análisis de los costes de farmacia por Grupos Relacionados de Diagnóstico', communication presented at the 13th Conference on Health Economics, 2–4 June, Granada, Spain.

Fernández, P. and C. García (1993), 'Iniciativas comunitarias y de la industria farmacéutica sobre mercado interior y competencia', communication presented at the 13th Conference on Health Economics, 2–4 June, Granada, Spain.

Fernández, P., M.J. Huertas and A. Flaquer (1992), 'Consecuencias del mercado único de medicamentos para la Industria farmacéutica', in S. Rubio (ed.), *Libro de Ponencias de las XII Jornadas de Economía de la Salud, 27–29 May*, Madrid, Madrid: Comunidad de Madrid, 179–90.

Franzi, A., L.L. Rodríguez and R. Llobet (1999), 'Impacto económico de la implantación de genéricos: estudio en 12 áreas básicas de salud', in G. López-Casasnovas and J. Callau (eds), *Libro de Ponencias de las XIX Jornadas de Economía de la Salud, 2–4 June*, [abstract only], Zaragoza. Huesca: Asociación de Economía de la Salud, 403–404.

García, C. and P. Fernández (1993), 'Innovación farmacéutica y competencia: precios de referencia', paper presented at the 13th Conference on Health Economics, 2–4 June, Granada, Spain.

Guerra, F. and J.C. Domínguez (1993), 'Consenso en el uso de medicamentos como instrumento de gestió', paper presented at the 13th Conference on Health Economics, 2–4 June, Granada, Spain.

Ibern, P. (1999), 'Copago farmacéutico: nivel de concentración en pocos usuarios y diseño de alternativas', in G. López-Casasnovas and J. Callau (eds.), *Libro de Ponencias de las XIX Jornadas de Economía de la Salud*, 2–4 June, [abstract only], Zaragoza, Huesca: Asociación de Economía de la Salud, pp. 409–10.

Larruga, J. (1999), 'Modelo de información personalizada, dirigida a los facultativos de atención primaria de la Comunidad Autónoma de Valencia, sobre alternativas equivalentes más económicas de la prescripción médica', paper presented at the 19th Conference on Health Economics, 2–4 June, Zaragoza, Spain.

Lobo, F. (1999), 'Medidas recientes del Insalud y otros servicios de salud dirigidas a orientar la prescripción de medicamentos hacia la eficiencia' in G. Lopez-Casasnovas and J. Callau (eds), *Libro de Ponencias de las XIX Jornadas de Economía de la Salud, 2–4 June*, Zaragoza, Huesca: Asociación de Economía de la Salud, pp. 393–400.

Lobo, F. (1993), 'Monopolio y competencia en la industria farmacéutica: los mercados de medicamentos genéricos', in *Libro de Ponencias de las XIII Jornadas de Economía de la Salud, 2–4 June* [abstract only], Granada, Spain. Barcelona: Asociacias de Economía de la Salud, p. 18–19.

Lobo, F. (1990), 'La evaluación económica, el registro y la intervención de precios de los medicamentos', in I. Mugarra and F. Antoñanzas (eds), *Libro de Ponencias de las X Jornadas de Economía de la Salud, 30–1 May–June* [abstract only], Pamplona, España: Pamplona: Asociación fde Economía de la Salud, pp. 232–4.

Martínez, J., A. Latorre, M. Ibarra and R. Huarte (1999), 'Prescripción de medicamentos genéricos en un área de salud de atención primaria', in G. López-Casasnovas and J. Callau (eds), *Libro de Ponencias de las XIX Jornadas de Economía de la Salud, 2–4 June* [abstract only], Zaragoza, Huesca: Asociacón de Economía de la Salud, pp. 405–406.

Ortún, V. (1991), 'La utilidad social de los medicamentos en España', in I. Mugarra and F. Antoñanzas (eds), *Libro de Ponencias de las X Jornadas de Economía de la Salud; 1990 30–1 May–June*, Pamplona, España, Pamplona: Asociación de Economía de la Salud, pp. 221–31.

Pinto, J.L., F. Sánchez and J. Rovira (1995), 'Uso del método de la evaluación contingente en la medición del bienestar social: aplicación al tratamiento farmacológico de la retinitis', in *Asociación de Economía de la Salud. Libro de Ponencias de las XV Jornadas de Economía de la Salud May* [abstract only], Valencia, España, Barcelona: SG Editores, pp. 372–5.

Rodríguez, B., M.J. Martín, N, Sáenz and A. Pozuelo (1999), 'Factores asociados al gasto farmacéutico', in G. López-Casasnovas and J. Callau (eds), *Libro de Ponencias de las XIX Jornadas de Economía de la Salud, 2–4 June* [abstract only], Zaragoza., Huesca: Asociación de Economía de la Salud, pp. 401–402.

Rovira, J. (1995), 'Temas controvertidos en la evaluación económica del sector sanitario', in Asociación de Economía de la Salud, *Libro de Ponencias de las XIV Jornadas de Economía de la Salud, 8–10 June*, Santiago de Compostela, Barcelona: SG Editores, pp. 199–224.

Rovira, J. (1992), 'La política farmacéutica ante el mercado único', in S. Rubio (ed.), *Libro de Ponencias de las XII Jornadas de Economía de la Salud 27–29 May*, Madrid, España, Madrid: Comunidad de Madrid, pp. 165–8.

Rovira, J., A. Kelety, J. Andrés, L. Tomás and M. Brosa (1992), 'Análisis coste efectividad de un nuevo fármaco para el tratamiento de la hipercolesterolemia', in S. Rubio (ed.), *Libro de Ponencias de las XII Jornadas de Economía de la Salud, 27–29 May*, Madrid, España, Madrid: Comunidad de Madrid, pp. 449–53.

Sacristán, J.A., J.C. Gómez and L. Salvador-Carulla (1997), 'Análisis coste-efectividad de olanzapina frente a haloperiodol en el tratamiento de la esquizofrenia en España', in L. Fidel and M.J. García (eds), *Libro de Ponencias de las XVII Jornadas de Economía de la Salud, 21–23 May* [abstract only], Murcia, Murcia: Asociación de Economía de la Salud, pp. 273–4.

Trillo, J.L., J.L. García and D.P. Comeche (1999), 'Creación de seudocompetencia en el sector farmacéutico hospitalario: aplicación de un procedimiento de adquisición centralizada de medicamentos en el ámbito de la Comunidad Valenciana, paper presented at the 19th Conference on Health Economics, 2–4 June, Zaragoza, Spain.

Index